"Somehow in this magical and very personal book, Russ and Allison have managed to convey Russ's delicious, soulful, and 'dogmatically flexible' style onto the page. This book most certainly IS Camino and most definitely belongs in your kitchen!"

—SUZANNE GOIN, chef and author of *Sunday Suppers at Lucques* and *The A.O.C. Cookbook*

"It is impossible to imagine how one translates the beauty which is Camino into a book. Somehow, Allison and Russ's labor of love shines through every image and every recipe . . . And now I'm off to make their herb jam."

—YOTAM OTTOLENGHI, author of *Plenty More* and co-author of *Jerusalem* and *NOPI*

"*This Is Camino* could not be more true to its name: it draws you in, and you can really feel the heart of the restaurant as you turn the pages. The book gives a beautiful glimpse into Russ and Allison's rustic, earthy approach—the very thing that makes Camino so exceptional."

—APRIL BLOOMFIELD, chef and author of *A Girl and Her Pig* and *A Girl and Her Greens*

"Camino is a lively, inviting restaurant with a primal open fire at its heart. And then there is Russ's cooking, which is unexpected, singular, and totally comforting. *This Is Camino* communicates all this in a way which will change how you bring people together in your homes to have fun and eat well."

—IGNACIO MATTOS, chef of Estela restaurant

EXCERPT FROM THE NEW YORK TIMES

"WHAT'S IMPORTANT BUT IS IMPOSSIBLE TO DESCRIBE IS THE STRENGTH AND UTTER BRILLIANCE OF HIS FLAVOR COMBINATIONS AND THE DOWNRIGHT SIMPLICITY OF IT ALL. MOORE HAS A PALATE THAT CANNOT BE STOPPED; EVERYTHING TASTES AS IF IT WERE CREATED TO GO WITH EVERYTHING SEASONING IT."

—MARK BITTMAN, the *New York Times*

For Thelma Hosun Moore,
the cutest, most generous, hard-ass
Korean lady, and favorite mom

THIS IS
CAMINO

RUSSELL MOORE + ALLISON HOPELAIN
WITH CHRIS COLIN

and Maria Zizka

Photographs by Yoko Takahashi

THIS IS
CAMINO

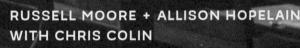

TEN SPEED PRESS
Berkeley

CONTENTS

RECIPE CONTENTS

INTRODUCTION

When we first started talking about a Camino book, the obvious question was how to show people the way we cook at Camino when we know that people do not have giant fireplaces in their homes. Our first solution was to not make a cookbook—to not have any recipes! To make a flip book! Or an art book! Or a zine!

After a little more thought, it seemed clear that the essence of our cooking isn't ultimately the fire. The fire's simply a (huge, roaring) means to an end. At its heart, Camino is about an approach to food, one that can happen anywhere. Neither Russ nor I are grandmothers, but fundamentally ours is grandmotherly cooking. Specifically, a frugal grandmother who grew up in the Depression, had plenty of style, kept a sweet vegetable garden, and could shake a good cocktail.

Grandmotherly cooking requires no special equipment. At our own home, we don't have a fireplace. We don't even have much of a functional kitchen. It's tiny, and our stove has a huge crack on the top that makes the burners too slanty to cook anything evenly. Our oven door doesn't even close all the way. Which is all to say this: Whatever you've got at home? Fine.

There was a time when what Russ and I had at home was *all* I wanted.

Back when Russ worked at Chez Panisse, he had a pretty great situation. Wonderfully talented coworkers. Six weeks vacation. And blissfully humane hours; he surfed four days a week. So when, after twenty-one years, he started to imagine something new, I wasn't sure so sure.

It wasn't the perks I feared we'd miss. It's that I don't like compromise and restaurants are full of small compromises. What if our restaurant said no to compromise? No non-organic produce, sure—but also no traditional waiter-busser hierarchies. No tablecloths. No martini glasses. No machismo. No pizza or burgers or pasta. No pigs from Iowa, even though they're great, and cheaper. There'd be no flowers on the table, no art on the walls. No bar stools, no Beefeater gin, no kids' menu. No alcohol with food coloring. (So long, Campari.) No alcohol from the "big two" distributors, for that matter. No encroachment on serendipity.

So what would it be? It'd be us: me, a landscaper whose restaurant experience consisted of eating at restaurants, and Russ, the guy who cooked our dinner over a backyard fire, atop that old rebar we lifted from a vacant lot. All those fancy Chez Panisse meals, but then at home he'd be out in the dirt, cinderblocks blocking the wind and neighbors wondering about the guy roasting goat over a fire.

Camino would be an extension of Russ bent over that fire—and, in a sense, of the Russ from way back, this half-Korean punk rock kid working the Texaco in Southern California. At sixteen he was hitching rides in the old Minutemen van, this barely-a-teen coughing up gas money for passage to whatever punk show was playing that night. What was playing, I suspect, was an escape from the stifling suburban jocks-and-cheerleaders tar pit of high school.

Why am I telling you about my husband's adolescence? Because you can draw a line from those years straight to the menu at Camino, three-and-a-half decades later. In his sweet and reserved way, he's the most defiant and strident person I know. (I stopped letting him read Yelp after someone referred to him as Stalin. He's wanted to top that ever since—Idi Amin maybe.) Restaurants are full of compromises and artifices, and Russ can't stand those things any more than his teenage self could've.

When Russ wasn't pumping gas and skipping prom, he was learning to cook at a nearby Italian restaurant. So when he decided to move to the Bay Area at twenty-two, a family friend suggested he reach out to some local eateries, including one with a name he couldn't spell—Chez something. He cold-called, got an interview with David Tanis and talked his way into a 6 a.m. tryout the next morning. He put his head down and cooked a staff breakfast for twenty people in ten minutes. This earned him seven hours of peeling garlic the next day.

It went on like this—two days a week, then a little more. Six bucks an hour. Each night he went home and researched all he'd encountered that day (what in the world did "corked" mean?). He was around grownups—film talk, art talk, wine talk, plus the cracking open of goat heads. He was hooked.

Me? This was not my path. I had not worked in a restaurant. So really my only exposure to restaurants was as the girlfriend of the chef at Chez Panisse. Not the strongest resume, maybe, but it was exposure to a restaurant as a beautiful lifestyle, one where you decide how you want to live and then make the restaurant around that.

Where Russ and I overlapped was simplicity. As talk of this theoretical Camino gathered steam, we envisioned a place that was real and comprehensible and beautiful and honest and good. We'd be that little Italian house in the countryside, with one light on and a little old lady cooking over one pot. She invites you to dinner, you take a seat—and you don't ask for grilled cheese and a Coke.

So, okay, we'd be a little Stalin-like, too, if Stalin offered a limited, strictly organic menu, cooked over a massive fire.

Most of all, though, we'd be a restaurant more theoretical than fixed. I mean, the food isn't theoretical—I promise it's real. But it changes every night. The essence of Camino isn't some signature dish, or stone tablet of perfected recipes. Camino is the thinking that led to those recipes, which will probably change again tomorrow night.

That last aspect—sort of funny when you're putting together a cookbook. Until now we've had nothing written down, even dishes we make repeatedly. Every year, rather than simply whip out the nocino recipe, we start from scratch, feel what the right amount of walnuts is. For Russ, everything lives in the strange, swirling cloud that is his head, and improbably that's a highly effective system.

The nocino thing? Sure, there are moments when I see it from the outside and it looks totally nutty. But there's a philosophy behind the nuttiness. At some level, every meal here needs to feel like it's being made for the first time. For Russ and for all our cooks, that wards off a certain rigidity that can creep into a kitchen. It ensures full engagement with ingredients and technique, and prevents autopilot. It keeps you loose and honest, if that makes sense.

For you, the reader, all this adds up to a cookbook that might feel unconventional at times. The recipes might not look like recipes you're accustomed to. You'll find Very Specific Feelings About How to Cook interspersed with instructions to go off and improvise. There are recipes that are suggested and then more suggestions on how to rearrange all the components into something else entirely. And in the middle of the book, you'll encounter something decidedly unorthodox—an intimate and highly candid look at how all this comes together at Camino over the course of a week.

Most of all, you will encounter hints for how to think about food like we do at Camino—to be dogmatically flexible in your cooking, to think ahead to your next meal, to take that little extra step to make your food the tiniest bit better, to enjoy yourself, and to not compromise.

—ALLISON HOPELAIN

CHAPTER ONE

CAMINO
BASICS

CAMINO BASICS

For every compliment Camino gets on our food, an ounce or two of gratitude goes to the last decade's global financial collapse.

Six months after we opened, the economy imploded. Even in the affluent Bay Area, folks started staying home. At Camino, we found ourselves with five cooks and too little business. You can't really send cooks home early on a slow night—on the paycheck level, that's sort of a mini economic implosion for them. So I had to find ways to keep them busy, not to mention use up the food going uneaten. It was a shitty situation to which we owe much of our success.

Slow days became project days. Projects, in turn, became our lifeblood. At first, it was easy stuff: preserving lemons, canning tomatoes, making jam. Then it grew. We started buying all this citrus from Didar Singh of Guru Ram Das Orchards. His fruit is sometimes ugly (he has this bruisy peach that has a real name, but we just call it "Didar's Ugly White Peach"), but it's just *better*. His fruit has this vitality—peel one of his oranges and you're covered in this amazing oil that comes bursting from the skin. So invariably I'd buy too much, and invariably we'd have extra. So we juiced them to make sorbet or for cocktails, we candied the peel, we even saved the syrup from candying the peel—and then didn't use it for years, until our bartender, Tyler, finally came up with a need for it.

It happened like this a lot those early days—confronted with unused ingredients and a rare chunk of free time, we'd start experimenting and preserving. Too much pig? We had to cure it: ham, and pancetta, and

lardo. Abundance of lard in the pantry? It became our cooking fat. Luckily, I came across a doughnut recipe that I could alter and make with lard instead of shortening—thanks, Marion Cunningham!

Our staff loves doing stuff like this. They're total hippies, always bringing in some new home fermentation creation, and our projects tap right into their kombucha-brewing, urban-homesteading gene. But they also tap into a larger philosophy of mine, one that gets at our very approach to cooking.

Maintaining a good kitchen means always having this floating sense of what you've got and how you can use it. It means not just thinking about today's mushroom dish, but tomorrow's consommé, which takes advantage of those lopped-off mushroom butts. And once you dial in your efficiency, it means you can buy more and more fun, interesting stuff from your various sources—because you've found a way to use it.

Allison sees it as akin to running an old-fashioned efficient household. And it's true, this stuff goes way back, and it's simple common sense. When you butcher your lamb, you're thinking about the little bits you can set aside for a future ragù. When you have leftover greens and herbs, you know that incredible, intense herb jam is possible. Chile sauces, preserved lemon, pickled walnut—these are by-product projects, the kind that sit happily until that perfect moment when they can add unexpected depth to your dish.

It shouldn't be a radical premise—and it isn't—but somehow too many home cooks, restaurant cooks, and a million cooking shows all miss this simple notion: A dish should begin with a glance in the refrigerator. And the pantry. And, okay, a tour of the farmers' market. But too often our thinking about food begins with that recipe your friend emailed you, rather than an assessment of what's on hand. A dozen ingredients are purchased, and at the end of the night half of them are only half used up, and two weeks later they're fished out of the back of the fridge and thrown away.

This isn't just wasteful. Planning a meal based on existing ingredients represents a profoundly different relationship to cooking altogether. It shunts you over to a more inventive and responsive way of thinking about your dishes. It makes you limber.

This first chapter is to help limber you up—to prepare you for thinking differently about cooking.

When we first opened, our flavors were super minimal. Austere, even—the only herb we had for a while was parsley. I didn't want a huge variety of ingredients lying around, and I didn't want to work with sources I didn't know. But as the stalled economy nudged us into all those projects, those projects nudged our dishes in new directions.

Today the walk-in and our back kitchen form the Camino Larder—our permanent collection, essentially. Tubs of fermented cabbage. Prunes soaking in brandy. A jar of pickle liquid. Some Seville orange marmalade. The vinegar barrel. And whatever someone's going to dream up next week. It's not glamorous. We're forever scrambling to make sure nothing's sitting on the floor when the inspector comes around. But in a sense—in some ways more than our fireplace—our larder is Camino's beating heart.

It's funny: For all our fanaticism about sourcing the freshest ingredients, we're just as obsessive about this funky old stuff gathering dust on our shelves. The two are inextricably linked in our kitchen—using duck fat in place of olive oil or sauerkraut juice for salt adds a subtle but crucial new dimension to our food, every bit as much as cooking with just-picked vegetables does.

This leads to another vital aspect of Camino's food: The Staples. The secret to this book lies in getting down the staples. All the grains we use are from Anson Mills in South Carolina—here is their phone number: 803-467-4122; and here is their website: www.ansonmills.com—stock up! They are the constant in an ever-changing menu. The Staples are the food items that we have at Camino all the time. They show up on the menu in one way or another every night—just never the same way. I'm not saying they are 100 percent interchangeable or that you should put pounded herb sauce on everything, but these are all flexible and indispensable to our food.

Also indispensible are some cooking methods that we use all the time and that appear over and over in these recipes. Some are super basic, some are unique to Camino, and some are as old as time. But they are all Camino basics—what I expect new Camino cooks to know, or at least pick up in the first few weeks on the job.

FRIED FARRO

Makes about 5 cups

I grew up eating white rice with dinner every night and continued doing so into adulthood. At Camino, it seemed weird to serve something as processed as white rice, and we wanted to offer more whole grains, so we started experimenting with different kinds of farro. We settled on Anson Mills's farro piccolo (also called einkorn), which is smaller than most farro available and doesn't have any of the husk removed (*non perlato*), so it is firmer and nuttier. Because we started out thinking of it as a rice substitute and I wanted to come at it from a non-Italian angle, I ended up frying it a little like fried rice. This particular farro, with its husk intact, can stand to be recooked without falling apart.

    2 cups unhusked farro piccolo

    Coarse salt and fine salt

    Olive oil

    2 cups sliced spring onion, leek, scallion,
    or red onion

    6 cloves garlic, thinly sliced

    A big handful of herbs (mint, basil,
    fenugreek, cilantro, or Italian parsley leaves),
    coarsely chopped

Preheat the oven to 375°F.

Toast the farro on a dry baking sheet until it smells nutty and turns a shade darker, about 7 minutes.

Put the toasted farro in a pot and cover with water by a couple of inches. Add a big pinch of coarse salt, bring to a steady simmer, and cook until the farro is tender but not super soft. Knowing exactly when the farro is done can be tricky. I usually end up tasting it five or six times while it's cooking. At first, it'll taste like a raw grain, as you might imagine, and then it'll soften a bit and seem to be almost done for a long time. It's done when the raw flavor is totally gone, but it is still firm, about 20 minutes. While you taste for doneness, you should also taste for saltiness. When the farro is done, drain and spread it out to cool to room temperature. It will be easier to fry if it is not warm.

Heat a cast iron pan or other large, heavy-bottomed pan over medium heat. Add enough olive oil to coat the bottom of the pan, then add the spring onion and a pinch of fine salt. Cook the onion until it's beginning to get tender and brown in some places, about 4 minutes. Add the garlic and stir quickly so it doesn't brown at all. Immediately add the farro, another splash of olive oil (enough to barely coat the farro but not make it greasy), and some salt, and stir. You want the farro to protect the garlic in the pan so that eventually the garlic is soft but not browned, or worse burned.

The farro will begin to brown and stick to the pan. Using a wooden spoon, scrape up the browned bits. Then don't touch it for a few minutes, let the farro stick, and then scrape it up again. Do this a few times until it's a little crispy. Add the herbs and continue to fry and stir. Cook for another couple of minutes and check for salt.

You can serve it immediately, or you could cook the farro hours ahead of time and reheat it in a heavy pan over medium heat. We heat it up in a clay pot in the coals. This adds another layer of crispy bits to stir into the farro.

VARIATION

Add roasted corn or Cooked Greens (page 13) when you add the herbs.

POLENTA
Makes about 6 cups

I know: who needs a polenta recipe? The instructions are right on the back of the bag. But here are some tips for making extra good polenta:

Use freshly milled polenta. We use white Otto File polenta from Anson Mills.

Ferment it a little by soaking it in water. If we have some whey on hand (the clear liquid that pours off your yogurt or ricotta), we'll add a splash of it to the overnight soak to help the fermentation along.

Skim the chaff. This helps make it more fluffy.

Cook it painfully slowly. We start it at 1:00 and it is just ready by 5:00. The folks at Anson Mills told me that I am radically overcooking it, but it really doesn't taste done to me before then. I know this seems like a lot of time to devote to polenta; you have to come up with some other cooking projects to do at the same time—maybe ragù (page 197), ratatouille (page 77), or pork cooked in milk (page 204).

3 cups white or yellow Anson Mills coarse polenta

1 tablespoon whey (optional)

Coarse salt

½ cup unsalted butter

Combine the polenta, whey, and 6 cups of water in a bowl. Cover and set aside at room temperature to ferment. This is best done overnight, but 4 hours or so will work fine.

When it's done soaking, skim off the chaff floating on the surface. Put the polenta and its soaking liquid in a heavy-bottomed pot set over high heat. Stir in a big pinch of salt. Polenta really wants to stick when started this way, so you actually have to stir it the whole time until it comes to a boil. Once it boils, turn the heat down as low as possible and continue to stir every few minutes. After about 10 minutes, the polenta will get very thick—almost too thick to stir. Add a splash of water to loosen it up a bit. I purposely start with not enough water so that I am forced to pay attention to what is happening in the pot (plus, then I never have to remember how much water I'm supposed to use). Continue to nurse the polenta along, adding a splash of water as needed. After an hour or so, start tasting, using the opportunity to check for both doneness and salt. Once the polenta is done, stir in the butter. If you add the butter too early, it seems to fry the grains a bit in an unpleasant way.

You can serve this right away or you can put it in a double boiler until dinner is ready. You can also spread the whole mass out onto a baking sheet and put it in the fridge. To reheat the cold polenta, just break it up a bit, add a splash of water, and heat it slowly on the stove.

RED LENTILS
Makes about 5½ cups

We rely on red lentils quite a bit at Camino. It started as a weird little addition to a composed salad at home when there was nothing left to cook and other dried beans would take too long. I found a bag of red lentils in the cupboard left over from the one time I made dal, so I cooked them a little like dal but way thicker. Red lentils are peeled so they cook quickly and easily turn into a purée. We mostly eat them warm, but if you need to add weight to a vegetable or fish salad, some red lentil mush can do the trick. If you serve these at room temperature, drizzle a little olive oil on at the end. You can add as much or as little ground chile as you like; just don't make them too plain—they can really taste boring if you don't spice them up a bit.

> 1 to 2 dried moderately hot chiles
>
> 3 tablespoons olive oil
>
> ¼ teaspoon brown mustard seeds
>
> 4 cloves garlic, thinly sliced
>
> 3 (⅛-inch-thick) slices unpeeled ginger
>
> ¼ teaspoon ground turmeric
>
> 2½ cups red lentils
>
> Salt

Tear the chiles into manageable pieces, discarding the stems, and place them in a spice grinder. Pulse a few times to create a coarse powder.

Heat a pot over medium heat. Add 1 tablespoon of the olive oil and all of the mustard seeds. Swirl them around and cover the pot. In a few minutes, you should start hearing them begin to pop (kind of like Lilliputian popcorn). Once the popping begins to slow, take the pan off the heat and remove the lid. Here's the tricky part: while everything is still hot, quickly add the garlic, ginger, and turmeric and stir immediately. You want the garlic and ginger to be coated in oil and you want the turmeric to sizzle a bit, but you don't want any of it to get brown. I really don't like burnt garlic and I especially don't like burnt turmeric. So, after everything sizzles in the hot pan for 15 seconds or so, splash some water in there to stop the cooking.

Now add the lentils, some ground chile, a bit of salt, the remaining 2 tablespoons of oil (so you have both cooked mustard-y oil and uncooked fruity oil), and enough water to cover by about half an inch. Turn the heat up and bring to a boil, then turn the heat down to a simmer, and stir to break up the clumps of lentils. Continue to cook, adding splashes of water here and there if the lentils start to get too thick and poke out of the liquid. But don't add so much water that the lentils get watery and soup-like—you can always add water later, but you can't easily take it out.

After 15 minutes or so, the lentils should begin to fall apart. This usually happens unevenly, so keep stirring and tasting for doneness (and of course, for salt, since you are tasting anyway). It's nice if there is a little texture left in the lentils, but there should be absolutely no raw flavor or crunch. It will look like a lumpy, bright yellow purée. The whole thing should take about 30 to 40 minutes.

To serve, you may want add a little more ground chile or olive oil. Red lentils can be made ahead, refrigerated, and reheated easily over medium heat with a splash of water.

GRILLED BREAD

This is not really a recipe but more like general advice about grilling bread. Grilled bread is a big part of Camino—we grill bread for brunch, toasts for bar snacks, and thick pieces for ragùs. We often grill a piece of bread, rub it with garlic, and put it at the bottom of a fish stew or other soup for a surprise. Sometimes we grill a thin slice of bread as a crunchy treat in a salad. The point is that leftover bread can be a valuable part of a meal.

My favorite way to grill bread is to brush a thick slice evenly with olive oil and grill it really hot. If the grill is not hot enough, the bread will dry out. When you do it just right, you end up with a soft interior and a crunchy exterior with some black spots. This is what you want to eat with roasted mushrooms or a bowl of soupy fresh shell beans. I mention brushing it evenly because if you just drizzle the oil randomly, the parts in between the oil will taste like stale bread once it cools off a bit—even if you're using fresh bread. Also, the hot grill is important because you want it to grill, not bake.

If you are already using a hot grill to grill something else, just clean the grate and make some space for the bread.

Cut the bread into slices that are a little less than 1 inch thick. If you're using a baguette, cut it on an angle so you have a larger surface area. Brush the slices on both sides with an even layer of olive oil.

Grill the first side for about a minute, until there are nice dark marks, then flip. (If you pick up the bread to check if it's done and then set it down on the grill again, you'll get fuzzy marks, which isn't the end of the world, but clean lines look better.) Cook the second side for another minute or so, until crispy on the outside with a few black spots but still soft in the middle.

CRISPY FLATBREAD
Makes 6 individual flatbreads

We make this flatbread in the wood oven, but it works very well in a regular oven on an upside-down cast iron pan. It's a good accompaniment to composed salads—or any salad, really.

    ¾ cup warm water (under 100°F)

    1½ teaspoons honey

    ¼ teaspoon active dry yeast

    ¾ cup whole wheat flour

    ½ teaspoon salt, plus more for sprinkling

    ¾ cup all-purpose flour, plus more for kneading

    Olive oil

Pour the water into a bowl and add the honey. Sprinkle in the yeast and stir to dissolve. Set aside in a warm place to bubble for a few minutes.

Once the yeast is alive and slowly bubbling, stir in the whole wheat flour and salt, then add the all-purpose flour in ¼-cup increments, stirring well between each addition. Once all the flour is incorporated, turn it out onto a lightly floured surface and knead it for 6 minutes. It's a good idea to set a timer for 6 minutes because, when kneading, sometimes 2 minutes can feel like 6 minutes and you really need the time for the gluten to develop.

Pour a splash of olive oil into a bowl, put the dough into the bowl, then flip it over so that all sides are lightly oiled. Cover and let rise for 2½ to 3 hours at room temperature or, better yet, overnight in the fridge.

Give the dough one little knead, then cut it into six equal pieces (about 2 ounces each). Roll each piece into a ball, set on a lightly oiled dish, then roll the balls to coat with the oil, cover, and refrigerate for about 30 minutes.

continued

Meanwhile, put a 10-inch (or larger) cast iron pan upside down in the oven and preheat the oven to 500°F or as hot as it will go. If you don't have a large enough pan, make your dough balls smaller.

Using as little flour as necessary, roll each dough ball out to a 10-inch round. You want them to be evenly thin, not thick around the edges like pizza. Perforate the dough with a fork in a few places to force it to rise in little bubbles all over rather than in one big bubble.

When the cast iron pan and oven are hot, drape one piece of dough over the upside-down pan and bake for a couple of minutes, until it puffs up, bubbles in some places, and starts to get brown. Flip, and bake for another minute or so on the second side, until it feels crisp and firm everywhere. Brush one side with oil and sprinkle with salt, then set aside to cool.

VARIATIONS

These are also good sprinkled with chiles, sumac, sesame, or nigella.

COOKED GREENS
Makes about 1½ cups

Olive oil

4 cloves garlic, peeled and sliced

10 cups greens (about 10 ounces, or from 1½ bunches), such as spinach, chard, or red mustard

Salt

Moderately hot ground chile, to taste (optional)

Heat up a pan over medium-high heat for about a minute. Swirl in enough oil to coat the bottom of the pan. Add the garlic and let it sizzle for a few seconds, but don't let it brown. Add as many greens as will fit and season them with salt and a pinch of ground chile, if you want. I don't usually try to make these greens spicy, but I like to give them just a little something. Cook, stirring occasionally, until the greens wilt and make space for more greens. Add the rest and cook for a couple of minutes, until all the greens are tender. If you're not using them right away, spread the greens out on a plate and let them cool.

CHILE SAUCE
Makes about ½ cup

I tend to think of dried chiles not as a spice or condiment but as a vegetable—a vegetable that happens to be dried. I'm lucky enough to get chiles that are dried by the farmers who grow them, so I can get them whole and I also know how old they are. We store whole dried chiles in sealed jars until we need them and then we grind what we need as we go.

Before Camino, I always used pre-ground smoky pimentón from Spain, but now I'd rather grind up whatever whole chile I can get from farmers I know, and then smoke another part of the dish to achieve that flavor in a different way. If you understand the flavor of the chiles you're working with, you won't be afraid create a cultural mash up of chiles that originate from different parts of the world. A lot of the chiles that we use are Mexican varieties, which makes sense for California farmers.

Anchos (sweet, bright, and medium hot, from Mexico)

Chilhuacles (almost smoky, a little bitter, and hottish, also from Mexico)

Pasillas (earthy and not very spicy, from Mexico)

Espelette (very bright and sweet, of varying spiciness and, really, good for everything, from the Basque Country)

Golden cayenne (steely, bright, and quite hot, from the U.S. and South America)

continued

Korean chiles (very hot and bright, clean)

New Mexicos (medium hot, sweet, and a little dusty, from New Mexico)

For this sauce, you will need to rehydrate the chiles in boiling water after you grind them. This softens them and helps incorporate them in the oil so you don't end up with separate chile flakes floating in oil. This is really good with fish, poultry, and eggs.

4 or 5 dried chiles (a single variety or a mix)

2 cloves garlic

Salt

5 tablespoons olive oil

1/2 cup very thinly sliced scallions or chives

Break up the chiles into manageable pieces, discarding the stems but keeping all the seeds and inner ribs. I'd rather include all the seeds in the sauce because they add complex bitterness and spiciness. That way you can use fewer chiles to deliver the heat (some of these chiles cost me $80.00 a pound!) and, if the sauce turns out too spicy, just use less of it. Grind the chile pieces in a coffee or spice grinder until coarse. It's good if they have a little texture, so don't grind them all the way to a powder. Put the ground chiles into a bowl and rehydrate them with a couple tablespoons of boiling water to make a dense paste—you don't want them to be swimming.

Using a mortar and pestle, pound the garlic with a pinch of salt. Scrape it into the bowl with the chiles. Add the olive oil, scallions, and another pinch of salt. Stir well to combine, then taste a small amount for seasoning.

This will last a couple days covered in the refrigerator, but the garlic flavor will get stronger.

VARIATIONS

If you are serving this with a fish stew, you can moisten the chiles with fish stock instead of boiling water. You can also use any vegetable or bean cooking liquid to give the sauce a little more depth.

Add any herb (mint, oregano, lovage, perilla, parsley, nepitella), or combine this with Pounded Herb Sauce (below) to make Chile-Herb Sauce.

Add toasted and slightly mortared sesame seeds.

Add raw tomato grated on a cheese grater.

All of the above.

POUNDED HERB SAUCE
Makes about 2/3 cup

2 cloves garlic

Salt

Leaves from 1 small bunch mint

Leaves from 1/2 small bunch oregano

1 small bunch chives, sliced

1/2 cup olive oil

Using a mortar and pestle, pound the garlic with a pinch of salt. Roughly (but quickly) slice the mint leaves, then immediately add them to the mortar. As soon as you cut the mint it will start to turn black, so to preserve the bright green color, quickly pound it into the garlic paste.

Add the oregano and chives, and then pound everything together. The herbs don't need to be perfectly smooth, but they should be pounded enough that the juices come out. Stir in the olive oil and a little more salt, then taste for seasoning.

This will last a couple days covered in the refrigerator, but the garlic flavor will get stronger.

NOTE

The herb stems can be used to make Egg Tea (see page 164).

LARDER

RED WINE VINEGAR

I got very excited about making vinegar when I first started cooking at Chez Panisse. My friend John Luther and I both went out and bought little barrels and convinced some folks at the Kermit Lynch store to give us wine left over from tastings. As a starter, I used a bottle of vinegar that had been sitting on my counter for a while that had developed a mother. That first batch wasn't very good, so I bottled it up, put the bottles under my house, and forgot about vinegar for the next fifteen years until we started thinking about opening Camino. I had this idea that I never wanted to buy vinegar—that we should make it all. So I scrounged under the house, found the old vinegar, and started a new batch with it. By the time Camino opened, we had accumulated three cases—just enough to open with. And with extreme frugality, we stretched that out until our first true Camino vinegar was ready.

Now we always have at least one batch going, and it's all from that original bottle from way back when. Every batch is a little different; sometimes a cook will accidentally grab a bottle from a new vintage and everything tastes different for a while until we figure it out.

Most of what I know about vinegar is from my own experience and my mistakes. The goal is to create an environment for bacteria to eat wine and turn it into vinegar. But if you have too high of an alcohol content in your barrel, it can kill all the good bacteria. To solve that problem, many recipes call for lots of water. But too much water makes watery vinegar, and I think what you want is the strongest vinegar you can possibly make. If you're making a salad with strong vinegar, you can use a higher ratio of oil to vinegar and use less vinaigrette overall—you still get the flavor without overdressing your salad.

Another way to control the alcohol level is to just start with lower alcohol wine. I don't make a huge effort to curate a perfect mix—we just use what is available, as long as it's not corked, including wine left over from tastings and from customers' unfinished bottles. The wine we serve at Camino is generally under 13 percent alcohol, which works out well for our barrel. A couple of years ago we did screw things up by including leftovers from a wedding party that brought their own wine. The wine was jammy and tasted a little bit cooked, but I thought just a small amount wouldn't hurt the vinegar. It did. That batch had a sweet and cloying quality that made it difficult to use.

You should start with a small oak barrel, about three gallons. Anything larger and you will become a slave to your barrel, and will have to give your vinegar away to passersby. Of the several varieties of oak available, we use American oak, which is the cheapest, though it does add an oaky flavor to your first batch. This flavor will disappear in future batches so it might be worth the savings.

To prepare the barrel, fill it with water and let it sit overnight outside or in the sink. Water will leak all over the place and you'll have to keep filling it up until the wood swells and the barrel becomes watertight. Empty the water and a drill a 1½-inch hole on each end of the barrel close to the top edge. The barrel will be lying on its side, so the "top" is where the bunghole is—the hole where you'll pour in the wine. You will need some sort of stand or blocks to keep your barrel from rolling around.

Cover the holes that you drilled with patches of cheesecloth to keep fruit flies out yet allow airflow.

You will need live vinegar to start your first batch. Most commercial vinegar has been pasteurized, which stabilizes it but also kills all the bacteria, so it will not work. You should find someone who is willing to give you some of their homemade vinegar. People will tell you that you need the vinegar "mother," which is just a blob of cellulose. It has some of the

continued

right bacteria, but using live vinegar makes it easier to control the ratio for your first batch.

For your first batch, I recommend that you make a self-esteem boosting and economical mini batch—self-esteem boosting because it's going to work and economical because you will need less live vinegar to start the process. After that you will start your vinegar with a little bit of your last batch, which is free.

The recipe is really just a ratio (and honestly, for our first six batches I didn't measure anything). I also use the universal measurement of the 750 ml wine bottle since this is all about wine.

> Ratio for first batch:
>
> 3 bottles of wine
>
> 1 bottle of live vinegar
>
> ½ bottle of water

Put everything in the barrel. Make sure the bung is closed and the cheesecloth is secure. After about 4 days, open the bung and smell—it should still smell like wine with a hint of vinegar. Shine a flashlight in the hole to see if the surface is hazy. If so, you are on your way—the bacteria have formed a veil on the surface and are at work. Don't disturb the veil by agitating it or adding more wine. Lots of recipes tell you to add wine as you have it on hand. I prefer to complete the process so that you have finished vinegar.

Now you are going to wait 4 months. While the starter batch is working, use those months to save leftover ends of bottles from dinner parties, combining them into bottles and corking them for safekeeping.

In 4 months, if it smells like vinegar, it's probably done. Use a straw with your thumb on one end to pull out a taste. If it tastes good (you shouldn't taste any alcohol), siphon out half a bottle of finished vinegar to use as your reward and leave the rest in the barrel. What's left in the barrel is your starter for your first real batch.

Pour the saved up leftover wine into your barrel at a ratio of six parts wine to one part water. You can continue with mini batches or you can go big. At Camino, we fill the barrel up all the way to the drilled holes.

For this and all your subsequent batches, you are going to siphon off all you can from the barrel into a bucket. Whatever you cannot get out of the barrel will be what you use to start your next batch. At this point the wood is impregnated with the bacteria so you don't need as much to start.

Sometimes the vinegar will have an acetoney, nail-polish-remover smell. You can get rid of this by aerating it before bottling. To do this, leave the vinegar in the bucket, stir it vigorously a few times a day, and keep it covered with cheesecloth between stirs. The smell should go away after a few days and then you will be ready to bottle it.

The vinegar will taste good right away but will be even better if you age it for a few months or years. I still have four bottles from that original batch left under my house that are now twenty-two years old.

PICKLED CHILES

We mostly pickle red chiles, such as ripe jalapeños, cayenne, and paprika. You can do single varieties or a mix. You can also use green jalapeños, which taste really good but end up looking a little dreary—a lot like canned jalapeños.

Take each chile and poke a hole in it with a skewer. The hole can be anywhere—the point is to create a path for the pickling liquid to get inside the chiles. To figure out how much brine you need, pour water over the chiles to cover and then pour that water into a measuring cup. The ratio for the brine is 1 tablespoon of coarse gray salt to 1 cup of water. Add the appropriate amount of salt. If you are not using coarse gray salt, you will have to adjust the ratio to taste. Once you have a few fermenting projects under your belt you will get a knack for how salty things should be.

Put the chiles and the brine into a pickling container—a crock or a wide-mouth jar will work. Toss in one head of garlic, cut in half horizontally, for every 2 pounds of chiles. The garlic flavors the brine and it also tastes good once it's pickled. Find a plate that will fit inside your pickling container to hold the chiles underneath the liquid. Then put a weight on it; we tend to use a mason jar filled with water, but anything heavy and clean will work. Cover the container with cheesecloth or a dishtowel and close it off with twine or a rubber band to keep the bugs out, and leave it out at room temperature.

After about a day, the chiles will start fermenting. You'll see little bubbles, which means all is going well. Then you just let it go at room temperature for a couple of weeks. Any part of a chile that's sticking out of the brine and is exposed to air will get moldy, so make sure they are covered by liquid. The surface of the liquid will develop a white mold that you can skim off—you won't be able to get all of it out, but don't worry, it'll be fine. The chiles will get more and more pickle-y the longer they sit out. I usually leave them out for about 2 weeks and then put them in the refrigerator. At this point, you can put them in a container with a lid. We've always used ours up within a year, but I imagine they will keep longer.

USES

Pickled Chile Sauce: Remove the chile stems and garlic skin then blend the pickled chiles, garlic, and seeds in a blender.

Pickled Chile Relish: Remove the stems, chop up the pickled chiles with the seeds. Add the herb of your choice (oregano, mint, basil, shiso) and a splash of olive oil.

You can also use the pickling liquid: We usually add a little bit to the next batch of pickled chiles, to inoculate it and get it quickly fermenting. We also might pour a splash of pickling liquid into rockfish stew—to give it a nice salty, tangy flavor—and we might use a little bit of it when making Chile Sauce (page 13).

SAUERKRAUT
Makes about 3 quarts

Like some other methods in this chapter, this barely counts as a recipe—it is really just a ratio of cabbage, salt, and time. Because there are only two real ingredients, the quality of salt is important. Coarse gray sea salt will make a subtle but significant difference in the flavor. If you use a different kind of salt, both the ratio and the flavor are going to change. Kosher salt, for example, is much saltier and has a slightly metallic taste that will affect the flavor of your kraut.

Sauerkraut is very basic fermentation: you create an environment that allows the bacteria you want to thrive while discouraging other bacteria. If you want to get really serious about fermentation, you should go out and get Sandor Katz's book *Wild Fermentation*— I use it as a reference all the time. He inscribed my copy of the book, "To Russ, Never throw it away. Love, Sandor." Which reminds me, don't throw away your leftover sauerkraut juice—you can add it to a beet soup (page 59) or use it to start your next batch of sauerkraut.

> 2 small, dense red or green cabbages (about 4 pounds)
>
> 2 tablespoons plus 1 teaspoon coarse sea salt

Quarter the cabbages, cut out the cores, and peel away any wilted outer leaves. Slice each cabbage quarter as thinly as possible. It's best if the slices are all the same thickness, but it's not such a big deal if they are different lengths. Take half of the sliced cabbage and half of the salt, and, with your hands, work the salt into the cabbage by squeezing and mixing thoroughly.

Put the salty cabbage into a ceramic crock or a wide-mouth glass jar (wide enough that you can put a plate or ramekin inside). Set the crock on the ground, put a pot lid or plate on top of the cabbage, and lean into it with all your weight to pack the cabbage down. Repeat with the salting, mixing, and packing process with the remaining cabbage. You want the cabbage packed in tight so that the liquid released over the next few hours will more easily cover all the cabbage.

Weigh down the cabbage by putting something heavy on the plate or pot lid you used to press it. (Usually we use a jar filled with water.) Cover the whole thing with a dish towel or cheese cloth and secure it with a rubber band or twine to keep the bugs out. Leave the crock out at room temperature in a spot that does not have a lot of temperature fluctuation. The cabbage will start to release its juices. After a day, check to see if there is enough liquid to cover the cabbage completely, with no bits sticking out. If not, prepare a solution of 1 teaspoon of salt in 1 cup of cool water and pour it over the cabbage until it is covered in liquid. Replace the weight and towel.

Check the kraut regularly, but don't worry if you forget to check for a few days and find mold starting to grow on the surface. Even if the brine does totally cover the cabbage, a few pieces usually float to the surface and get moldy; just remove them.

I like to taste the sauerkraut every few days to see what it's doing. Each batch is a little different, so we go by taste to decide when the sauerkraut is done fermenting. It's actually really tasty in the early stages. After about 3 days, it will taste like raw cabbage with a little bit of a pickle flavor. But you should leave the sauerkraut out to ferment at room temperature for at least 2 weeks, by which time it will taste strong and pickle-y. The cooler your kitchen, the slower the fermentation process will be. When the sauerkraut tastes good to you, remove the weight, cover the crock, and put it in the refrigerator, where it will keep for months. You can transfer the sauerkraut to a smaller container if you need the space in your refrigerator.

HERB JAM

Makes about 3 cups

Herb jam is a great example of how Camino started trying to use up the seemingly unusable parts of vegetables in order to get the most out of them, and then became dependent on that end product—herb jam! Now, somehow, herb jam is on the menu almost every day, and it seems like there is always a steamer full of greens and herbs going in the back, making the kitchen smell like a mysterious country far from here. And it's how I don't feel bad that I spend too much money on vegetables or if I stupidly commit to too many farmers. It is actually *how* I get to spend so much on vegetables. It's also a really good entry point to a waste-free/closed system way of cooking, because every time you buy vegetables, you already have all these ingredients on hand. And it's a great secret weapon to give your food a deeper, more complex flavor. It can be added to yogurty salads or used in our favorite bar snack, aged sheep's milk cheese and herb jam toast.

This is a take on a Paula Wolfert recipe that appeared in her book *The Slow Mediterranean Kitchen*. Paula's recipe calls for specific herbs and greens, but we end up using almost any and all greens, especially those that are at the end of their lives.

It's nice if you use a combination of sweeter greens and stronger greens, plus lots of different herbs (don't use rosemary or sage—they'll take the herb jam in a weird direction).

SWEETER GREENS

Spinach	Cauliflower leaves
Beet tops	Chard leaves and stems
Outer lettuce leaves	Kale

STRONGER GREENS

Fennel tops	Wild nettles
Carrot tops	Outer chicory leaves, like radicchio or escarole

HERBS

Any mint	Chives
Any oregano	Scallions
Basil	Lovage
Savory	Fenugreek (not too much)
Thyme	Cutting celery

1½ pounds various greens and herbs

6 cloves garlic, unpeeled

1 to 2 dried hot chiles

Olive oil

1½ tablespoons cumin seeds, toasted and ground

¼ cup pitted black olives (we use local Kalamatas but niçoise or dry oil-cured olives would work fine)

Lemon

Put the greens and herbs and garlic cloves all together in a steamer set over medium-high heat, and steam until tender, adding water as it evaporates. This could take 20 minutes or 2 hours, depending on what greens you're using. Some of the hardier herb stems will never get tender, so you can remove them later—basically you can't overcook it. Remove both the greens and the garlic from the steamer. Set the garlic aside and chop up the herbs and greens very fine.

Tear the chiles into managable pieces, discarding the stems but keeping the seeds, and place them in a spice grinder. Pulse a few times to create a coarse powder. Heat a pan over medium-high heat and add a splash of olive oil, all the chopped greens, a pinch of salt, the cumin, and the chile. You are trying to develop a

continued on page 26

deep flavor by cooking most of the moisture out of the greens; this will take about 10 minutes. Stir the herb jam mixture often as the water evaporates, as it will want to stick.

Turn the heat off but leave the mixture in the pan. Peel the steamed garlic and mash it into the pan along with the olives. Mix everything up and taste; add salt as needed, a good splash of olive oil, and more chile if it isn't spicy enough.

Herb jam can be stored in the refrigerator, tightly covered, for about 5 days. Right before serving, add a squeeze of lemon.

PRESERVED LEMON

For years, I thought of preserved lemon as a strictly North African ingredient. But at Camino we sneak it into dishes, often in such small amounts that you wouldn't even know it is there. It can add a layer of brightness and lift to a dish without overpowering it. Because preserved lemon is so salty, I often use the chopped pulp to replace some of the salt required in a dish.

Preserved lemon will last for a long time, so it's worth making a big batch when your neighbor brings you lemons that nobody wants. Any variety will work, including Meyer. We like Lisbon lemons specifically grown by Didar from Guru Ram Das Orchards—they are more lemony and the skins are particularly oily; I don't know if that is because of the variety or because of Didar.

Wash the lemons and cut them into quarters vertically, leaving them attached at the stem end so they open up into four pieces. Shove a nice big pinch (almost a tablespoon) of coarse salt into each lemon. Pack as many salted lemons as possible into a jar. Squeeze juice from more lemons and pour it in the

jar to completely cover the lemons. The more tightly packed your lemons are, the less juice you will need. Weigh down the lemons so they stay under the juice level (a ramekin usually works). Cover the jar with a piece of cheesecloth or a dishtowel and a rubber band or some twine to keep the fruit flies out. Leave the jar at room temperature, checking it every so often to make sure all the lemons are still covered in liquid. If mold develops on the surface, just skim it off. After about 1 month, when the lemon skin has softened and the flavor is strong and fermented, put it in the fridge where it will keep at least a year.

Use the salty juice from this batch to start your next. You'll still have to add more fresh lemon juice to cover the lemons, but it will get the process going faster. If you are really a hippie, you can add some of the salty juice to a hibiscus agua fresca. (If you're reading the Larder section you're probably a hippie, so just go ahead and do it.)

NOCINO

Makes about 1 gallon

Nocino is an Italian after-dinner drink that we make every year. It is simple to make but takes patience—like two years' worth of patience. The first thing you need is a source for green walnuts. Find a farmer who grows walnuts; he or she will probably sell you some nuts when they are still green (usually mid-June). They should be full size but tender enough to easily cut with a knife. Be aware that the juices from the walnuts will turn everything greenish black for a couple of weeks: your hands, the cutting board, your kitchen counter. I have an aversion to gloves, but if you don't, you will probably want to wear them. Try nocino on vanilla ice cream or just sip a little bit at the end of a long dinner. We also use it in our Amaro Cocktail (page 246).

7 pounds green walnuts

Zest of 2 oranges

Zest of 1 lemon

1 tablespoon whole juniper berries, crushed

1 teaspoon whole allspice, crushed

5 whole cloves

5 stems of myrtle (optional)

1 gallon high-proof neutral spirit (we use 172-proof spirit made from biodynamic grapes), or the most neutral vodka you can find

3 cups sugar

Cut the walnuts in half and put them in a large glass jar (agua fresca jars work well and look good). Add the citrus zest, juniper, allspice, cloves, and myrtle, and cover the jar with a tight-fitting lid or plastic wrap.

Put the jar in a sunny part of your kitchen or outside. Let it sit for at least 2 months and as long as 4 months. Strain the mixture and discard all the solids. Combine the sugar with 3 cups of water, bring to a boil and let cool. Start by adding two-thirds of the simple syrup to the strained liquid, then taste it. You will likely use all of the simple syrup but keep in mind that the bitterness will ease while the nocino is in the bottle. You have to try to taste through the bitterness to figure out how sweet you want it. I don't like it very sweet, but you need it to be sweet enough or you'll never drink it. Once you feel you have it right, put the nocino in bottles, cork them, and lay them on their sides in a cool dark place for another year and a half to two years. In Italy, the rule of thumb for nocino (started in June) is that it is ready to taste the following Christmas but not actually drinkable until Easter. It will start out very bitter and will slowly change. I really think it is better left for one more year. And, sadly, we have found it's good for about five years and then it starts to decline. So wait . . . then drink up.

INGREDIENTS AND METHODS

SALT

New cooks at Camino find our salt situation confusing: our salt is less "salty" and there is usually a period of palate adjustment for them to go through. I have thought about this a lot—perhaps too much—but it really matters which salt you use. I'm not claiming that I can always tell the difference in a dish, but using good quality salt is one of the many little decisions that add up to something better. Perhaps the difference it makes in a dish is unknowable—maybe it is at the homeopathic level—but when you taste salts side by side the differences are very clear.

We have three different salts at Camino, each with its own purpose:

COARSE CELTIC SEA SALT OR SEL GRIS: This is coarse, minerally, wet, gray sea salt, which has more going on than just saltiness—there is a sense of the ocean! We use this for anything liquid—soups, sauces, polenta, vegetables cooked using the Oil and Water Method (see page 30), and so on. We use it for anything pickled or fermented—sauerkraut, dill pickles, pickled chiles: all the pickling recipes in this book are ratios of water and coarse Celtic sea salt. If you are using a different salt you will have to adjust the ratio of salt to water. We also use it for curing ham, lardo, or pancetta. It's tricky to use because the grains vary in size, but the flavor is great. We also grind it slightly in a food processor and use it as our table salt. Please try it next to kosher salt—you'll find that it is less salty but has more flavor. It will change your life.

FINE CELTIC SEA SALT: This is coarse Celtic sea salt/sel gris that has been dried in an oven and ground finer. It is a little easier to use because the grains are uniform, but the drying process takes away some of the oceanic flavor. We use it for seasoning meat, fish, salads—anything that's not liquidy.

REFINED SEA SALT: This salt is clean with no defining flavors. We use is for salting cooking water that we are going to throw away. We also clean our cast iron pans with it.

COOKING FATS

One of the most confusing things about the Camino kitchen for a new cook is cooking fat. I really want cooks to think about what they are cooking before deciding which fat to use. I also want them to be aware of cost when making their decisions. Deciding how much of which kind of cooking fat to use is part of being mindful of waste—waste of product and waste of flavor.

OLIVE OIL: Good olive oil is expensive, so you don't want to waste any of the flavor. A lot of the recipes in this book call for starting with some olive oil, adding more during the cooking process, and using some to finish the dish. This gives more layered olive oil flavors—cooked oil and fresh oil.

I like our food to feel like it's from California, so using California olive oil is a good start. We use three different olive oils, all extra-virgin: one that is fruity and peppery for dressing salads, in chile sauce and strong herb sauces, and for finishing cooked dishes; one that is prettier and a bit lighter for sweeter herb sauces, herb salad, or anything that is more delicate; and the workhorse oil (a little less expensive but still tasty), which we use for marinades and cooking—including the Oil and Water Method (see page 30)—for brushing on bread and vegetables for grilling, and so on.

RICE BRAN OIL: It's good to have a clean, flavorless refined oil with a high smoke point for hot sautéing and frying. Peanut oil is also good as long as none of your friends has a peanut allergy. Anytime we call for rice bran oil in this book, you can use whatever flavorless refined oil you have in your cupboard. (And when you are done with that bottle, try out some rice bran oil.)

ANIMAL FATS

When you buy whole animals, you can't help but think of every part of them as being equal. If I pay $4.75 a pound for a pig, it is $4.75 for fat, $4.75 for shoulder, and $4.75 for loin. I don't throw away the loin and I don't throw away the fat. We always look for ways to use a little animal fat here and there to make it economical to buy expensive animals.

LARD: When you have pigs, you have lard. Somehow lard has a bad rep. (Maybe the phrase "lard ass" is partly to blame?) What I like about it is that a little goes a long way to add depth to a dish. It works very well for sautéing vegetables over high heat that are going in a braise and it's great for browning meat.

DUCK FAT: Why does duck fat have a better rep than lard? I'm not sure, but I, like the rest of the world, really like it for roasting or frying potatoes. We also use duck fat for sautéing vegetables over high heat and browning meat, just like lard. It sometimes just depends on what we have on hand. Perhaps the best use of duck fat is for preserving various duck parts (see Duck Hearts, Gizzards, and Wings Confit, page 179).

OIL AND WATER METHOD

Blanching vegetables is a very restauranty technique that I try to avoid. Restaurants often use it as a way to cook large amounts of vegetables ahead so then they can reheat them quickly right before serving. But the waste has always bothered me—first off, all that cooking water. And then when you drain the vegetable, you also throw away all the vegetable flavor that got pulled into that water. Not to mention the salt! And then how do you reheat the vegetable? Butter and more water? In some other medium like stock that doesn't taste like the vegetable at all?

The Oil and Water Method came about for the times when we don't want to grill vegetables—either because there is no space in the fireplace or because we want them a little juicier. And I wanted a way to cook vegetables ahead without pouring the precious vegetable flavor down the drain. This method creates a flavorful liquid in which to cook the vegetable, resulting in a delicious vegetable and a delicious liquid. You can rapidly reduce the liquid immediately after cooking to make a sauce or you can rewarm the vegetable with its cooking juices in a pan on the stove or a clay pot set over coals. If you have cooking liquid leftover, it is great for poaching eggs or you can add it to water for cooking dried beans or lentils—you'll find something to do with it. Here's the idea:

In a wide, heavy pan, heat up just enough water to cover your vegetable of choice by about two-thirds. Add a big splash of olive oil, a handful of herb stems or leaves, a few cloves of smashed but unpeeled garlic, and a big pinch of coarse salt. (If you're going to use the liquid as a sauce, peel and slice the garlic.) Bring the mixture to a rolling boil and add the vegetable in one layer. You may need to cook the vegetable in a few batches, which is preferable anyway, as the cooking liquid improves—though more than three rounds makes the liquid a bit mucky and sweet. Cook until done, stirring often. The idea is to have just enough liquid to get everything cooked without diluting the flavor. If it seems really easy to cook everything evenly, you have too much water: you should be stirring and flipping and tasting the whole time—this is active cooking!

If all goes well, the vegetable and the cooking liquid should both end up with perfect seasoning. Vegetables that take a long time to cook, like cardoons or burdock, will require less salt because they will be cooking longer—remember, the liquid is reducing the whole time so you have to think about how that will affect the saltiness. This also means that if you are doing more than one batch, you should check the liquid for salt at each round to see if it's getting too strong—you may have to add a splash of water.

Once the vegetables are cooked, lift them out with a slotted spoon or strainer and set them aside in a bowl. If you are serving them right away, pick out any herb stems from the liquid, turn up the heat and reduce until the liquid thickens slightly. Spoon the liquid over the vegetables and serve.

If you are serving later, spread them out to cool at room temperature. Cool the cooking liquid to room temperature separately, then store the vegetables in the cooking liquid. To reheat, bring the mixture to a boil. Continue boiling for a moment—long enough to create an emulsion between the oil and water—and serve with some or all of the liquid.

With this method, it is hard to retain the bright green color of green legumes, such as English peas, fava beans, and green beans. To help with this, you will need to cook them really quickly and, if you are not using them immediately, scoop them out of the liquid, spread them out on a plate or tray, and put them in the refrigerator to quickly cool.

STOCK AND SAUCE

Stocks and sauces are tricky subjects for this book. They are so essential to how we cook and to what ends up on your plate at Camino that I feel I have to include them. That said, I'm not sure I would make stock and sauce at home. But this book is not about how I cook at home (if it were, there would be a long chapter about yogurt and granola and all its variations). This book is about how we cook at Camino, and how we cook in a grandmotherly and economical way. And how, when you get whole animals, you have bones and those bones have value—not to be wasted.

Many restaurants make stock every day and they buy extra bones to do it. We don't. We make stock from the bones of the animals whose meat we serve for dinner. Using bones from whole animals at home will be easy with chickens and ducks and fish. Lamb and pork bones will be more challenging if you're not buying whole animals or animal shares, but your butcher will sell them to you—maybe even give them to you.

BLOND STOCK: This is made by simmering raw vegetables and uncooked bones and scraps in water. It is usually made from poultry but can be made from any animal. At Camino, we use it for soup or to replace water when we are making a meat braise.

The classic vegetables for stock are onions, celery, and carrots. My favorite ratio is one part onion to one part celery and carrot combined. Leeks can also be used, but include them in the onion section of the ratio. Cut everything into large slices—you're going to cook these for a long time so there's no need to cut them small. As far as quantity goes, less is better, but you are shooting for five parts bones and scraps to one part vegetables (including onions). Too many vegetables will make your stock sweet.

Put the cut vegetables in a pot and put the bones and scraps on top of them. Barely cover with cold water. Bring to a simmer (but not a boil) over high heat, then turn the heat down to low. Using a large ladle, skim off some of the fat and foamy stuff that comes to the surface. Don't dive in with the ladle: hold it level with the surface of the stock and move it around, letting the fat and foam fall into it. Once you've given it a good skimming, throw in a small handful of herbs—it's easier to skim without stems floating around. The classic herbs for stock are parsley stems, thyme, and bay, but you can also consider using winter and summer savory or a small amount of lovage or cutting celery. I usually add a crushed garlic clove or two (this is a good place to use the super small cloves you don't want to peel). I don't add peppercorns at this stage—if the final dish needs pepper, I'll add it at the end. I was traumatized at a young age by reading Richard Olney's thoughts on adding pepper to liquids too early; read *Simple French Food* if you want to be similarly shaken. Keep the stock at a gentle to medium simmer and skim it when you walk by or when you notice an accumulation of fat; about every 15 minutes

continued

or so should do. For poultry stocks, continue cooking for 3 to 4 hours. Pork, lamb, or goat stock can go for 5 or 6 hours; beef stock can go as long as 8 to 12 hours if you want a really gelatinous texture. Fish stock is made like a blond stock except that the vegetables are cut thinner and sweated for a few minutes because the cooking time for the stock is much shorter, about 45 minutes to an hour.

Strain the stock first with something with larger holes to get all the big pieces out, then strain with something finer—this is actually easier than just straining it once through something fine.

You can refrigerate the stock if you are going to use it in a few days, or freeze it for up to a month.

BROWN STOCK: This is similar to blond stock with the additional steps of browning the vegetables, roasting the bones and meat scraps, and deglazing the pan to make a roastier stock that you can use to make sauce.

Roast the bones and meat scraps in a roasting pan in a 450°F oven until brown. While the bones are roasting, brown the vegetables in a stock pot—the same vegetables as for blond stock with the possible addition of tomato if it makes sense for the final dish. Once the vegetables are brown, add the roasted bones and scraps to the stock pot. Cover with cold water and bring to a simmer over high heat. Skim, and add the herbs.

While the stock is heating up, deglaze the roasting pan. Ladle in enough water to barely cover the bottom of the pan. Heat the roasting pan on the stove to loosen the browned bits. Scrape them up with a wooden spoon and add the liquid and the browned bits to the stock pot. Deglazing is critical because much of the flavor and color of your stock comes from these pans.

Continue the same routine of simmering, skimming, and straining as for blond stock.

SAUCE: This is made by reducing brown stock. This seems like an indulgence at home. But we do it all the time at Camino, so I feel like I have to include it. Plus, it's something of a lost art, a holdover from fancy French restaurants of the 1970s. If you are into it, consider reducing brown stock to make sauce for grilled meats—we do this because, for one, we have a constant supply of bones, but also because we always rest meat after we grill it. Obviously, the meat is going to cool while it's resting, but a ladle of sauce will heat it right up so it's ready to serve.

To make sauce out of brown stock, add a glass of wine for every gallon of stock—red or white depending on the final dish. Reduce over medium-high heat, skimming often so the fat doesn't emulsify into the stock, which dulls the flavor. Continue reducing until the sauce is thick enough to coat the meat but is short of sticky. Season with salt.

We also use brown stock to reinforce meat braising juices for sauce. Braising juices on their own are already seasoned, so you can only reduce them so much before they become too salty, therefore they are always a little thin for sauce. Reducing braising juices with the addition of brown stock lets you make the most luxurious sauce because it has both the body from the bones in the brown stock and the complex seasoning from the braise. In this book, for the recipes where we would make sauce from brown stock and braising juices at Camino, it's given as an option rather than a required part of the recipe. You'll see the suggestions in Pork Shoulder Cooked with Milk, Lemon, and Myrtle (page 204), Slow-Cooked Duck Legs with Savoy Cabbage, Prunes, and Duck Cracklings (page 178), and Slow-Cooked Lamb Shoulder with Greens, Yogurt, Chiles, Ciantro, and Basil (page 194). It is an extra step for an indulgent improvement in your dinner, but is absolutely not necessary.

At Camino, we don't make vegetable stock. It always seems too sweet to me and I'd rather use water. I also like to use the cooking liquid left over from the Oil and Water Method (see page 30) in place of vegetable stock, because it gives you the singular flavor of that vegetable without the sweetness.

BREADCRUMBS

I'd rather you didn't make any of the recipes in this book that require breadcrumbs if it means you are going to buy fresh bread just for that one recipe. Please make breadcrumbs with leftover bread!

Cut up whatever ends or slices you have, put them on a baking sheet, and dry them out in your oven heated just by the pilot light. Depending on the ferocity of your pilot light, the bread should be rock hard after a day or two. Grind it in a food processor and store the crumbs in one of the many empty yogurt containers you have laying around. Don't refrigerate. If somehow you don't use them, and the crumbs begin to get moldy, throw them out—you gave it a good shot!

P.S. Use any kind of bread that you have.

TOASTED SESAME SEEDS

Warm up a pan over medium heat. Add the sesame seeds and turn the pan down to just above low. Shake the pan once in a while until the sesame seeds begin to get a little color, then shake the pan constantly because they can easily burn. Cook the sesame seeds until they are a few shades darker and very aromatic. When the sesame seeds are done they should fall apart easily when rubbed between your fingers.

If you are toasting black sesame seeds I suggest doing it mixed with some white sesame seeds so you can see what's going on.

CHAPTER TWO

VEGETABLES

VEGETABLES

I love when I come across the words "Organic when possible" in that sophisticated little font at the bottom of a menu. Really? When possible? In the Bay Area, it's always possible.

I'm stubborn about this. I haven't bought a non-organic vegetable since the last millennium. Pay five cents more per pound. Make another phone call. Or go without that vegetable for two more weeks. It's just not that hard.

At Camino, we're trying to give people an enjoyable meal. But it just doesn't make sense to make the world worse for it. If that dinner is going to dump more petrochemicals in the water and deplete more soil and put small farmers out of business with more Monsanto monocrops—well, I should just get a job that pays well instead.

Which makes me sound driven by principle. But it comes down to something more elemental than that. When you come to Camino and have a vegetable, you should be excited about it and I should be excited about it. That excitement has a thousand threads—groovy soil balance and responsible aphid management being just a couple of them. And those threads all connect; that's the thrill of a restaurant. It's the thrill of buying produce from interesting people doing interesting things, and of getting the best flavors as a result, and of navigating the challenges baked into those decisions. Shortcuts erode that thrill.

A big chunk of my life is devoted to getting produce for the restaurant. I could buy everything from a distributor—a dedicated organic distributor, no less—in just one phone call. But I don't see how you can write a strong menu if you're not interacting directly with farmers and knowing exactly what's going on with their produce. As I write this, peaches have been around at the market for a month—but I don't want them yet, because I'm familiar enough with them, and with certain looks on certain farmers' faces, to know that the varieties available are too sweet and low acid at this point. There's no shortcut for that information.

Writing a new menu each night is central to our approach. It means we don't get locked in with a certain vegetable, which in turn lets us support small farmers better. This sounds straightforward, but it's rare. I remember going with Allison to a fancy restaurant, where we had this amazing dish involving a vegetable I shall not name, which they grew in their garden. I was blown away. Later, touring their garden, I asked what they'd do when that vegetable ran out.

"Oh, we'll just buy some from the distributor," they said.

What? Seriously? Here was this terrific and absolutely loaded restaurant saying they're fine with produce that's less fresh and that's outside their relationship with their garden. It absolutely negated the wonderfulness of that dish for me. I kept thinking, *Why not just think of a new dish?*

Flexibility is just as essential in our treatment of vegetables as in our procurement of them. I once snapped at a seasoned cook for cutting roasted peppers before we'd nailed down the details of the dish. He was doing exactly what you're supposed to do in a restaurant—getting a leg up by prepping a food that's always prepped the same way. Except not at Camino. Everything's up in the air here until it's not. I spent my whole adult life learning the cooking traditions that bring the best out of each vegetable—and now I work just as hard to branch out from those traditions. The more mutable we can keep things, well, the crazier things will be for us. But they'll also be the better and more interesting—for us and for everyone we work with and feed.

When we get a vegetable I don't know, I experiment a lot to get acquainted with it. We started using burdock a few years ago. It's this root that's often pickled and served in futomaki— that's all I knew about it. So we just bought a box and started messing with it in every possible way. I never want someone to whip a phone out and research it. Ruins the moment. At last, we tried shaving it thin and frying it. It was great. I later realized that's already a thing—it's what everyone did in the 1980s, but I like the process of figuring it out ourselves.

And, of course, nothing makes me happier than experimenting with one vegetable while using up what remains of another. A few months ago I found myself thinking about cold beet soup. I didn't know what I wanted to do, exactly, so I just had one of the cooks cook me some beets. Evening was approaching and, still without a plan, I was heading reflexively toward borscht. But I think borscht is best with a meat stock, and this needed to be a vegetarian dish. So I wandered into the walk-in, which is often where the solution lies.

On one of the shelves was a bunch of sauerkraut—and sauerkraut juice—that we weren't sure what to do with. It hit me that I could use the juice as the salt for the beets. It was the most exciting thing in the world to me. I added some cabbage to keep it from being too strong, and some sauerkraut, and brought it to a boil. Then I started worrying it would be too stark, like a tonic. Back to the walk-in. This time I saw all these mushroom butts, which we hadn't gotten a chance to use for consommé yet. So I chopped them all up, tied them in cheesecloth—I didn't want the actual mushrooms in there, just their flavor—and brought them to a boil in the soup. A little salt, some extra pickling juice—it was the best thing I'd made in a long time. We played it like it was borscht, with crème fraîche and grated horseradish, and made it six days in a row.

Some days our food is better than other days. I think that's okay. I don't want to make the kinds of compromises necessary to change that. I want our diners to have a wonderful plate of food every time—but are we ever going to be as consistent as some of those three-star places? No way. I'm glad for that. To me, it means we're doing right by our vegetables—and, I think, right by everyone who comes into contact with them, too.

AVOCADO, PUNTARELLE, AND RADISH SALAD WITH POPPED MUSTARD SEED AND PRESERVED LEMON

Serves 4 to 6

Puntarelle is a Roman chicory valued for its light green crunchy stems. In Rome, it is *always* cut into strips and soaked in ice water to make the stems curl. And it is *always* dressed with anchovy, lemon, and garlic. We cut and soak the puntarelle just like the Italians do, but we dress it like we are Californians who have Tunisian and Indian friends.

Puntarelle is a little bitter so you want to dress it with something strong like the Italians do, with anchovy, or like we do, with preserved lemon and mustard seeds. For this salad, we make two dressings, one for the puntarelle and radishes, the other for the avocado. I like the avocado to have a dressing without acid; and this one uses all of the preserved lemon—pulp and peel.

    1 head puntarelle (about 1½ pounds)

    1 bunch radishes

    1 large clove garlic

    ¼ preserved lemon, including pulp

    2 lemons

    Olive oil

    1½ teaspoons brown or yellow mustard seeds

    1 small shallot or spring onion

    Salt

    2 avocados

    Pepper

You are going to use all the light-green-colored parts of the puntarelle, including the heart, which looks like mutant asparagus from outer space. Break off the stems of the puntarelle at the base of the plant. Trim off all the dark green leaves, cut the stems into 2-inch lengths and julienne them into thin strips. Put the strips in ice water so they curl. Cut the heart into

the same size strips as the stems and add them to the ice water. Discard any tough parts. Slice the radishes thinly and set aside.

Notice at this point that you have puntarelle greens and radish tops that are not going into this salad. You can cook the bitter puntarelle greens with garlic and olive oil and put them on a toast with Duck Hearts, Gizzards and Wings Confit (page 179) or some aged sheep's milk cheese. Or you can use them and the radish tops in a frittata, or to make Herb Jam (page 23).

For the dressing for the puntarelle and radishes, pound the clove of garlic in a mortar and add the chopped pulp of the preserved lemon. Juice 1½ of the lemons directly into the mortar with the preserved lemon and garlic. Stir to mix.

Heat a small pan over high heat for a few seconds, add enough olive oil to cover the bottom of the pan, and add the mustard seeds. Swirl the pan until the mustard seeds begin to pop, cover the pan so the seeds don't escape, and reduce the heat to low. After about 30 seconds, you'll hear the popping slow. Pour the seeds and oil into a bowl to cool for a few minutes. Once cool, add the seeds and oil to the lemon mixture and add more olive oil so you have about three parts oil to one part lemon juice.

To make the dressing for the avocado, slice the preserved lemon rind into very thin slices about ¼ inch long. Slice the shallot the same size. Barely cover with olive oil.

To make the salad, take the puntarelle out of the ice water and spin it in a salad spinner. Put it into a bowl, add the sliced radish, and pour over some of the preserved lemon–mustard seed dressing. Taste it before adding salt because the preserved lemon pulp might be enough. Add more dressing, lemon, or oil as needed. I think it's nice if it's not too acidic, so you taste the preserved lemon.

Slice or scoop the avocados out of their skins onto a platter and season with salt and pepper. Spoon the preserved lemon peel–shallot dressing over them. Set the dressed puntarelle and radishes alongside.

TOMATO SALAD WITH YOGURT AND HERB JAM

Serves 6

1 small clove garlic

Salt

1 teaspoon Red Wine Vinegar (page 17)

Herb Jam (page 23)

Olive oil

6 tablespoons whole milk yogurt

3 large tomatoes (about 1 pound)

½ pint cherry tomatoes (about 6 ounces)

3 small scallions, white and green parts

Lime wedges, for serving

Peel the garlic and pound it with some salt in a mortar. If your tomatoes are perfect, you may not need to add any vinegar to the dressing at all. If your tomatoes are less than perfect, splash the vinegar right into the mortar. Add ¼ teaspoon of herb jam and a few tablespoons of olive oil.

Spoon the yogurt onto a platter (or divide it among individual salad plates). Spoon a couple of tablespoons of herb jam onto the yogurt in random little plops. It's nice if you get a bite of salad with some herb jam in it and then on the next bite you don't.

Cut the cores out of the large tomatoes, cut the tomatoes vertically into slices, and set them on top of the herb jam and yogurt in a single layer. Season them with a good amount of salt. I think tomatoes taste better when they're a little saltier than you think they need to be.

Slice the cherry tomatoes through their north and south poles (to keep the juices inside) and season with salt. Pour the dressing over them and taste. Adjust with oil, vinegar, and salt, as needed. Spoon them over the tomato slices.

Split the scallions lengthwise, if they're big, and slice them thinly on the diagonal. Scatter them over the tomatoes. Serve the salad with wedges of lime on the side, for squeezing on the tomatoes at the last moment.

SMASHED CUCUMBER WITH CHILES AND MINT

Serves 6

2 pounds thin-skinned cucumbers, such as Persian or Japanese cucumbers, stem ends trimmed

Coarse salt and fine salt

1 clove garlic

½ lemon

½ lime

Leaves from 2 sprigs spearmint

1 spring onion, or ½ bunch scallions

3 tablespoons olive oil

A small handful of other herbs, such as chervil, anise hyssop, sorrel, or perilla

1 or 2 Pickled Chiles (page 19), chopped, or dried moderately hot chiles, ground

1 tablespoon Toasted Sesame Seeds (see page 33)

Crispy Flatbread (page 11)

Rinse the cucumbers and dry them well. Toss them in a bowl with enough coarse salt to lightly coat. Rub each cucumber to rough up the skin a little bit, then set them aside for a few minutes.

Put the cucumbers on a work surface and use a pestle or the heel of your hand to whack them. You don't want them to completely fall apart, but you do want to break them up a bit. With a knife, split them lengthwise, then cut crosswise on the diagonal into chunky pieces. Return them all to the bowl and season with fine salt. The cucumbers need to be strongly seasoned because they are cut into such big pieces.

continued

Pound the garlic with a pinch of fine salt in a mortar. Juice the lemon and lime directly into the mortar, then slice the spearmint and add it as well. Stir a bit to mix. Pour the minty, garlicky citrus juice over the cucumbers. Trim the roots of the spring onion, but keep the green tops attached. Split lengthwise, then slice crosswise on the diagonal into very thin slices. Add them to the cucumbers along with the olive oil, other herbs, and pickled chiles, and toss well. The idea is for the smashed cucumber pieces to be really spicy and salty on the outside but fresh and clean on the inside. Taste a few pieces and then let them sit for at least 15 minutes, and up to several hours.

Just before serving, sprinkle the toasted sesame seeds over the cucumbers. Serve with crispy flatbread.

———

GRILLED BELGIAN ENDIVE WITH FRESH TURMERIC AND WALNUTS

Serves 6

There is just one little moment of trickiness with this sauce: the garlic and fresh turmeric should sizzle and cook in the hot oil without browning—or, even worse, burning. If you keep a glass of water within reach, it should be no problem. A splash of water helps cool down everything and it also helps disperse the turmeric flavor and color.

Olive oil

4 cloves garlic, thinly sliced

1 thumb-size piece fresh turmeric, peeled and cut into a fine julienne

1/8 teaspoon nigella seeds

1/4 cup walnuts

Salt

4 heads Belgian endive

1 lime

Preheat oven to 350°F.

Build a fire to grill the Belgian endive.

Spread the walnuts on a baking sheet and toast them in the oven until they are a shade darker, about 8 minutes. Once they are cool, wrap them in a dish towel and peel some of the skins off. Chop them coarsely and set them aside.

To make the sauce, heat a small pan over medium heat. Add enough olive oil to coat the bottom of the pan, then add the garlic and turmeric and immediately begin to shake the pan so that the garlic and turmeric sizzle. You want the turmeric and garlic to spend a moment or two in the hot oil, but you really don't want them to get brown at all. Once they have sizzled for a few seconds, add the nigella, give the pan another quick shake, and add a couple of tablespoons of water. The whole thing should bubble for another few seconds, and all the liquid will turn bright yellow. Pour the contents of the pan into a bowl, using a rubber spatula to get as much out of the pan as possible. Add a pinch of salt, let cool for a moment, then add the walnuts and another couple tablespoons of oil. Set aside.

To grill the endive, rake the coals under the grill for medium-hot grilling. Remove any brown or wilted outer leaves from the endive heads and cut them lengthwise into quarters. Brush all sides with olive oil and sprinkle with salt. Depending on the size of the endive, they should take 12 to 15 minutes to cook.

Grilling Belgian endive can be difficult because it is fairly dense and also a little bit sweet. That means it wants to get brown really fast without cooking all the way through, but you also don't want the endive to be pale and gray. Ultimately, it should have a little crunch, but not a lot. To achieve this, you want the endive to spend most of the grilling time on the two cut sides so the heat can reach the interior and not too much time on the leafy side, where it will brown too quickly. You also should check when you first turn them to see how fast they are browning. You can

continued

always move the endive to a different part of the grill if it is going too fast or too slow. Or, if you are using a grill with some access, like a Tuscan grill, you can spread the coals out more thinly or pile them up under the vegetables. Remember, if you are paying attention, you can control everything almost immediately on a grill by moving the coals.

One more thing. The endive will look best if you have one clean set of grill marks on each side: that means you can move the endive quarters when you flip them to a different side, but try not to move them on the same side: they'll taste fine but they won't look as nice.

To serve, place the grilled endive on a platter. Spoon the sauce over the top and squeeze a little bit of lime juice over as well. This dish also tastes good at room temperature. If you serve it that way, wait until the last moment to add the sauce and squeeze the lime.

――――

KABOCHA SQUASH AND GRILLED NEW ONION SALAD WITH YOGURT, POMEGRANATE, AND ALMONDS

Serves 6

This is a salad with a lot of different flavors and textures. I like the combination of the earthy, nutty kabocha with the bright, tangy flavors of yogurt and pomegranate. At Camino, we put a few myrtle leaves in the water that is used to steam the kabocha. They give this subtle, piney flavor to the squash. But they can totally be omitted if you don't have access to myrtle. (I mean, who does?) I prefer the denser gray kabocha, but green or red will work.

  1 small kabocha squash (about 2 pounds)

  Salt

  2 spring onions

  Olive oil

  ½ cup pomegranate juice

  ¼ cup almonds

  ½ bunch parsley, stemmed

  2 sprigs oregano, stemmed

  1 clove garlic

  ⅓ cup whole milk yogurt

Preheat oven to 350°F.

Build a fire to grill the spring onions.

Peel the kabocha with a vegetable peeler, then cut it in half and remove the seeds. Cut into ¾-inch-thick wedges, sprinkle with a pinch of salt, and arrange in a single layer in a steamer. Steam until just tender, about 20 minutes, then let cool to room temperature.

Cut the spring onions in half lengthwise, leaving the roots intact to hold them together. Rake the coals under the grill for medium-hot grilling. Brush both sides with olive oil and sprinkle with salt. Place the spring onions cut side down on the grill and cook them until they are satisfyingly brown and have nice, dark grill marks, about 4 minutes. Turn them over and grill for another few minutes on the second side. Move them to a cooler part of the grill and pile them into a little tangle to steam for 3 more minutes. Remove from the grill and let cool.

Boil the pomegranate juice in a pot until it is thick and has reduced to about 1 tablespoon. While the pomegranate juice is reducing, spread the almonds on a baking sheet and toast them in the oven until they are a shade darker, about 8 minutes. Once they are cool, taste them to make sure they are crunchy. If not, pop them back in the oven for a few more minutes. Chop them coarsely and add to the reduced juice along with the parsley, oregano, a pinch of salt, and enough olive oil to cover the nuts and herbs.

Peel the garlic and pound it in a mortar until smooth. Mix with the yogurt.

Spoon the garlicky yogurt onto a plate and arrange the steamed kabocha wedges on top. Drape the grilled spring onions over the kabocha, then spoon the herby, nutty, pomegranatey mixture on top.

THE LUXURY OF HERBS

People ask where the inspiration for our dishes comes from. The answer, in many cases: across the street, past the old video store, and up the hill a ways.

We have a lot of excellent neighbors at Camino. We have one particularly awesome neighbor who, not long after we opened, came by and asked if we'd be interested in any herbs. She had a big yard, and apparently an inattentive neighbor with a big yard, too. Absentmindedly, I rattled off some exotic names and never thought of it again.

Until several months later, when this kindly woman showed up bearing *rau ram*, anise hyssop, fenugreek, summer savory, lovage, and more. The flavors were insane. Fresh fenugreek! I'd never really cooked with it. We started experimenting, and in very little time fresh herbs—the freshest, the local-est—had become a core component of Camino's menu, and something people associated us with.

Plenty of places use fresh herbs—what's the big deal? At Camino, I think part of the big deal comes down to mindset. We think of our herbs the way other restaurants think of foie gras: as a luxury item. The height of luxury, to us, is a salad of just fresh herbs. Chervil, sorrel, and anise hyssop, for instance, thrown together with Persian mint, tarragon, and maybe chrysanthemum. And when we're cooking with herbs,

we often cook with them from the start of the recipe, rather than just throwing them on, garnish-like, at the end.

Like any luxury, this one is born of rareness. Historically, it was no small thing to possess all of these herbs at the same time, each fresh and bright in flavor. Combined, they are just exquisite. I'll never stop feeling super excited about being able to put them in a bowl together. There's an inherent fanciness to herbs; they know this in Korea and in Mexico. Good *pho* places know this, with their piles of *rau ram*, basil, and cilantro. Chris and Tim, the herb growers up the hill, know it—you should see their yard.

There are some easy ways to acquaint yourself with an herb. Start by tasting them raw and separately. Mix them with a frittata, or a scrambled egg. Butter lettuce is great for highlighting what an herb tastes like.

SHEEP'S MILK RICOTTA GRILLED IN A FIG LEAF WITH HERB SALAD AND TARRAGON TOAST

Serves 6

For this recipe, your grill needs to be hot enough that the fig leaves burn fairly quickly so you get the smoky coconut flavor from the leaves before the cheese gets too soft. You'll need ricotta that has been drained in a basket so it is firm enough to slice. If you can't find drained ricotta, you can use loose ricotta but you should bake it instead of grilling it. Line each of six ramekins with a fig leaf, add a scoop of ricotta, and bake it in a 500°F oven until the leaves burn on the edges.

3 stalks green garlic

Olive oil

Salt

3 sprigs tarragon, stemmed

Bread for grilling, cut ¾ inch thick

A handful of mixed picked herb leaves, such as Persian mint, parsley, chives, basil, purple basil, or chervil, for the ricotta packets

1 pound sheep's milk ricotta

Black pepper

6 fig leaves

3 handfuls of mixed herbs, such as chervil, Persian mint, sorrel, anise hyssop, cilantro, or parsley, for the herb salad

Lemon juice

Build a fire to grill the ricotta.

While the coals are getting ready, prepare the green garlic for the toast. Trim the roots off the green garlic and cut off the leaves about an inch past where they branch. Remove any tough outer layers. Split the stalks lengthwise, then rinse them under running water. Slice them on the diagonal ⅓-inch thick.

Heat a small pan over high heat. Pour in enough olive oil to liberally cover the bottom of the pan, then add the garlic and some salt. Stir it once, then immediately add a splash of water to prevent burning. Cook the garlic for a few minutes, until it is tender. You can add another splash of water if the liquid is evaporating too quickly and the garlic isn't done yet. The goal is to have bright green, tender garlic that isn't brown at all. Just before the garlic is done, add the tarragon, then spread the green garlic-tarragon mixture on a plate to cool.

Chop the herbs for the ricotta packets. Cut the ricotta into six equal pieces that can each be wrapped up almost entirely in a fig leaf. Brush the cheese with olive oil, season with salt and pepper, and sprinkle with the chopped herbs. Fold the fig leaves around the cheese, shiny side facing in. Don't worry if some corners of cheese are sticking out. Brush the cut sides of the bread uniformly with olive oil.

When the coals are ready, rake them under the grill for hot grilling. Set the packets on the grill, folded side down. Cook until the edges of the leaves start to burn, about 3 minutes, then carefully flip and grill the second side for another 2 minutes. Don't worry if the leaves start to unfurl a little. Grill the bread at the same time, about 1 minute on each side, until it's crispy on the outside with a few black spots but still soft in the middle.

To serve, put one packet on each plate, peel back the leaves a little bit and drizzle some more oil on top of the cheese. Spread the green garlic-tarragon mixture on the grilled bread and add a piece to each plate.

Pick the herbs for the salad, leaving some of the tender stems, especially chervil and parsley—this will help the salad feel fluffier. Tear the leaves of stronger herbs, like anise hyssop and sorrel. Combine the salad herbs in a bowl and dress with just enough oil to barely coat. Sprinkle with a pinch of salt and a little lemon juice, then delicately toss everything together so that each leaf is lightly dressed and put a handful on each plate.

Don't eat the fig leaf!

BUTTER LETTUCE SALAD WITH HOMEMADE VINEGAR AND HERBS

Serves 4 to 6

Because this salad is so simple, it can be really difficult to get right. There is no place to hide. Every step of making it is important, from how you wash and dry the lettuce to how you toss the lettuce with the vinaigrette. We only make this salad with perfect butter lettuce from Blue Heron Farms, our own vinegar, and delicious California olive oil from our friends at Pacific Sun.

Our vinegar is strong and flavorful, so we use a higher ratio of olive oil to vinegar in our dressing. This helps create the right consistency to coat the lettuce leaves well with less vinaigrette. If the vinegar you're using isn't super strong, you'll have to up the amount of vinegar to get the flavor right—another reason to make extra sure your lettuce leaves are dried well.

   1 large butter lettuce head, or 2 smaller heads

   1 small clove garlic

   Salt

   Red Wine Vinegar (page 17)

   Olive oil

   A small handful of chopped soft, sweet herbs, such as chervil, mint, anise hyssop, tarragon, or chives, in any combination

   Black pepper

Trim the base and remove the outer leaves of the lettuce, reserving them for another purpose. (We save them for sautéing with peas, which is one of my favorite classic combinations, and, of course, herb jam!) Trim a little bit more off the base and let the leaves fall into a large bowl of cool water. Continue trimming and gently pulling the head apart into individual leaves, trying not to manhandle the lettuce. Swish the leaves around in the water to release any dirt. You can dry the lettuce using the Frenchie-roll-them-up-in-a-towel method, but it's really hard to get the leaves all the way dry—which is what you want here. I think a salad spinner works well if you don't fill it up too much, so do it in batches. After spinning the lettuce dry, tear the biggest leaves in two and throw all the lettuce into a bowl with a towel in the bottom, then cover with another towel just to soak up any last drops of water. Chill the clean lettuce until you're ready to serve the salad.

To make the vinaigrette, pound the garlic with a pinch of salt in a mortar. I always make the vinaigrette right in the mortar by stirring in a splash of vinegar and then adding the olive oil. Because Camino vinegar is super strong, I add about four times as much olive oil as vinegar, but your ratio might be different. I think it tastes better if it's not emulsified, so don't bother with a whisk. After you stir it, dip a piece of lettuce into the dressing and taste it for acid and salt. Adjust as needed.

To dress the salad, toss the herbs into the bowl of lettuce. Sprinkle a little salt and a few grinds of pepper over the leaves. Using a small ladle, start by dressing the lettuce lightly. The goal is to just barely coat every leaf. Gently but thoroughly toss the salad with your hands, touching every leaf at least once, then taste, and add a bit more vinaigrette and another pinch of salt, if necessary. Serve right away.

MATSUTAKE MUSHROOM AND FRESH FLAGEOLET BEAN RAGOÛT WITH OYSTERS AND WILD NETTLES

Serves 4 as a fancy first course

Until recently I had not used matsutake mushrooms that much—I mostly thought of them as a Japanese ingredient. But since they grow locally, I imagined a uniquely California scenario for this dish: a dusty, hungry, failed gold miner hiking in the Sierra foothills discovering a patch of this strange piney mushroom near a patch of annoying stinging nettles. There was nothing else for dinner, so he put his rusty pot over the campfire and put the mushrooms and wild nettles in it, along with a can of beans. A fellow miner came by the campsite with a few oysters he foraged out of the San Francisco Bay, so they tossed those in, too.

Back to reality, I realize the chances are remote that you are going to come across matsutake, wild nettles, and fresh flageolet beans at the same time, but there's a short window when these ingredients overlap around here. Wild nettles are the same as stinging nettles, but they lose their sting on contact with heat—just be careful handling them before you cook them—some people are more sensitive than others. Although the inception of this dish started with Forty-Niners and panning for gold, it is actually quite fancy. The matsutake add an almost briny flavor to the beans that is echoed by the oysters. Because of the distinctive flavors, you definitely want to serve this dish on its own—or maybe with some Crispy Flatbread (page 11).

12 ounces fresh flageolet beans in the pod

3 cloves garlic

1 bay leaf

Salt

½ bunch scallions

8 ounces matsutake mushrooms

A big handful of wild nettles

12 oysters

Olive oil

Preheat your oven to 500°F or as hot as it can safely go.

Shell the flageolet beans and place them into a small pot. Smash but don't peel one of the garlic cloves and add it and the bay leaf to the beans. Cover with ½ inch of water, add a pinch of salt, and place over high heat. Once the beans come to a simmer, turn the heat down and continue to cook until tender, about 10 to 15 minutes. You want these beans a little soupy, so if they start poking out, just add more water. The beans and broth should both taste seasoned at this point. Set the beans aside while you get the rest of the ingredients together.

Slice the remaining two cloves of garlic. Trim and clean the scallions and cut into 1-inch lengths. If they are large, split them in half first. If you already have a fire going for some reason, you can grill the scallions, but I wouldn't start a fire just for them. So if not, sauté the scallions and sliced garlic together for a couple of minutes over medium heat. Spoon them into a 10-inch *cazuela* or other baking dish.

To clean the matsutake, scrape them with a knife and give them a wipe with a damp cloth, if they need it. Slice them thinly and lay them over the scallion-garlic mixture. Cut the wild nettles into 2-inch pieces and set them on top of the mushrooms. Pour the flageolets and all their juices over everything. Shuck the oysters, pouring the oyster liquor over the beans. Set the shucked oysters aside. The mixture should be loose but not soupy. If it is dense and dry, add a small splash of water.

Put the *cazuela* in the oven and bake until the juices just come to a slight simmer, about 12 minutes. Check the seasoning, then add the shucked oysters. Cook for another 2 minutes and taste again for seasoning. Drizzle a couple of tablespoons of olive oil over the top and serve directly from the baking dish.

FRIED HEN-OF-THE-WOODS MUSHROOMS, SCALLIONS, AND HERBS WITH YOGURT AND GREEN GARLIC

Serves 6 as a first course or 4 as a main course

The vegetables and herbs are all fried in an Indian pakora batter based on the method and ratio I stole from Niloufer Ichaporia King's book, *My Bombay Kitchen.* But I change up the spice mixture every time I make it (because I can't actually follow a recipe!). You can serve this as a snacky first course or as a main course with Red Lentils (page 10) or Cooked Greens (page 13).

> 1 cup brown rice flour
>
> 1 cup garbanzo flour
>
> ¼ teaspoon baking soda
>
> Salt
>
> 2 dried moderately hot chiles
>
> 1 teaspoon fennel seeds
>
> 1 teaspoon black peppercorns
>
> 1 cluster hen-of-the-woods mushrooms (maitake)
>
> 1 bunch scallions
>
> 1 small stalk green garlic
>
> 1 cup whole milk yogurt
>
> Rice bran oil or other neutral oil, for frying
>
> Bubbly water
>
> Handfuls of herbs, such as chrysanthemum leaves, cutting celery leaves, piccolo fine basil, or Italian Parsley

Prepare the batter by tossing together the rice flour, garbanzo flour, baking soda, and ½ teaspoon of salt.

Tear the chiles into manageable pieces, discarding the stems but keeping the seeds, and place them in a spice grinder. Pulse a few times to create a coarse powder. Grind the fennel and peppercorns in the grinder as well, and add them and the chiles to the flour mixture.

Trim the base of the mushroom cluster and break it up into petals. The bottom stems shouldn't be much thicker than ½ inch. Trim the scallion roots and peel away any outer layers that look bad. If your scallions are very young, you can fry them whole. Otherwise, cut them into 3-inch-long pieces. Set aside a few of these for the yogurt sauce.

To make the yogurt sauce, pound the garlic with a pinch of salt in a mortar and pestle. Stir it into the yogurt, along with a pinch of ground chile. Slice the reserved scallions and add them to the yogurt.

Pour at least 3 inches of oil into a heavy-bottomed pot and heat to 350°F.

While the oil is heating up, toss the mushrooms with a pinch of the flour-spice mixture to coat them a little because otherwise they can get a bit soggy. Then add enough bubbly water to the mixture so that it has the consistency of thin pancake batter. When the oil is hot, dip a few mushrooms in the batter, shake off the excess, and drop them into the oil. If you add too many at once, the temperature of the oil will drop too low, so start with just a few. Once you drop them in, don't touch them for a moment, until the batter sets, then use a skimmer to flip them over and cook them until they're evenly browned, about 3 minutes. Lift the fried mushrooms out and let them cool on a rack set on a baking sheet. If your scallions are whole, batter them and twirl them into the oil one at a time so you end up with a swirly shape. If they are cut, drop them in the oil and try to get them to stay clumped together. Scallions fry pretty quickly, so it should only take a couple of minutes for the batter to be golden brown and set. Once you've fried all the mushrooms and scallions, add a splash of bubbly water to the batter to make it a little bit thinner. You want the herbs to be very delicately coated. Dip the herb leaves and drop them into the hot oil. The herbs take the least amount of time to fry, maybe only a minute or so. While you're frying, be sure to keep your eye on the temperature of the oil—it should

continued

stay right around 350°F. If you happen to be making this for a large party, you should make two different batters: one for the mushrooms and scallions and a thinner one for the herbs. That way you can keep frying all night long.

Sprinkle salt over the fried mushrooms, scallions, and herbs, and serve them warm with the yogurt sauce for dipping.

USE PAKORA BATTER TO FRY:

Chrysanthemum leaves to tuck into an herb salad

Fish, such as lingcod, salted lingcod, or fresh whole anchovies or smelt

Lemon slices

Artichokes, thinly sliced

Cauliflower, sliced

Whole asparagus, peeled

SAUERKRAUT SALAD
Serves 6

½ small Savoy cabbage (about 12 ounces)

Salt

Rice bran oil

2 teaspoons yellow or brown mustard seeds

1 stalk green garlic, or 1 clove garlic, sliced

3 to 4 cups Sauerkraut (page 20)

Salt

Quarter the cabbage, cut out the core, and peel away any wilted outer leaves. Slice the cabbage as thinly as possible, put it in a bowl, and season lightly with salt. Toss to combine, then set aside to soften for about an hour.

Heat a small pan over medium heat for a minute. Pour in enough oil to coat the bottom of the pan, then add the mustard seeds. Swirl the pan until the mustard seeds begin to pop, cover the pan so the seeds don't escape, and reduce the heat to low. After about 30 seconds, you'll hear the popping slow.

The pan will be really hot, so let it cool a little before adding the garlic. The garlic should sizzle, but don't let it get brown at all. If the garlic looks like it is going to brown or burn because the oil is still too hot, add a splash of oil to cool everything down.

Take a big handful of the sauerkraut, squeeze out excess brine, and add it to the salted cabbage, mixing to combine. Continue adding enough sauerkraut to make a 50/50 proportion of raw cabbage to sauerkraut. Mix together and taste for seasoning. If the salad is too salty, you can add a bit more sliced Savoy cabbage. When the seasoning is right, add the popped mustard seeds and taste again. Serve at room temperature with leftover roast meat or Pig's Head and Trotter Fritters (page 210) with a little of the mustard seed-garlic mixture spooned over the top.

CHILLED BEET AND SAUERKRAUT SOUP WITH HORSERADISH AND CRÈME FRAÎCHE

Serves 6

4 or 5 large beets (about 1¾ pounds)

Salt

1 large fennel bulb, or 2 or 3 smaller bulbs

1 large yellow onion

8 or 9 cloves garlic

½ pound green or Savoy cabbage

Olive oil

1½ cups Sauerkraut (page 20), preferably red sauerkraut, because it looks better

1 cup sauerkraut liquid (see page 20)

Mushroom butts (optional)

Red Wine Vinegar (page 17)

Crème fraîche

1 small piece fresh horseradish, peeled

Black pepper

Preheat the oven to 375°F.

Wash the beets and trim only their stem ends, leaving a little bit of the stems attached. If you cut into the beet, the flavor will leach out while it roasts. Crowd the beets in a single layer in a roasting pan, season with salt, and pour in about an inch of water (a little less if the beets are small and a little more if they're large). Cover the pan tightly with aluminum foil and roast the beets until a skewer slides easily through them, about an hour.

When the beets are cool enough to handle, peel off their skins and trim away any fibrous root ends. Cut the beets into ½-inch cubes.

Trim the fennel, reserving the outer leaves for another purpose, such as Herb Jam (page 23). Dice the fennel and onion into pieces that are a little bit smaller than the beet cubes. Slice the garlic thinly. Slice the cabbage thinly to resemble the size of the sauerkraut.

Set a large pot over medium heat, then pour in enough oil to cover the bottom of the pot. Add the diced fennel and onion and a pinch of salt, and cook the vegetables until they start to soften. Next, add the sliced cabbage and garlic, and cook for a couple of minutes. Add the beets, the sauerkraut, and ½ cup of the sauerkraut liquid. Pour in enough water to barely cover, then add a splash of vinegar. If you have mushroom butts, this is the time to tie them up in a piece of cheesecloth and add that to the pot. Turn the heat up and bring the soup to a boil, then lower the heat and simmer for 5 minutes. Chill the soup.

Once it is cold, taste for seasoning. You want it to taste a little undersalted, because the soup is best when you can add some of the remaining raw sauerkraut juice, using it to season as you would use salt.

Serve with a spoonful of crème fraîche, a little grated horseradish, and a few grinds of black pepper.

COMPOSED SALADS

We have a version of this on the menu often—mostly when I think the menu needs something a little more complex. That said, composed salads are fun!—almost snacky. Because they're three salads sharing a plate (four has too many flavors, two is too skimpy), the possibilities are endless.

In the back of your mind, you need to think about the balance of flavor, texture, weight, and raw versus cooked. And in the way back of your mind, you want to think about that single carrot languishing in the fridge and whatever grilled meat you had for dinner last night. Because each element is really only a third of the dish, it doesn't take too much of anything to pull it together. In fact, you can get away with a really small amount of something if you make it strong or spicy.

Each component should be interesting on its own but even better with a couple other salads to go with it. For example, it would be hard to plow through an appetizer-size portion of smoky eggplant, but it's great when set off by carrot salad and fire-roasted peppers.

Besides the recipes below, you can use all sorts of things as your third ingredient, including:

Leftover grilled meat

Herb Frittata (page 167)

Yogurt, or yogurt with Herb Jam (page 23)

Herb Salad (page 50)

Sliced tomato

A small amount of Salted Lingcod (page 117)

The radish salad from the Whole Roasted Petrale Sole recipe (page 120)

Hell, even a piece of the petrale!

Red Lentils (page 10)

Like I said, endless possibilities.

All these recipes are geared toward serving six people as one-third of each plate—in other words, smallish amounts meant to be combined with other things. In reality, I would make more with leftovers in mind—these are all easy to scale up.

Keep in mind that all of these should be served at room temperature or slightly warm. Definitely not cold. Don't forget the Crispy Flatbread (page 11).

These all serve 6 as part of a composed salad.

———

CARROTS WITH CARAWAY, SESAME, CHILES, AND LIME

1/2 teaspoon caraway seeds

2 cloves garlic

Salt

Olive oil

2 tablespoons lime juice

3 large carrots (about 12 ounces), peeled

1/2 teaspoon Toasted Sesame Seeds (see page 33)

1 dried moderately hot chile

Toast the caraway seeds in a pan until they are a shade darker.

Using a mortar and pestle, pound the garlic with a pinch of salt. Set aside a quarter of the garlic paste in a small dish and cover with olive oil. You can use this later for fine-tuning the flavor. Pour the lime juice into the mortar and stir to combine.

Slice the carrots into a fine julienne—it's important that they are not too thick because you want them to wilt a little. You can use a mandoline if you are not afraid of it like I am. Put the carrots into a bowl and use your hands to toss them with the lime and garlic and some salt.

Break up the caraway seeds a little using a mortar and pestle or a quick pulse in a spice grinder. Sprinkle them and the sesame seeds over the carrots.

Tear the chiles into manageable pieces, discarding the stems but keeping the seeds, and place them in the spice grinder. Pulse several times to create a coarse powder. Add to the julienned carrots, toss to combine, and taste for seasoning. If the salad is too acidic, add a splash of olive oil. If it tastes flat, add a bit more garlic paste or chile powder. You can serve it right away, but it will improve if you let it sit for half an hour

MASHED BEETS WITH MUSTARD SEED

3 large red beets (about 1 pound)

Salt

Rice bran oil

1 teaspoon brown or yellow mustard seeds

2 cloves garlic, thinly sliced

3 tablespoons whole milk yogurt

½ lemon

Preheat the oven to 375°F.

Wash the beets and trim only their stem ends, leaving a little bit of the stems attached; if you cut into the beet, the flavor will leach out while it roasts. Crowd the beets in a single layer in a roasting pan, season with salt, and pour in about an inch of water (a little less if the beets are small and a little more if they're large). Cover the pan tightly with aluminum foil and roast the beets until a skewer slides easily through them, about one hour.

Meanwhile, heat a small pan over medium heat for a minute. Pour in enough oil to coat the bottom of the pan, then add the mustard seeds. Swirl the pan until the mustard seeds begin to pop, cover the pan so the seeds don't escape, and reduce the heat to low. After about 30 seconds, you'll hear the popping slow.

Remove from the heat and let cool, uncovered, for a minute or so.

When the beets are cool enough to handle, peel off their skins and trim away any fibrous root ends. Cut the beets into large chunks and place them in the bowl of a food processor. Blend until smooth, scraping down the sides as needed (you can use a potato masher instead of a food processor; the mashed beets will be a totally different texture—rougher but still really good). Add the popped mustard seeds, yogurt, a big squeeze of lemon juice, and some salt. Taste for seasoning.

SMOKY EGGPLANT

If you are already grilling, this is an opportunity to extend the fire into the next meal or two. Not to say that I would ever have a plan for the next day, but it's like money in the bank to have some smoky eggplant kicking around—it has a lot of uses. Plus you are not wasting the heat of the coals, and it's quicker and easier than you would think. You can serve this as part of a composed salad, maybe with fire-roasted peppers, greens, or carrot salad. You can also smear a little underneath a tomato or cucumber salad or serve it with poached eggs, farro, and yogurt.

3 globe eggplants

2 cloves garlic

Salt

1 lemon

A handful of mint leaves

Olive oil

A handful of cilantro sprigs

Nestle the eggplants directly into a pile of hot coals. About every 5 minutes, turn the eggplants, moving them to a new spot—the eggplant will have smothered the coals a little. Cook until they are soft and have

continued

collapsed. A small eggplant will take somewhere around 15 minutes to get to this stage; a large one will take closer to 20 minutes.

Let the eggplants cool, then peel away all the skin with your fingers or a small paring knife. It should be pretty easy to get most of the burnt skin off, but a little fleck of black here and there is fine. Pull the eggplants apart into big pieces, put them in a strainer, and let them drain for at least 10 minutes. (Or, if you happen to have actually cooked the eggplant after your other fire dinner, as in the above scenario, and feel like going to bed rather than dealing with them, you can let them drain overnight in the fridge.)

Pound the garlic and a pinch of salt in a mortar. Squeeze the lemon juice directly into the mortar. Pick the mint leaves, lightly crush them in your hand, and add them to the garlicky lemon juice.

Put the drained eggplant in a bowl and pour in a generous splash of olive oil, some salt, and a couple of tablespoons of the garlicky lemon juice (leaving the mint leaves behind). Coarsely chop the cilantro leaves and stems and add them to the bowl. Stir and taste; I try to avoid mixing it too much because then it all becomes a smooth purée, and I like it to have some texture. If the eggplants aren't very sweet, you'll want to add another tablespoon or so of the garlicky lemon juice and some additional oil.

────

FRESH GARBANZO BEANS WITH SAFFRON AND GREEN GARLIC

As I write this, my long-time garbanzo farmer seems to have given up on the farming game. It's a sad time at Camino. Organic garbanzos are difficult to find, but I'm sure someone will take up the cause. Not only are fresh garbanzos difficult to find, they are also difficult to shell—they only have one or two beans per pod. But don't let all this negativity stop you—they are also the

best legume out there. You are going to use the Oil and Water Method (see page 30) for this, concentrating on having the perfect amount of delicious liquid left at the end of the cooking time.

> Pinch of saffron (about 10 threads)
>
> 2 stalks green garlic
>
> 1/2 dried moderately hot chile
>
> Olive oil
>
> 2 cups shelled fresh garbanzo beans
>
> A few leaves of lovage, summer savory, or mint

Soak the saffron in a couple of tablespoons of boiling water for at least 10 minutes.

Cut off the green garlic tops right where they start to branch off. Peel one outside layer and trim the roots. Slice on the diagonal into 1/8-inch pieces. Break up the chile into five or six biggish pieces.

Put about 3/4 inch of water in a shallow pan along with a pinch of salt, the broken-up chiles, the green garlic, the saffron, and a splash of olive oil. Bring to a rolling boil and add the garbanzo beans. You want to cook the beans as fast as you can to retain the green color and flavor, so keep the heat cranked up. After a minute or so, start tasting. Garbanzo beans are done when the starchy flavor is gone, but there is still a little crunch. When you think they are getting close, add the lovage or other herbs. As you are tasting for doneness, add water occasionally if needed. But not too much—at the end you really want just a little water clinging to the beans. Once they are done, pour them out into a shallow dish to cool.

FIRE-ROASTED PEPPERS

During the hour or so while you are building a fire to cook dinner, this is the time to sneak in some peppers. Peppers are the one thing I think you can cook while the coals are still a little flamey. At Camino, we also cook these at the end of the night when there are coals left from cooking dinner. In other words, there is a lot of flexibility with peppers because you are trying to burn the skin. With that in mind, you'll need thick-fleshed peppers, so there is something left after you blacken them—bell peppers or Corno di Toro peppers, but not Gypsy or Flamingo.

Once some coals are spilling off around the base of your fire, set some peppers directly on them and nestle them in a bit right next to the flame. With long tongs, turn the peppers when each side is almost completely black. As the peppers blacken, throw them into a pot with a tight-fitting lid to steam. The skin burns so quickly in the fire that the flesh has no time to cook, so they need a little time to soften up.

After the peppers have steamed for about 10 minutes, take them out of the pot to cool a bit.

There are a million hair-brained ways to peel and seed roasted peppers, but I think I have the easiest method. The pain-in-the-ass part is the seeds, not so much the skin. Start by splitting all the peppers vertically, and then use a small knife to scrape all the seeds out into a pile. Clean the seeds off the counter, rinse your knife, and once you are seed free, pick up the peppers and peel the blackened skin off with your hands. Little black bits will stick here and there, which I think is okay. Don't be tempted to rinse them with water, because you will lose all the flavor.

You can cut or tear the peppers into any size you want. I personally like all shapes except the universally accepted ½-inch strip (see Punk Rock, page 666).

To use the peppers in a composed salad, splash them with enough olive oil to coat and some red wine vinegar. Season them with salt and the torn leaves of some sort of herb (my favorites are Persian mint, spearmint, oregano, or any kind of basil). You can also add a smidge of pounded garlic, and sometimes I'll add sliced garlic, more for flavoring than for eating.

Like with any marinated vegetable, it's best to taste, adjust the seasoning, and then come back in 20 minutes and taste it again. You will probably have to add more salt and vinegar.

If you are using the peppers as part of a hot dish, I think it's best to omit the vinegar and up the garlic.

GREENS WITH PRESERVED LEMON

1⅓ cups Cooked Greens (page 13)

½ Preserved Lemon (page 26)

2 tablespoons olive oil

Give the cooked greens a quick chop with a knife—there shouldn't be any long, stringy pieces—and put them in a bowl. Scoop out the pulp of the preserved lemon, chop finely, and set aside—this part of the lemon is very salty, but it tastes good. If you are making the cooked greens just for this salad, you should undersalt them a little bit so you have an excuse to use this pulp later to adjust the seasoning—it will give you a deeper flavor than just plain salt. Cut the preserved lemon peel quarters lengthwise into four long pieces, then cut each piece crosswise into ⅛-inch-thick slices. Add the sliced lemon peel to the bowl with the greens. Drizzle in the olive oil and toss everything together. Taste and add the lemon pulp if needed to adjust the seasoning.

VEGETABLE MAIN COURSES

We take the vegetarian main courses at Camino very seriously—often challenging ourselves to sway non-vegetarians into ordering them. We often include a Camino Egg (page 164)—a poached or fried egg would work great, too—to these dishes because it's nice to have something that's not starchy or sweet but that adds a little luxurious texture to the dish. I don't see it as replacement for meat but more as the thing that can pull the whole dish together.

ROASTED BLACK TRUMPET MUSHROOMS WITH CARDOON GRATIN AND CAMINO EGG

Serves 6

4 or 5 large cardoon stalks (each 2 to 3 feet long)

½ lemon

2 fresh or dried bay leaves

1 stalk green garlic, or 4 cloves garlic

Salt

3 tablespoons butter

3 tablespoons all-purpose flour

8 ounces black trumpet mushrooms

Olive oil

4 cloves garlic, thinly sliced

6 prepared eggs (Camino Egg, page 164)

With a sharp knife, trim off any leaves from the cardoons and peel the outside layer, removing the strings that run up the stalks. Remove the white, fuzzy membrane on the inside of the stalk by scraping it with the knife or wiping it off with a towel. As you go, put the cleaned cardoon stalks into a bucket of water with half a lemon squeezed into it so they don't turn black while you finish cleaning the rest.

Cut the cardoons into pieces that will fit into your pot. You'll definitely want to use a stainless steel pot, otherwise the cooking liquid will turn black. Pour in enough water to barely cover and add the bay leaves, garlic, and some salt. Bring to a simmer and cook until the cardoons are tender all the way through with just a little firmness but not a crunch. Start checking for doneness after about 10 minutes and keep an eye on the water level, topping it off if it drops too low. The thinner stalks will, of course, be done sooner and you'll have to pull them out. The thickest stalks might take an hour to cook. Drain the cardoons and save the cooking liquid.

Preheat the oven to 500°F.

Melt the butter in a heavy-bottomed pan set over low heat. Add the flour and stir. Cook over low heat for several minutes. Bring the cardoon water back up to a simmer, add a couple ladlefuls of it to thin out the roux. Then, while whisking the rest of the cardoon water, pour the flour-butter-liquid mixture back into the pot. Increase the heat so that the liquid simmers. If it is too thick, add water until it is the consistency of gravy and keep stirring and cooking until the raw flour taste is completely gone. This is a vague concept and it's not always easy to tell when it's done, but I find that it usually takes about 15 to 20 minutes. When it is done, remove it from the heat and strain the sauce to make it smooth. Taste for seasoning. If the sauce is too salty, add a splash of milk or water.

Cut the cooked cardoons on the diagonal into 2-inch pieces. Crowd them in a single layer in a 9-inch baking dish. At this point, you could add an herb like savory, but if you really want to taste the cardoons, it's better to leave it out. Pour the sauce over the cardoons and bake for about 30 minutes, until the gratin is brown and bubbly.

While the gratin is baking, clean the mushrooms: split them in half vertically, and run your thumbnail along the inside to remove any pine needles and obvious dirt. The tip of the mushroom stem can be woody, so tear off any parts that feel tough. To really clean the mushrooms, you will need to drop them into a bowl of water, swish them around, and then let them settle for a minute. Pick out any pine needles that float to the surface. Lift out the mushrooms and drop them into another bowl of water. Swish them around and let any dirt fall to the bottom of the bowl. Continue moving the mushrooms from one bowl of clean water to another. You may need to do it three times or ten times; it just depends on how dirty the mushrooms are. Once you get to the point where the bowl of water has no sand or grit at the bottom, wash the mushrooms one more time just in case. Lift the mushrooms out of the bowl and put them in a colander to drain (you don't want to pour them directly into the colander because then you are just pouring dirt back on the mushrooms).

Black trumpets cook really quickly, so you want to cook them on high heat, but you have to be careful not to brown the garlic. Heat a pan over high heat for a couple of minutes. Pour in enough olive oil to barely coat the bottom of the pan. Add the garlic to the hot oil and let it sizzle for just a second. Quickly add the mushrooms and season them with a little salt—a bit less salt than you think you should because you're going to reduce the liquid later on and it'll get saltier. Cook, stirring often, until the mushrooms stop releasing their liquid, about a minute. Pour the liquid into a small pot, keeping the mushrooms in the pan, then return the pan to the heat. Add another splash of olive oil and a little more salt. Keep stirring and cooking the mushrooms until they are wilted but still have some texture, about 1 minute more. When the mushrooms are done, put them on a plate so they don't continue to cook while you make the sauce.

Boil the reserved mushroom juices over high heat. The liquid will bubble ferociously and start to look like tar. Cook until thick. It's easy to burn so be careful. It'll taste like super concentrated soy sauce.

Using a spatula, divide the gratin into six potions and scoop it onto each plate, trying to keep the browned part on top. Put the Camino Egg (this is the opportunity to use the cardoon leaf in your Egg Tea,

see page 164) next to the gratin and scatter the black trumpet mushrooms on top of the gratin and the egg. Drizzle the reduced mushroom juice over the egg.

NOTE

If you have any mushrooms and reduced mushroom juices left over, make a chicory and black trumpet mushroom salad and add the juices to the vinaigrette.

EGGPLANT-TOMATO-MINT GRATIN WITH FRESH BLACK-EYED PEAS, FRESH FENUGREEK, AND GRILLED ARTICHOKES
Serves 4 to 6

It's less important to get medium-size artichokes than it is to get good artichokes. Look for tight heads, and if there is any stem (hopefully there is), make sure it's firm and not rubbery. The artichokes are cooked using the Oil and Water Method (see page 30) and then are finished on the grill. Grilling the artichokes gives crunch to an otherwise fairly soft dish, but you could also cut them in smaller pieces and use the cooking liquid to rewarm them on the stove. Either way, save the cooking liquid because you are going to use it to cook the black-eyed peas.

If you can't find fresh fenugreek, this will be equally good with spearmint or Persian mint. Fresh fenugreek has an earthy flavor that will remind you of curry, but it tastes greener and milder than fenugreek seed, which is used to make to make actual curry.

EGGPLANT GRATIN
Olive oil

2 small yellow onions, thinly sliced

Salt

Cloves from ½ head garlic, sliced

1 bunch spearmint, stemmed

continued

4 smaller globe-type eggplants, like Listada
de Gandia or Rosa Bianca (about 1¼ pounds)

4 large tomatoes

ARTICHOKES

6 medium artichokes

½ lemon

6 cloves garlic, unpeeled

2 bay leaves

2 sprigs summer savory, winter savory, or mint

Olive oil

Salt

BLACK-EYED PEAS

1 pound fresh black-eyed peas, shelled
(approximately 2 heaping cups)

1 sprig summer savory

2 bay leaves

8 cloves garlic

½ bunch scallions, trimmed and thinly sliced

Small handful of fenugreek or mint leaves

Olive oil

Coarse salt and fine salt

Preheat the oven to 400°F.

Heat a pan over medium heat, pour in enough olive oil
to cover the bottom of the pan, then add the onion and
season with salt. Cook until softened but not browned,
then add the garlic and cook for a couple more minutes.

Coarsely chop the mint and quickly stir it into the
garlic and onion. It will stay relatively green if you
move fast and toss it around in the pan immediately.
Cook for another moment, then spread the minty
onions and garlic in the bottom of a 10-inch round
baking dish or equivalent.

Eggplant skin can be tough, so use a vegetable peeler
to peel off 2-inch strips of skin, leaving ⅓-inch-wide

stripes of skin in between. Slice off the stem ends,
then cut the eggplant horizontally into ⅓-inch-thick
rounds. Cut the cores out of the tomatoes and slice
them ¼ inch thick.

Build a fire to grill the artichokes.

While the coals are getting ready, assemble the
gratin. Make one layer of overlapping eggplant
slices, propped up and arranged like shingles, on
top of the minty onions and garlic. Brush liberally
with olive oil and season with salt. Make the next
layer with tomato slices, leaning them against the
eggplant slices, and season them with salt. Continue
alternating eggplant and tomato layers until you've
filled the dish, remembering to brush the eggplant
layers with olive oil. I also salt each layer as I go
(rather than salting everything ahead) so I can
gauge the salt level as I assemble to dish. And I like
to place the tomatoes so you can see them poking
out from between the eggplant layers. Cover with
foil and bake until tender, about 45 minutes. At this
point, remove the foil and use a brush to baste the
top of the gratin with the juices that have collected
in the dish. Cook for another 20 to 25 minutes until
brown, basting it every 5 minutes or so and taking
care to retain the eggplant-tomato pattern. When
it's done, the gratin will be nice and brown on top.

While the gratin is baking, cook the artichokes using
the Oil and Water Method (see page 30). Peel the
outer leaves of the artichokes until you reach the
tender pale green ones on the inside. Cut off the tips
off the leaves. Trim the very bottoms of the stems to
see how tough they are. If they're tough, keep cutting
until you hit the relatively tender part. Carefully pare
a thin layer of skin off the stem and the base of the
artichokes. Cut the artichokes in half lengthwise and
scoop out any choke. Toss the cleaned artichokes in
a bowl of water with the juice of the half a lemon to
keep them from turning black.

Lightly smash the garlic cloves but don't peel them.
Put them in a pan large enough to accommodate the

continued

artichokes in one layer—you may need to cook them in batches. Add the bay leaves and savory. Add about an inch of water to the pan along with a big splash of olive oil and some salt. Bring the oil and water mixture up to a boil and taste for seasoning—the artichokes will taste as salty as the water when they are done, so adjust accordingly. Add the artichokes to the pan and cook at a medium boil until tender. Since the artichokes are poking out of the water a bit, stir often while they cook to keep them moist. If you are doing two batches, you may have to add a little bit of fresh water to the pan. Once the artichokes are done, scoop them out of the liquid and spread them out to cool before grilling. Save the cooking liquid for the black-eyed peas.

While the artichokes are cooling, put the black-eyed peas in a pot, and add the artichoke cooking liquid. If the liquid does not cover the beans, add enough water to barely cover.

Bring the beans to a gentle simmer. Cook until they are creamy on the inside but not mushy, 15 to 20 minutes. While the beans cook, add water as needed to keep them barely covered in liquid. As they cook, taste the beans for doneness and the water for salt—by the time the beans are done, they will be as salty as the water.

When the beans are done, rake the coals under the grill for medium grilling. Lightly coat the artichokes with olive oil, sprinkle with a little salt, and place them cut side down on the grill. Let them go for 3 or 4 minutes, then check to see if the underside is browning. Once they are a satisfying brown color, flip them all over and grill the other side. Once both sides are brown, they are ready to serve.

Reheat the beans in their liquid, adding the scallions, fenugreek (or mint) and another tablespoon of olive oil. Bring the liquid to a boil and let it reduce slightly until the cooking liquid has some body to it.

To serve, put the black-eyed peas in a shallow dish and scatter the grilled artichokes on top. Serve the gratin in its baking dish.

KING TRUMPET MUSHROOM PARCELS WITH GREENS AND GRILLED RUTABAGA
Serves 6

This recipe is adapted from Yotam Ottolenghi's recipe for wild mushroom parcels from his book *Plenty*. We made these for a party for Yotam when the book was released in 2011, and we haven't stopped making them since. They are fun and elegant as a middle course with a slice of sheep's milk ricotta, or you can serve as a main course with polenta or farro, cooked greens, and grilled rutabaga.

Speaking of which: 2012—Year of the Rutabaga! Maybe you missed this, but for an extremely small group of Riverdog Farm customers, rutabaga were the talk of the town. Seriously, for months and months they were the most delicious vegetable you could get. Camino customers were exclaiming, "This is the best potato I have ever had!" In early days pitching this book to a publisher, I couldn't stop talking about rutabaga. I was met with an eerie silence and an uncomfortable smile which only egged me on. I mean, I was talking about *GRILLED rutabaga*! Grilled! They passed on our book, but luckily a more adventurous publisher rolled the dice, so I am able to present to you: Grilled Rutabaga—way better than mashed.

All kidding aside, its best to buy rutabaga after there has been cold weather, because that's when they're sweeter.

1½ pounds king trumpet mushrooms

2 cloves garlic

Olive oil

A handful of chervil

A handful of parsley leaves

Splash of absinthe

Splash of white wine

Salt

continued on page 74

GRILLED RUTABAGA

4 small rutabaga (about 1½ pounds)

Coarse salt and fine salt

1 teaspoon whole allspice

1 teaspoon black peppercorns

Olive oil

Cooked Greens (page 13)

Fried Farro (page 8) or Polenta (page 9)

Preheat the oven to 500°F.

Build a fire to grill the rutabaga.

Trim the bottom ½ inch off the mushrooms and save for a million other uses, such as Chilled Beet and Sauerkraut Soup (page 59) or Roast Duck Consommé (page 180), or to add to a meat braise. Cut the mushrooms lengthwise into ⅓-inch slices and place them in a bowl.

Pound the garlic and some salt in a mortar, then pour a couple of tablespoons of olive oil directly into the mortar, and stir. Coarsely chop the chervil and parsley leaves and scatter them over the mushrooms. Pour a splash of absinthe and a splash of wine over the mushrooms, scrape in the garlicky oil, and season everything with salt. Before you assemble the mushroom parcels, bake a few mushroom slices on their own to test the seasoning.

Cut six 18 by 18-inch pieces of parchment paper. Divide the mushroom mixture evenly among the six pieces. Gather the parchment around the mushrooms, give it a little twist, and tie it snugly with string—the mushrooms will release a lot of liquid and you don't want to lose any of it, since it will create a nice sauce for the rest of the dish. Bake for about 10 minutes. You should be able to see liquid bubbling inside the parcel and it should be hot to the touch.

Peel the rutabagas, making sure to get under the thick skin. Simmer them in salted water until you can easily push a skewer through them, about 20 to 30 minutes. Once cooked, they are pretty fragile, so lift them out of the water gently. Let cool and then cut them crosswise into ½-inch-thick slices.

Grind the allspice and peppercorns in a spice grinder or with a mortar and pestle. Brush both sides of the sliced rutabaga with olive oil and season with salt and some of the pepper-allspice mixture.

Rake the coals under the grill for medium-hot grilling. When the grill is hot, about 5 minutes, put the rutabaga slices on and cook them for a couple of minutes. Don't nudge them or move them around or else the grill marks will turn out fuzzy. Check one slice after a couple of minutes and when there are solid, dark grill marks, flip the slices and cook the other side for a few minutes.

To serve, place the grilled rutabaga and greens and polenta or farro on individual plates. Serve the parcels on a platter so guests get to choose their own. Then they can untie the parcel and when they empty the mushrooms out, the juices will make a sauce for the rest of the dish.

RATATOUILLE COOKED IN THE FIRE

Generously serves 6 to 8

Ratatouille is a Provençal vegetable stew that is traditionally cooked in a pot on the stove. It's delicious, but it's even better when each vegetable is cooked separately over a fire and then mixed together. I like each vegetable to be distinct and for their juices and the fire's smokiness to tie them together. We use untraditional spices and herbs—cumin, coriander, fenugreek, saffron, mint, basil—and we change them up all the time.

I like ratatouille best as a main course with a Camino Egg (page 164), Polenta (page 9), and some spicy Cooked Greens (page 13). We sometimes serve it as side dish to grilled fish, lamb, or poultry. It's also great as part of a composed salad the next day, cooked into an omelet, or served with rice. Because cooking ratatouille in the fire is such an ordeal, you should make enough to do all of the above.

1½ teaspoons cumin seeds

2 teaspoons caraway seeds

2 teaspoons coriander seeds

1 teaspoon fenugreek seeds

Pinch of saffron threads (about 15)

4 to 6 summer squash (about 2 pounds)

4 or 5 torpedo or red onions (about 1 pound)

2 globe eggplants (about 1¾ pounds)

4 peppers (about 1 pound), such as Gypsy, Flamingo, or Corno di Toro

Olive oil

Salt

5 or 6 yellow onions (about 1¼ pounds)

6 large tomatoes (about 2 pounds)

Cloves from 1½ heads garlic, sliced thin

2 big handfuls of herb leaves, such as Persian mint, piccolo fino basil, or parsley

Build a fire and while the coals are getting ready, you can start your prep work.

Toast the cumin, caraway, and coriander seeds in a pan until they're a shade darker. Take the pan off the heat and add the fenugreek, tossing it around to warm it but not really toast it at all; browned fenugreek tastes bitter. Put all the spices in a grinder along with the saffron threads and pulse into a coarse powder.

Trim the stem ends of the summer squash and cut lengthwise into ⅓-inch-thick slices. Trim both ends of the torpedo onions, peel, and cut into ⅓-inch rings. Since eggplant skin can be tough, use a vegetable peeler to peel off 2-inch strips of skin, leaving ⅓-inch stripes of skin in between. Slice off the stem ends, then cut the eggplant into rounds that are a little bit thicker than the squash and torpedo onion slices, as they will shrink a little when you cook them. Slice the peppers in half lengthwise, pull out the seeds and ribs, and slice lengthwise again into quarters.

Keeping the torpedo onion slices intact, brush the onions, squash, and eggplant with olive oil on each side and season with salt and with the spice mixture. With the peppers, it's easier to just toss them in a bowl with olive oil, salt, and spices. All these vegetables will be easier to grill once the salt has softened them a bit, so let them sit for at least 20 minutes.

While the other vegetables are softening, roast the yellow onions in the coals. The coals are probably not quite ready for grilling yet (still a little flamey), but they'll be far enough along for the onions. Nestle the onions, whole and unpeeled, directly in the coals. Cook them until they're completely black and a skewer slides through them without much resistance, about 30 minutes. Use tongs to flip them over every once in a while so they cook evenly.

Once the coals are ready (no more flames), you can start grilling the vegetables. If you have a big enough grill, you can grill all the vegetables at the same time, but you will need a medium-hot area for the

continued

squash, tomatoes, torpedo onions, and peppers and a slightly cooler area for the eggplant. If you have a small grill, you can cook each vegetable one at time—brushing and wiping your grill in between each new vegetable and replenishing your coals so you maintain a medium-hot grill for most of the vegetables, cooking the eggplant last on the descending coals. The tomatoes are a little more flexible with the grill temperature, so you can tuck them in between other vegetables; I prefer them on a hotter grill because then you can get some black spots on them. In any case, when you are grilling so many different vegetables, you have to stay organized and on top of it. I'm messy about a lot of things, but not this.

Grill the squash slices close together and at a slight angle. Let them cook for a few minutes without moving them, then check one slice to see if it has nice, dark grill marks. When it does, flip all the squash and cook the second side for another few minutes. As the vegetables are done cooking, move them all to a baking dish to cool a bit. They will start releasing juices as they cool and you want to save all this liquid for later.

Pull off the stems from about two-thirds of the tomatoes, but leave the cores in. Without any oil or seasoning, put the whole tomatoes right onto the grill, stem side down. Cook them until they begin to soften on that one side, about 4 minutes or so, before turning them over and letting them cook for another couple of minutes. Cook them until they just start getting soft—if you let them go too long they will turn to mush and fall through the grates.

Grill the peppers skin side down for about 5 minutes, checking to see how brown they're getting, then flip and cook the second side. If the peppers brown too quickly but still feel really raw and crunchy, you can pile them up on top of each other right on the grill—that way they'll steam a little bit.

You want to keep the sliced torpedo onions intact, so be careful setting them on the grill. Once they have grill marks, flip them over—still being careful, but they will start falling apart at this point—and cook for a few more minutes. Once they have grill marks on the second side, use a spatula to pile them up on a cooler part of the grill to steam, letting the rings fall apart.

You're going to cook the eggplant slower than the other vegetables and on a cooler grill because you want nice marks on the outside *and* you want to ensure that it is cooked all the way through to the inside. Grill the eggplant just like the squash, but slower, over cooler coals, and poke at it more often to make sure that it is getting tender. There is nothing worse than undercooked eggplant.

Honestly, grilling the eggplant is the hardest part of ratatouille. And, honestly, I never let anyone except my co-chef Michael grill eggplant at Camino. And, since we are being honest, we almost always roast the eggplant in the wood oven instead of grilling it. Which is to say that you can put it on a parchment-lined baking sheet and roast it in your oven at 400°F until it is brown and tender.

After all the grilled vegetables have cooled off a little bit, dice everything into similar size cubes, roughly 1/3 inch. The tomato will be a big mess, but don't peel it, and try to keep as much of the juice as you can. For the roasted (now entirely blackened) yellow onion, use a knife to peel away the black skin and dice the onion. A little fleck of black here and there is okay. Put all the diced vegetables back into the dish with the collected juices.

Heat a pan over medium-low heat, add a good amount of olive oil, and then add the garlic and some salt. Cook it slowly for a couple of minutes until it softens, but don't get let it get any color. Add the garlic and its oil to the dish with the vegetables. Cut the remaining tomatoes in half and grate them on a box grater over the dish. The skins should end up in your hand and the raw tomato pulp and juice should go into the ratatouille. Coarsely chop the herbs and add them to the dish. Gently mix everything together and taste for seasoning, adding a bit more salt, herbs, or spice mixture if it needs it. Just before serving, heat up the ratatouille in the dish set right on the grill.

CAMINO

CAMINO

Chrysanthemum frittata with tomato and fresh anchovy salad   11
Avocado toasts with coco nero beans, parsley and cutting celery   10
Smoked quail with roasted figs, grilled roman squash and mustard seeds   14
Butter lettuce salad with homemade vinegar and herbs   8

Grilled local squid and albacore with pickled chile broth and scallions   15
Sheepsmilk ricotta grilled with myrtle; with cucumbers and herb salad   12

Lamb leg à la ficelle, grilled loin and slow-cooked shoulder with
fresh flageolet and butter beans, greens and chiles   28
Wood oven-baked ratatouille with green beans, farro, wild nettles
and an egg cooked by the fire   24
Grilled whole local sardines and pan de zucchero with potato gratin,
roasted tomatillos, jalapeños and mint   24

Fiscalini cheddar   7

September 20, 2013

Bread available
upon request

Corkage   20

An 18% gratuity will be added for parties of 6 or more.

Poached eggs with fresh shellbean ragout, smoky
hen-of-the-woods mushrooms and pounded mint   10
Wood oven-baked ling cod brandade with fennel and olive
and garlic-lovage toast   13
Grilled whole sardine with ratatouille and carrot salad   11
Grilled pancetta, butter lettuce and tomato sandwich
with green bean and radish salad   13
Stoneground oats with brown butter, maple syrup
and almonds   7
French toast with fruit compote, hazelnuts and crème fraîche
Tunisian orange cake with Barhi dates and yogurt   8

September 15, 2013

CAMINO COLLECTIVE: AUTHOR DINNER PARTY

Omnivore
Books

CHAPTER THREE

A WEEK AT CAMINO

Hang around a restaurant long enough and eventually you more or less work there. Not in any remotely helpful sense—just that you start absorbing the rhythms and catastrophes and triumphs and grilled squid as your own. So it only made sense to start writing this.

I'd been lurking at Camino, helping with the writing of this book you're holding, when it started becoming clear that individual recipes only capture one tiny aspect of the place. More so than with most restaurants I'd seen, the essence of this one lived not in a single meal but in the carefully ordered chaos that produced it.

So we decided I'd write about that—instead of just dipping the cup in the river here and there, we'd try to show the river itself. What follows is a week in the life of Camino, starting now, on this rainy Wednesday.

—CHRIS COLIN

WEDNESDAY

9:55 A.M.

Camino's closed Tuesdays, so Wednesdays have a first-day-of-the-week feel. Everyone takes stock—sees what produce remains, reflects on the reservations for the next few nights, looks ahead. But none of that has really begun yet. The place is still on this wet morning, Oakland gray and gloomy outside the big wall of windows. It's the kind of gloom that brings out the coziness of a warm, unlit restaurant in the first stirrings of its day.

The walk-in is a riot of eggs and limes and crabs and kale and massive pink slabs of ex-pig. Boxes of fresh asparagus sit outside the door, smelling like dirt and spring. Nearby, a broad shelf holds a dozen dusty mason jars—Allison calls it "our weird shelf"—containing watermelon jam, pickled cabbage rolls, pickled walnuts, and other experiments brought into existence at one lull or another.

It's a lull now. Only a couple bodies move here and there, checking idly on inventory; the restaurant's medieval, Volkswagen-size fireplace is inert. But the quiet is the coiled kind, that same hush that signals a tidal wave is coming.

9:58 A.M.

It comes. From nowhere a swarm of humans materializes, moving with studied precision. In a blink, five dozen chairs are wordlessly transported to the newly cleaned dining room floor. The trim and tidy co-chef, Michael, starts setting up his station. Rachel, with her pierced lip but mild New England reserve, is sharpening her knives.

A massive and complex machine has sprung to life, its assorted parts coming online one by one: plates clanging here, flatbread getting underway there. At the white-hot nucleus, of course, are Russ and Allison. RussandAllison. One word, a single entity equal parts seriousness, quirk, precision, whimsy, mellowness, and good clothes.

The plan is to lurk here for a week. Lurking at Camino is a little like lurking in the ER: Wherever you stand, no, don't stand there. Don't annoy the woman carrying the sharp thing, or the hot thing. Don't tip over the heavy thing. Or worse, don't misperceive the subtle and impossibly delicate thing, that which nudges perfectly good food to another level entirely.

10:35 A.M.

Managing a restaurant's million moving parts—we don't get to see this in cooking shows. There's the Oakland fisherman to email about crabs, that celery to use because Russ bought some from the Catalan Family Farm; he just likes them. That woman is coming by to discuss the Alzheimer's fundraiser. Allison must manage assorted non-food flavors—organize the visit from that Muscadet maker later this week, balance waiter personalities out on the floor, make sure the dishes are paced right for the larger parties.

Meanwhile, that schoolteacher who sells Russ those Peruvian ground apples—he's coming by. And that neighbor from up the street? She's been growing Persian mint in her yard, which Russ prefers to spearmint in certain salads; she's coming by, too. And as always, there's the weekly orders of two large beasts, which need to feed several hundred humans over the coming six days, without waste, without running out, without failing to meet their potential.

Somewhere in there, Russ will start thinking about tomorrow's menu.

10:42 A.M.

Russ, generally in motion, pauses a moment near the cold station, "I want to make consommé," he says.

11:10 A.M.

A big man with a bushy white beard strolls into Camino. Jim Reichardt, of the great Reichardt duck dynasty, is just back from France. Despite a hectic morning's schedule, Russ greets him and they spend the next few minutes scrolling through Paris photos. These aren't Louvre or Notre Dame snapshots—the two men are looking at some pressed duck Reichardt was served. Pressed duck assessment moves on to general poultry gossip. If you have good relationships with farmers, you get good stuff, Russ tells me later—and good duck is one of his favorites. He'll figure out what to do with it later. Just get the good duck.

12:40 P.M.

Travis McFlynn, the youngish fellow who makes Camino's Spanish-style *cazuelas*, drops by to take orders. He makes ceramics for Alice Waters and other chefs, too. Apparently there is such a thing a celebrity restaurant ceramicist.

12:55 P.M.

Pigs range in size up to a hundred pounds—but Russ, when ordering, never specifies how big a beast he wants. A code of enforced serendipity governs Camino.

"I hate planning," he says.

"He *can't* plan," Allison clarifies.

1:30 P.M.

Cooks' meeting. The staff gathers in the dining room, nibbling on a light lunch while Michael leads the conversation. Should the Savoy cabbage that accompanies tonight's Dungeness crab come in strips or pieces? In what manner shall the turmeric be fried? How much farro's in the walk-in? To an outsider, it's striking how much remains up in the air—even theoretical—just hours before the first customers arrive. But the vibe is mellow. Michael's calm and quiet, almost inaudible at times. He idly picks Russ's brain about the chicken ballotine that might come to pass later this week.

The vibe is mellow but not casual. The thinness of Monday's soup hangs in the air. Minutes before the doors opened, Russ had realized the broth hadn't thickened sufficiently. Frantic innovation prevailed, Russ blending some mushroom butts and rice. But it wasn't forgotten. Tonight's chicory salad, made with homemade vinegar and aged sheep's milk cheese, seemed like it could come together or not—would the chicories be too bitter? Consensus was, let's get it to come together. Cooks' meeting adjourns, back to stations.

Russ is reflecting on duck, which isn't on tonight's menu.

"I really want to make consommé," he says.

1:42 P.M.

Michael has come up with a smoked sardine and carrot salad for tonight, with smoky lentils and fresh turmeric.

2:43 P.M.

A day at Camino can be broken into two halves: prefire and fire. Everything that occurs in the first half feels almost speculative. The writing of the menu, the sharpening of the knives, the preparation of the stock—these morning activities feel essential but nevertheless abstract. The idea of a hundred diners entering the stone-still space and demanding food in a matter of hours? Inconceivable. Then there is fire and everything changes.

The first fire starts in the oven, a few yards to the left of the central fireplace. Then, once the wood has been preheated—preheating helps minimize smoke—the main fire is lit. The sweet smell of almond and cherry wood instantly suffuses the entire restaurant. It's a primitive force in a modern setting. Over the week to come, two dozen diners, occasionally under the excuse of using the restroom, will wander up to the butcher block and stare, transfixed. Cara tells me the starers often have questions, but don't quite know what they are. "How do you keep the flames going ... up?" one fellow asked. "Physics," Cara replied.

2:50 P.M.

Rachel, who's been chopping green garlic tops, asks Cara if she'd like the leftovers. Sure, Cara says. It's a classic Camino moment. First of all, everybody's winging it—seldom does a recipe emerge. Second, there's the matter of what Cara will do with these nubs—last I checked, such things go in the compost bin. She informs me that no such thing would happen at Camino, especially not when eggs are being prepared. Instead of just using water, the cooker of the egg uses water infused with herbs. Egg Tea, they call it.

2:52 P.M.

Michael's slicing ginger for the pork, which will sit atop garbanzo beans. If there's something cozier than an almond and cherry fire crackling ten feet away, with the quiet chop-chop-chop of knives on a chopping block, and the hearty smell of beans in a giant pot, while cars pass by on wet streets, it's hard to think what it is.

3:02 P.M.

Nothing is wasted, Rachel explains. Over the course of the week every other cook will say the same. All restaurants say this, but it happens at another level here. One of Camino's signature creations, the marvelous herb jam, is made from the ends of used-up herbs. Orange peels are gold. Yogurt containers are Tupperware. Broken pots aren't discarded, but used to hold fire tools. The staff brings in the torn-out subscription envelopes from their magazines at home; these get commandeered for tip envelopes.

3:13 P.M.

Imperceptible lull. Start in on the ballotine for later this week.

4:15 P.M.

Madeleine's slicing scallions for the ricotta dish. Cara opens the oven, brushes her gratins. A pork leg has gone on the grill, the first piece of meat to do so today. The fire's high and intense.

4:16 P.M.

Michael makes a quick adjustment to the fire, then adds a dozen and a half quartered Belgian endive, seasoned and oiled, to a grill to the right of the fire. Soon he'll push them closer together so they can steam a bit. Their ultimate fate is to join some grilled asparagus, bitter grapefruit, mint, and sesame for a dish Russ says would never fly at Chez Panisse. "Sesame and citrus! Too weird! But it's delicious, and funny."

4:17 P.M.

Cara fries the burdock she peeled, to go on top of the crab. It glistens, golden brown and fine—almost hairlike. "It's funny, doing burdock like this," Russ says.

4:18 P.M.

Becca, the hostess, works a feather duster around the room.

4:45 P.M.

Waiter meeting. The waiters plus Becca and Allison gather in front of the bar as Michael goes over the menu. Savoy spinach isn't the same as spinach. The burdock is fried at a low temp, has a consistency that might be called tacky. There's a new waiter in the group and Michael explains classic Camino flatbread. The wine list is reviewed. A brief theoretical digression unfolds, on the subject of a particular bird occasionally on the menu. "'Squab' is a trick to make you think you're not eating pigeon," Allison notes. "We say 'pigeon.'"

She goes on to add a note about the oysters: Discourage diners from eating the greens they're served on. How? someone asks. "Tell them, 'They're not delicious. If you eat them you'll think we're bad cooks.'" Class dismissed.

5 P.M.

Tasters. A knot of cooks clusters around Russ at the butcher block. Russ dips a finger, declares Michael's sauce "a little . . ." Here he makes a "flat" gesture. He suggests adding a little misdirection—toasted coriander seed and cilantro? Michael nods.

He moves on to the chicory salad, with homemade vinegar and aged sheep's milk cheese. This time there's no gesture. It's just not right. The restaurant opens in half an hour. The salad will be remade three times in that window until finally he signs off.

5:30 P.M.

Brian adjusts the lights.

5:32 P.M.

Allison readjusts the lights.

7:50 P.M.

Dinner's in full swing, but a section of Russ's mental real estate is occupied by the crate of Seville oranges in the back of the kitchen. He started using the fruit last year, after a glut had sent down the price—he

ordered a bunch and forced himself to get acquainted. Now they're back and he's discovering ways to braise meat with them, make marmalade, and incorporate them into drinks at the bar. This is Camino in a nutshell, or one of its nutshells: enforced creativity with new ingredients.

Not everyone leaps at these projects. Occasionally, a cook will come through whose follow-through and enterprise are lacking. These qualities are cornerstones of good cooking, certainly of Camino cooking. These cooks don't last here long.

THURSDAY

9:30 A.M.

Prep meeting. The big slots for the night are filled: lamb, rockfish, oysters. A vegetable dish is needed and Russ notes the abundance of artichokes, plus puntarelle and chervil. As it happens, he says, they'll all work well together. Done. New dish invented.

Wait, I say, explain your idea process.

"My process is, I just see myself cooking it," Russ replies. "That's it. I see a picture of it in my head."

9:42 A.M.

Russ wants to make consommé this week. To do so, he'll need two blond stocks—chicken, duck—plus a bunch of leftover mushroom butts. ("It's not a big seller. I just want it. It's the fanciest thing we do, and it's Allison's favorite dish.")

This leads him into Tetris mode, trying to make all the moving parts fit together just right, a puzzle of time and space and traffic and cost and the whims of human appetites. Given that he intends to serve lamb on Friday and Saturday (he'll use the leftover meat for a ragù on Monday—most restaurants would buy a dedicated shoulder for a ragù), will there be too many meaty things in proximity?

"Maybe if we blow through a lot of chicken tonight, we can make a different soup with the leftovers," he calculates aloud. "But if there's a lot leftover, we can do consommé on Sunday. Or we could serve the ragù on the weekend and consommé on Monday . . ."

The stakes are high, Russ says later. If the chicken goes bad before it can be sold, "it's a big deal. It's depressing and wasteful and I just feel shitty about it."

9:53 A.M.

Somehow, despite these complexities, this is considered a slow day. Camino thrives on these. Slow days are project days. Vin d'orange. Curaçao. A shrub, excavated from a 1908 book on cocktails. All these drinks employ the Seville oranges. Last week, someone accidentally juiced a bunch of the Sevilles, thinking they were Valencias. This person has now been forgiven. Sort of.

10 A.M.

Russ is cooking on the line today, taking on the chicken and the artichoke dishes. He's particularly excited about the latter. "It's indulgent."

NOON

The pig Russ ordered? Its head is cooking in a vast pot, the tongue in a pot of its own. Jess, one of the newer cooks, is getting a lesson from Russ. The temperature, he explains, should be just higher than that of poaching—look for a few bubbles, where with poaching there'd be none. But don't crank the heat or the meat will dry out.

1:05 P.M.

Michael makes banh mi sandwiches for staff lunch. He does this from leftovers and they're better than any ever created. His secret: homemade garlic mayonnaise, the sweet carrots from yesterday's sardine dish, endive from yesterday, sesame, some particularly flavorful slices of pork, flatbread steamed gently into buns and, of course, chiles and cilantro.

The staff devours these, sips tea, plucks artichokes and segues into the cooks' meeting. Russ decrees that the word smoky will help move his chicken dish. He wants to sell the hell out of it.

4:24 P.M.

Russ stands at the fire, delicately picking through chervil while Rachel hacksaws the back legs off a lamb. Russ leans over and shows her his technique for counting the ribs, cutting between the eighth and ninth.

4:25 P.M.

Marx, it must be said, would love how utterly different the line operates here. Instead of a prep cook doing some small part all day, never seeing the final product, everyone has his or her own project that they see to completion. Cara's cutting the pork belly for the pancetta. Jess is making flatbread. Madeleine's learning to cut the skin off a pig. Russ leans the other way, patiently explains how to hold one's hand to apply the right kind of pressure against the skin.

Rachel trades her hacksaw for a cleaver, goes at the lamb's spine. There follows a series of heavy hacks and finally a satisfying thwock, down to the cutting board.

4:32 P.M.

Over at the bar, Tyler is stirring the vin d'orange, the sugar having released oil over the course of the day. He'll also make use of the leftover syrup from the kitchen's candied blood orange peel, and the leftover egg whites from when the kitchen uses yokes for ice cream.

5 P.M.

Tasters. A little sloppy, Russ says gently, referring to Madeleine's salad. She used the wrong grapefruit, and chopped too much parsley in advance—it'll oxidize, Russ says, chop as you need it.

Rachel gets critiqued, too: Her rockfish dish needs less tomato in the broth, plus better plating. Russ nudges some asparagus around, removes some cabbage to make it cleaner. Then he pulls cabbage from the dish entirely. Too salty, too much monotony.

"There should be more space for the crab butter to pop," he says.

Rachel agrees. "A lot of people would've loved it how it was, but I'd have gotten bored of it halfway through."

5 : 30 P.M.

Brian adjusts the lights.

"I guarantee Allison will readjust these in two minutes."

5 : 32 P.M.

Allison readjusts the lights.

9 P.M.

The chicken—the smoky chicken—is selling really well. Slight inner smile detectable in Russ.

10 : 24 P.M.

When a cook doesn't make the cut—and most wash out—it's generally not for poor knife skills or a limited grasp of French cuisine. It's enterprise that keeps your paychecks coming at Camino.

Someone on the line doesn't fully have it.

The rain has tapered off, the fire's been extinguished, and the last diner has left when Russ pulls aside one of the cooks. A few months in, it's clear she's not enough of a self-starter. Her staff meals lacked enterprise; her projects get abandoned sometimes. Russ breaks the news to her in the small, cookbook-lined office. It's friendly and not entirely a shock. Then she's gone.

FRIDAY

9 : 30 A.M.

Prep meeting. Lauren has an idea for a burdock and artichoke dish. Russ likes it—but has aesthetic concerns.

"Both of those foods want to turn ugly. What if you lay some nettles in there?"

Agreed.

10 : 14 A.M.

Yesterday's pig head is today's fritters. They'll go in a salad.

10 : 33 A.M.

Consommé tomorrow. Russ wants to butcher the ducks today, so their carcasses are available for stock.

12 : 29 P.M.

A new waiter will be auditioning tonight. As Allison explains, it's a tough gig—the ideal candidate needs the know-how that comes from fine dining, but the easygoingness of a more casual place. The guy who's coming has many years of experience, has the potential to slip right in. Allison's optimistic.

1 : 30 P.M.

Cooks' meeting. A cheese called columbine is on the menu. Russ worries briefly about the word's associations.

4 : 45 P.M.

There were no nettles for Lauren's promising-but-colorless burdock and artichoke dish, but she's going for it anyway. "Super ultra hippy-looking," observes Russ after her third attempt.

5 : 30 P.M.

Brian adjusts the lights.

5 : 32 P.M.

Allison readjusts the lights.

"The trick is to look at the bald heads. If I see a glare, the lights need to come down."

7 P.M.

The Friday night vibe is fully in place. Lou Reed is playing quietly, a leg of lamb is twirling in front of the fire, and nearly all the seats are already full. A group of fifteen is on the horizon and Allison's making sure space will open up at the right time. She's also got an eye on the auditioning waiter. He's mature and professional but diffident at times, tentative. "He's really sweet," one of the waiters says to me, "it sucks he's not going to cut it."

10:55 P.M.

He doesn't. Otherwise the evening's a success. The fire is out and the staff has dribbled out to one of the communal tables for dinner and decompression. Talk turns to whether Russ would get "a Korean exception" from the obligation to join a gang, should he ever go to prison.

The restaurant's closed at this point, but eight parties in the room are still going. Each of them had Lauren's burdock and artichoke. It was delicious, but Russ was right; the color was gray and uniform, like a black-and-white movie. Regarding its appearance, Lauren is the most critical of all. Russ says the self-criticism is worth more to him than getting a dish's hue right.

SATURDAY

11:15 A.M.

The Camino brunch was invented to open the restaurant up to a broader demographic. Indeed, this morning's clientele includes a dozen kids of varying ages and temperaments. Russ stands at the edge of the salad station, assessing.

"It's under control. Let's go."

We file out the back door and climb into his pickup.

11:35 A.M.

There's no farmer's market better than the Berkeley Farmer's Market, Russ says. He arrives armed with a dolly, a mental list of what remains in the walk-in, plus a general openness to whatever looks good.

The grapefruits look good. Russ buys two bags from Didar and his wife, Didar, of Guru Ram Das Orchards, in Capay Valley. Both wear long ponytails under baseball hats. The grapefruits are a gamble—some will likely have some frost damage—but the Didars have been giving him great stuff since his Chez Panisse days.

The recent frost is just one concern. Trini from Riverdog Farm says they've gotten seven inches of rain recently, but that's still below half of where they should be. As a result, no sweet corn will be planted next season. Russ is crushed. This represents a major financial hit for the farm, plus no corn for Camino—he typically buys a hundred pounds a week. "It's a crowd-pleaser, and it's great for vegetarian dishes, good to grill. We'll need to figure out a replacement," he says. He buys rutabaga, green mustard, King Richard leeks, green garlic, cilantro, and asparagus but he does so in a funk.

Next, two more flats of asparagus from the Kaki Farms folks, from a town called Gridley—it'll tide Camino over till peas and favas are in season. The mention of peas sends Russ into a reverie. "You can have truffles or foie gras, but a perfect bowl of peas? Hard to beat."

1:36 P.M.

Cooks' meeting. There shall be no crab butter in the grilled rockfish and little gems with pickled chiles and crab broth—too many strong flavors, Russ felt; let the chiles have a little space. As for the burnt nut ice cream with chocolate and cream, it's revealed that the hazelnuts, pecans, walnuts, and almonds have all been mixed together. Russ clucks. "We needed the space in the back," someone replies. Conversation swings around to Michael, who dined at a San Francisco restaurant last night. "Fine. Boring. But fine—well-seasoned," he reports, shrugging. Knowing nods all around.

2 P.M.

"The stupid ragù and the stupid consommé are weighing on me," Russ sighs.

3:15 P.M.

Chris, the neighbor from up the street, comes by to drop off some homegrown flora from her yard and, well, her neighbor's yard. Persian mint, anise hyssop, *yacón*, lovage, sunchokes, and weird things like mashua, a tuber-forming nasturtium relative.

4:44 P.M.

Lauren has her hands in a bowl of onions and a furrowed brow. It's furrowed for a good two minutes, which is two hours in non-kitchen time.

"I can't decide if I ground the coriander, cumin, caraway, and black pepper enough," she finally says. She's a friendly woman in outer space–themed leggings. "Very little is ever definitive," she adds. "The menu changes every night. You want to trust your judgment, but of course you're also trying to guess what Russ will like."

4:50 P.M.

Fred Niger Van Herck, a Frenchman with pale eyes and salt-and-pepper hair, drops in to give notes to the waitstaff about such things as the breaking of the musk and the nuances of biodynamic farming. Van Herck is a winemaker from Domaine L'Ecu, a fifth-generation winery in Muscadet. He passes around samples of his crisp and complex whites, some of which will appear on the menu. Allison is carrying two bottles to the back when one slips out of her hand. Life goes on.

5:25 P.M.

A dozen broken bottles couldn't dampen Russ's mood. He's chopping duck carcasses into chunks, to expose as much surface area as possible for the browning. While Van Herck discussed Muscadet, Russ rolled up his sleeves and butchered fifteen ducks. There's a spring in his step—he's actually bouncing. The duck will roast with chicken and quail bones. The consommé will be done by tomorrow night.

5:30 P.M.

Brian adjusts the lights.

5:32 P.M.

Allison readjusts the lights.

SUNDAY

11 A.M.

There's something about Camino's dining room that feels vibrant and warm even with a less-than-full crowd. That's what today's brunch has brought, so Russ feels reasonably comfortable escaping for a bit, to hit the Temescal Farmers' Market. He grabs another tea—he is seldom without a glass—and we almost achieve escape velocity.

11:02 A.M.

We're nearly at the door when Russ begins to worry aloud. Might Sam run out of carrots? There are only three people on the line this morning, so the margin for error is narrow.

There's this to think about, and a dozen other things, but essentially Russ is stalling. I recognize it—the chefly equivalent of loitering in the hallway after dropping one's kid off at kindergarten. At last, he's convinced everything's under control. Into the truck, off to Temescal.

11:40 A.M.

Russ is cooking tonight and has a hole in his chicken dish. He's hoping to find something at the market to fill it—something the cut the "softness" he feels in the plate. Also, they ran out of lamb sauce last night and

dipped into the chicken sauce. So they're low. Plan is to make a roux and a giblet gravy to stretch it. "Which feels very Sunday night anyway," Russ notes.

11:46 A.M.

We slalom the crowd, hitting Sun Rise Farms for a couple crates of grapefruit, skipping Pinnacle's cauliflower—looks good to me, but Russ, from ten feet, spots mini florets. He also walks past a good deal on butter lettuce. "It's good, but this other farm will have *incredible* butter lettuce in two weeks, and I wouldn't want a customer to think this is what our butter lettuce tastes like."

12:19 P.M.

Back in the truck, loaded up with onions and marjoram and celery but with nothing to fill the hole in Russ's chicken dish. Wasn't that the point? He's weirdly calm. "I'll have to get creative," he says with a shrug.

12:40 P.M.

We see it from all the way out on the street. Brunch is a madhouse.

12:42 P.M.

Inside there isn't an inch of slack. Sam, Michael, and Danny are on the line, whipping from fire to knife to egg pan to plate and back at a speed I, personally, haven't reached in years. It looks like Charlie Chaplin speed. Jaws are set, words clipped.

"A1–44?

"A1–44."

"We're good on puntarelle."

"Don't hold back on A9."

"I'll take 3 on B1."

1 P.M.

The madhouse is growing, not shrinking. A dozen people are lined up at the bar, two-deep, with more bodies on the sidewalk, in the drizzle. I ask Michael what's going on.

"People like brunch."

2 P.M.

No diminishment in the insanity, but the tidal wave—that's what it is—doesn't seem to trouble the cooks. It's almost strange. I find myself thinking of this certain breed of horse found in Iceland. Pushed to a certain speed, its so-called fifth gait, the animal actually runs smoother, the way sports car people tell you their Porsches and Ferraris handle better above 70.

2:15 P.M.

The tidal wave at last subsides, after delaying the cooks' meeting half an hour. Two hundred and thirty people, Allison reports. Busiest brunch ever, not counting Mother's Day.

Still nothing to fill Russ's chicken dish slot. Rachel proposes a fennel salad. Russ makes a face.

3 P.M.

Russ is teaching Lauren—till recently a vegetarian—the Camino approach to meat. They roast a lamb leg, then learn to carve it. "Nobody knows how to carve these anymore," Russ says. "We slice it here, rather than doing cubes. It's old-fashioned. I like it. Gives you a bigger yield, too."

5:23 P.M.

Last-minute change at tasters, customers already at the door. Russ tells Michael his dish needs to change—the radishes had gotten too tough in the roasting. Russ's solution: a raw radish salad.

5:30 P.M.

Brian adjusts the lights.

5:32 P.M.

Allison readjusts the lights.

6:30 P.M.

It's going to be a slow evening, everyone agrees—it's Oscar night, so the Bay Area will be eating popcorn at home rather than venturing out.

7:30 P.M.

So much for Oscars. The place is packed, stays that way till almost 10. By the end of the night, everyone's that odd mix of drained and wired.

MONDAY

9:30 A.M.

It's Little Bird Monday and Russ is wondering what will sell. At last, the lamb ragù is on the menu, as is crab and the consommé. Russ chuckles. "What a funny menu."

Talk at the prep meeting turns to the artichokes from last night. Perhaps they need more acid? Michael and Russ joke about cooking them in flour and water—a *blanc*—and everyone titters. A week in, an artichoke-infused version of gallows humor has taken root. Finally, Russ suggests tossing them with turmeric which, while not an acid, is an anti-inflammatory. Everyone makes a dude-just-dropped-some-science face.

10:02 A.M.

Russ is happy. The walk-in has been cleared out nicely. Madeleine is prepping vegetables for the raft, for the consommé; she'll skim the duck and quail fat off next.

2 P.M.

A visit from Thad Vogler, who designed Camino's bar program and whose exacting approach to spirits borders on religion. He's a massively tall man, with a crisp white shirt and a wry, sad smile. Ostensibly, he's here to talk to the waiters and bartenders about cognac, armagnac, and brandy, but his chats double as all-purpose sermons.

"Why do I like spirits? Time travel," Vogler says. "When I drink a cocktail that I know was drunk two hundred years ago, I feel a connection to history, and to place. That's what it can do."

Starting from the position that alcohol must be treated as any other farm product, too, Vogler installed in Camino not just a dry rigorousness about making principled decisions at the bar but also an enthusiastic one. For the next forty-five minutes, the crew gets pumped learning about agricultural subregions of France, and the history and places where a few new bottles come from.

8:12 P.M.

Russ and Allison, in a somewhat rare moment, are sitting together in their own dining room, eating a leisurely dinner of their design. This is also the final meal of my week at Camino, and we eat as Camino-ly as possible. Herb jam toast. Oysters. A small plate of young sauerkraut. The ragù. Not one but two quail dishes. The consommé. (Regular bowl or Chinese bowl? Allison and Russ argue the merits of each.)

Brian, the manager, joins us for an eight-minute discussion of what to drink with various dishes, and in what order to eat them. (Beer must accompany the ragù, everyone agrees.) We start with one of the new brandy experiments from the bar, involving, miraculously, gin and apple brandy.

The next hour of deliciousness is, in a sense, the week itself, distilled into food form, drawing to its close. Tomorrow is Tuesday—no Camino. Allison tells me they'll sleep in, do some dishes, do some laundry, and generally be somewhere besides here. Then they'll invariably pop in to Camino. They'll extract themselves, grab Chinese food or Korean food, maybe see a movie. Then back the next morning to start again.

CHAPTER FOUR

FISH

FISH

I hate fishing. You bring the sandwiches and just sit there on the pier, thinking about the sandwiches.

But fish? I've loved fish since I was a kid, when a whole bass or bonito was the ultimate treat in my family. It was always whole fish. Which made my dad a nervous wreck—if I got a Filet-O-Fish from McDonald's, he'd warn me to be careful of the bones. But my mom was the opposite, so it was bone-in fish all the time. If you did get a bone caught in your throat, she wouldn't bat an eyelash. She'd shrug and say, "Eat more rice." Bone-in fish is a juicy, delicious, fatty, fun mess.

We make fish as hard for ourselves as humanly possible. Only local fish, we decreed on day one. This arbitrary rule imposes limitations, and limitations spawn creativity. You have to get inventive, and a deep set of skills develops around that inventiveness. We're fans in general of making life hard for ourselves—absurd edicts abound at Camino.

What does this mean for our customers? No monkfish. No scallops. Yes lingcod, yes crab, yes salmon, yes rockfish. The occasional smelt, the rare sand dab. Some nights we can only get squid.

People assume it's about *sustainability, locavorism*. Nope. We serve local fish for the same reason you order vodka in Moscow and ride a camel in Egypt: it's about connecting with a place. You wouldn't order Alaskan halibut in Hawaii. You'd get *aku* from the old guy selling it out of the back of his pickup. Similarly, you order Bay Area fish when you're in a Bay Area restaurant. Life's just more fun that way.

That's not to say I don't also care about sustainability. When I first started writing menus as a chef, fish was the first item where I thought systematically about my impact on the world. I found that to be a great responsibility. I did tons of research into how different species are doing, and how they're caught. Right off the bat it was easy to veto shark's fin, shrimp, and Atlantic cod. But the list kept growing. No bottom-trawled petrale sole—only hook-and-line or purse seine.

Only fish from here. Seems straightforward to me, but the fish market guys give me endless shit about this rule. *Hey, which fish is local?* I'll ask. "The striper's local." *Really?* "Well, to us it's local, because it's caught by this great guy doing great sustainability stuff . . ." *Cool, but that's not local—that's something else.* There's a lot of confusion in the seafood industry, even from the folks who aren't trying to deceive you—and, by the way, most of them are trying to deceive you.

The constant question of what's available throws the menu into chaos. Some fish grills well and some doesn't. If we have a fish that needs to be cooked in the wood oven, that means the vegetarian dish must come off the grill; everything shifts. Every night is a puzzle.

For the fish that handle fire nicely, there's still the matter of convincing new cooks not to grill too fast. If you have those iconic grill marks on your fish, there's a good chance you've dried it out, and all you're going to taste is the fire, rather than the delicate fish flavor. People often think that's what grilled fish has to taste like. But the truth is, once you learn to control the coals and the fire, grilled fish can taste like so much more. It can taste fancy. It can taste like a place—ideally nearby—and it can taste like a certain time of year. And in my case, it can taste like childhood.

BAKED OYSTERS WITH ABSINTHE AND BREADCRUMBS

Serves 4 to 6

Since we only serve local fish and shellfish at Camino, oysters from Tomales Bay have a pretty regular spot on the menu since they are plentiful much of the year. We rarely serve them raw. Restaurants that serve raw oysters often have dedicated shuckers working in a station dedicated to raw seafood. If we were to serve raw oysters we would have to totally rearrange our cook line and hire another cook (hard enough to staff the place as it is!). Plus it makes sense for the fireplace restaurant to cook oysters using the fire.

At Camino, we bake these oysters in the wood oven, but you can just as easily bake them in a regular oven. We serve them with different side salads—red daikon, fennel, *yacón*—as a little accompaniment.

    ½ large fennel bulb with fronds

    1 stick unsalted butter, softened to room temperature

    1 scallion

    6 mint leaves

    Splash of absinthe

    ¾ cup Breadcrumbs (see page 33)

    Salt

    24 oysters

Preheat the oven to 500°F (or as hot as your oven will go without burning your house down).

Trim the fennel, reserving a handful of the fronds for the filling and saving the rest of the fronds and the stems to line the baking dish. Finely dice the trimmed fennel bulb, then sauté it in 1 tablespoon of the butter for about a minute. Add a splash of water and cook until tender, about 2 more minutes.

Split the scallion lengthwise, then cut it into fine slices. Finely chop the mint and the handful of fennel fronds. Work them together with the scallion,

cooked fennel, absinthe, breadcrumbs, a pinch of salt, and the remaining butter. If the butter is not well incorporated, you will end up with pools of melted butter in the oyster shells.

Shucking oysters is more a matter of finesse, not strength so approach it gently and with a little caution. Fold a dishtowel and set it in the palm of your non-dominant had. Place the oyster, cup side down, on top of the dishtowel with the narrow, hinged end pointed toward you. Without using much force (because you are pointing the knife directly at your hand), finesse the tip of your oyster knife into the hinge. It helps if you wiggle both the knife and the oyster slightly to help the knife find its way in. Once the tip is in, give it a twist—the shell will release with a pop. Often, a little piece of the shell will break off—wipe your knife clean before going back in. Pry open the top shell and run the knife across the inside of the upper shell to cut the abductor muscle, located on the right side of the round end. Discard the top shell. Hold the oyster steady from this point on so you don't spill the liquor—you want it to keep the oyster moist while you bake it. Run your knife across the inside of the bottom shell to cut the other side of the abductor muscle. If the oyster isn't loose you may need to run your knife around the edge. Remove any bits of shell or detritus that fell in.

Set the shells carefully in a baking dish lined with the rest of the fennel stems and fronds to hold them upright. Put about a tablespoon of the breadcrumb mixture on top of each oyster and bake until the breadcrumbs are brown, approximately 6 minutes.

THREE GRILLED SQUID DISHES

We serve squid at Camino fairly often because it is our main local cephalopod, caught right in Monterey Bay without a lot of bycatch.

Common wisdom is that you need to cook squid either hot and fast or slow and long or else it will be rubbery. When *grilling* squid, the rules are a little different. You want a hottish bed of coals, but to avoid the creepy texture of warm undercooked squid, you want to make sure that the inside of the squid body has time to cook without the outside getting charred. In other words, not that hot and not that fast. It should take about 5 to 7 minutes, depending on the size of the squid. The tentacles will take the same amount of time if you cook them on a slightly cooler area of the grill as they are spindly and tend to burn.

SOME HINTS:

Skewer tentacles and bodies separately.

Put the skewer through the tail end of the body.

Skewer both tentacles and bodies with a little space between them so they will cook evenly.

Make sure your grill is clean, brushed, and wiped with a dry towel.

Make sure your coals are hot with absolutely no flames.

And a little personal mysticism for which I receive a lot of eye rolling from my own crew . . . I like to point the opening of the squid body toward the fire so that heat swirls in and cooks the interior while you are grilling the outside.

After you skewer the squid, brush the bodies and tentacles with a little bit of olive oil and sprinkle with salt on both sides (and sesame seeds or chiles if you are using them). Place the bodies on the hot side of the grill with the opening pointed toward the fire (see Grill Setup page 132). The tentacles should go on the part of the grill that is just a whisper cooler, with legs pointing away from the fire. Grill until the bodies puff up and the undersides turn from gray to reddish brown, about 3 minutes. Then flip the squid over, keeping the opening of the bodies toward the fire and the tentacles away from the fire. Cook until the other side changes color and there are no translucent spots (even between the tentacles).

GRILLED SQUID WITH TOMATOES AND KOREAN PERILLA
Serves 6

Korean perilla is related to shiso, but it is a little stronger and more bitter. It's also harder to find, so you can substitute shiso.

> 1 clove garlic
>
> Salt
>
> Olive oil
>
> 1 pint cherry tomatoes
>
> ½ bunch scallions, sliced thinly, including all the white and green parts
>
> Handful of Korean perilla leaves, cut into thin strips
>
> 1 or 2 large ripe tomatoes
>
> 1 dried hot chile
>
> 2 pounds squid, cleaned

Pound the garlic with a pinch of salt in a mortar. Stir in a couple of tablespoons of olive oil.

Slice the cherry tomatoes in half through the north and south poles and put them in a bowl. Season them with a little salt, the scallions, the perilla, and the garlicky oil. Mix, taste, and adjust the seasoning.

Core and slice the large tomatoes and spread them on to a platter.

continued

Tear the chile into manageable pieces, discard the stem, and grind to a coarse powder in a spice grinder.

Brush the squid with olive oil and sprinkle with salt and a pinch of ground chile. Grill as on page 112.

Right when the squid are done grilling, season the large tomatoes with salt and more ground chile. Slide the squid off the skewer on top of the sliced tomatoes. Spoon the juicy cherry tomato and perilla mixture over the squid.

GRILLED SQUID WITH CUCUMBERS AND ANISE HYSSOP

Serves 6

2 cloves garlic

Salt

1 small spring onion or shallot, thinly sliced

3 or 4 limes, or 2 lemons

1½ pounds cucumbers (any combination of Mediterranean, lemon, Armenian, Japanese, or, the hard to find, Italian pickling melon)

3 tablespoons olive oil, plus more for brushing

Small handful of anise hyssop leaves (including flowers, if any), or substitute mint, chervil, tarragon, basil, or summer savory

2 pounds squid, cleaned

1 tablespoon Toasted Sesame Seeds (see page 33)

To make the dressing for the cucumber salad, pound the garlic and a pinch of salt in a mortar. Add the spring onion, juice the limes directly into the mortar, and stir.

Peel the cucumbers. When we are using a variety of cucumbers, we slice each one in a different shape. I think it helps reinforce the different flavor that each one has and it's whimsical. Mediterranean or Japanese cucumbers look good split in half lengthwise and

cut diagonally in thick slices. If you're using lemon cucumbers, it's nice to cut them so they look like little lemon wedges. I usually leave the seeds in unless they are really big or bitter. Put the cucumbers in a bowl and season them with salt. Pour in the olive oil and a few spoonfuls of the garlicky lime juice. Tear or slice the anise hyssop (or whatever herb you're using) and toss everything together. Taste and adjust the lime, salt, and olive oil as necessary. Set the cucumber salad aside while you grill the squid. Be sure to taste it again before you plate it.

Brush the squid with olive oil and sprinkle with salt and sesame seeds. Grill as on page 112.

When the squid is done, spread the cucumbers on the plate, leaving a little juice in the bowl. Slide the squid off the skewer onto the cucumbers and spoon the remaining cucumber juice over the squid.

GRILLED SQUID WITH FRESH TURMERIC, CHILES, AND RADISHES

Serves 6

Olive oil

1 clove garlic, sliced

2 thumb-size pieces fresh turmeric

Salt

1 bunch radishes

1 dried moderately hot chile

1 small lime

2 pounds squid, cleaned

Heat a small pan over medium heat. Add enough olive oil to coat the bottom of the pan, then add the sliced garlic and turmeric and immediately begin to shake the pan so that the garlic and turmeric sizzle. You want the turmeric and garlic to spend a moment or

continued

two in the hot oil, but you really don't want them to get brown at all. Add a couple of tablespoons of water to the pan, and let them sizzle for a few seconds. All the oil and liquid should turn bright yellow. Pour the contents of the pan into a bowl and use a rubber spatula to get as much out of the pan as possible. Add a pinch of salt, let cool for a moment, then add another couple tablespoons of olive oil.

Tear the chile into manageable pieces, discard the stem, and grind to a coarse powder in a spice grinder.

Trim the radish root ends and leaves, leaving an inch or so of stem attached. If the tops are exceptional, you might consider leaving a leaf or two. Slice the radishes lengthwise into thin slices. If they're small and not very dense, you might want to cut them into quarters.

Season the sliced radishes with salt and sprinkle with ground chile. Add the turmeric-olive oil mixture, squeeze in some lime juice, toss well, and taste. Set the radish mixture aside while you grill the squid. Brush the squid with olive oil and sprinkle with salt. Grill as on page 112.

Slide the squid off the skewers onto each plate. Spoon the radish-turmeric mixture over the squid, and serve.

GRILLED SARDINES AND ASPARAGUS WITH CITRUS, CHILES, AND SESAME

Serves 4

If I had to pick a fish, I'd pick sardines every time. The opening menu at Camino had goat, egg, and sardines as the three main course options. My friend Cal told me I was nuts—that goat would be too challenging and *then* what would people have to turn to? Sardines?!

Fresh-out-of-the-water sardines are full of clean, oceany flavor. If sardines look at all suspicious at the market, don't get them. Sardines, like mackerel, blue fish, and other oily fish, degrade quickly.

If you are new to sardines, take this bit of advice: try to pull the filets off the spine before you begin eating, or all the little bones will get tangled up in the flesh and I will not be able to win you over to sardines—you will have to order the goat.

16 or 20 fat asparagus stalks

8 whole sardines, scaled and gutted

Olive oil

Salt

1 tablespoon white and black sesame seeds, toasted (see page 33)

5 or 6 mild chiles, such as pasilla

2 cloves garlic

1 bunch mint

½ bunch cilantro

1 bunch chives

2 sprigs tarragon

3 cups assorted citrus segments (from about 3 pounds of citrus, such as orange, blood orange, grapefruit, or pomelo)

Build a fire to grill the sardines.

Break off the woody ends of the asparagus and peel each stalk from the flower all the way to the end. I like fat asparagus because there is more of the sweet interior and less of the grassy skin. You can grill fat asparagus from raw, but it is pretty much a shriveled mess at the end. So even though I hate blanching, I'm going to give you blanching instructions for asparagus because, at the end of the day, it is actually better this way. The rule of thumb is lots of very salty, rapidly boiling water. You want to keep the temperature of the water high when you add the asparagus so that the blanching happens super quickly and the asparagus retains its bright green color and flavor.

Blanch the asparagus in salted water until bright green and slightly crunchier than you want—a really fat asparagus might take a little more than a minute. Spread the stalks out on a baking sheet and let cool.

Lightly brush the sardines with olive oil and season them with salt and a big pinch of sesame seeds. Toss the cooled asparagus stalks with enough olive oil to coat them, then sprinkle with salt and sesame seeds.

Break up the chiles into manageable pieces and grind them in a spice grinder to a coarse texture. Rehydrate the chiles by mixing them with a couple tablespoons of boiling water.

Pound the garlic and a pinch of salt with a mortar and pestle until it is a roughish purée. Chop the herbs. Mix the chiles, garlic, and herbs with enough oil to make a thick but pourable sauce. Add a pinch of salt, and taste.

Rake the coals under the grill for medium-hot grilling. Sardines have particularly delicate skin, so make sure your grill is well-seasoned.

After the grill heats up, put the sardines on the grill over medium-high heat and cook until fairly brown, then carefully flip them over and grill on the other side. Larger sardines will take 3 or 4 minutes on each side; smaller ones about 2 minutes on each side. Grill the asparagus at the same time as you are grilling the fish because you need the same temperature grill. The asparagus should take about 5 to 6 minutes.

Spread the citrus on a platter and lightly season it with salt. Place the hot sardines and asparagus on top of the citrus. Spoon over some of the herby chile sauce and sprinkle the rest of the sesame seeds over the top. Serve the remaining sauce on the side.

This would be particularly good with Fried Farro (page 8).

SALTED LINGCOD

We don't buy salt cod because it comes from Atlantic cod, which a) isn't local and b) is totally overfished. But I really like salt cod, so we decided to make our own version by salting our local lingcod. The flavor is a little different and it has a finer texture, but it's delicious. I make a habit of buying a little more lingcod than I need so that we have some to salt.

First, remove the skin and pinbones from your lingcod filet or have your fishmonger do it for you. Put the fish in a baking dish or other non-reactive platter and coat it evenly with coarse salt. Put a plate on top of the fish as a weight. Cover the fish with parchment paper and refrigerate. Flip the fish over every two days and pour off any liquid that has collected.

The amount of salt you use depends on how soon you are going to use the fish. If you are planning on using it in just a few days, salt it only a little more heavily than you would for grilling fresh fish. If you want to keep it for a week or more, go heavier on the salt. The fish will get dryer and funkier the longer it ages. If you salt it very heavily, it will keep in the refrigerator for a month. If you are a really serious fish preserver, you can take it out after a month, wrap it in cheesecloth, and hang it in a cool, dry area. We usually keep it in the refrigerator anywhere from 3 days to 2 weeks. After two weeks, the texture is firm but not totally dry. If you're grilling it for a salad or a fish stew, soak it for a few hours to make it less salty. If you're making brandade (see below), you can rely on the poaching to remove enough of the salt.

LINGCOD BRANDADE AND BRANDADE FRITTERS
Serves 6

2 sprigs parsley

3 fresh bay leaves

7 cloves garlic, 5 peeled

1 1/2 pounds Salted Lingcod (preceding recipe)

1/2 cup milk

1 small russet potato

Black pepper

continued

2 tablespoons cream

¼ cup olive oil, plus more as needed

4 egg whites, or 2 whole eggs

Breadcrumbs (see page 33)

Rice bran oil

Put the parsley, bay leaves, and a couple smashed and unpeeled cloves of garlic in a pot. Set the salted fish on top, pour in the milk, and then add enough water to barely cover the fish. (If I didn't have any milk in my fridge, I wouldn't go out and buy it just for this. It'll be fine with only water.)

Bring up to a gentle simmer (don't let it boil—if the fish cooks too hard it will get a cottony texture). The time it takes to heat it up to a simmer should be enough to cook the fish all the way through, but if there are some thicker pieces that are not done yet, turn off the heat and let them sit in the hot liquid until they are opaque. Take the fish out of the liquid and break it up into big pieces.

Ideally, you're going to use this milky liquid to cook the potato, but taste it first; if it's too salty, you can just boil the potato in water.

Peel the potato and cut it into big chunks—you don't want the potato to absorb too much liquid, so pretty big pieces are ideal. Put them into a smaller pot with the remaining cloves of peeled garlic and pour in just enough milky liquid to cover, leaving behind the herbs and unpeeled garlic. Bring to a boil, then turn down the heat so that the liquid simmers, and cook the potato until it's done.

Strain the boiled potato and garlic and pass them through a food mill or use a potato masher to get them pretty smooth (don't overwork them or they'll turn gummy).

Break up the fish into biggish flakes, picking out any bones you find, and add them to the mashed potato and garlic. Grind some black pepper over the top and

stir in the cream and olive oil. Stir everything together and lightly smash up the bigger pieces of fish. Taste for seasoning. If it seems dry, you can add a little more olive oil. At this point, you have brandade, which you could bake in the oven until brown and serve with garlic toast and a radish-preserved lemon salad.

Or you could make fritters . . .

For fritters, chill the mixture for about 15 minutes to firm it up and make it easier to handle.

Whisk the egg whites just until they're a little frothy. (If you don't have a few egg whites lying around, waiting to be used, left over from making ice cream or mayonnaise or something else, you should just use whole eggs, yolks and all.) Scoop up ping pong ball–size pieces of the brandade, dip them in the egg white, shake off the excess, and roll them in the breadcrumbs. Set the breaded brandade on a plate and refrigerate them until you're ready to fry.

Heat the rice bran oil to 340°F. Carefully lower in a few pieces at a time and fry them until they form a nice, hard crust, about 3 minutes. Serve hot as a snack with lemon wedges or with a puntarelle salad.

GRILLED SALTED LINGCOD AND ROCKFISH STEW WITH SAFFRON AND MINTY GARLIC TOAST
Serves 6

Ideally, you use the scraps (head, tail, fins) of the fish you are serving in the soup to make the stock, but if that is not possible, you can get them from your fishmonger. Be sure to remove the gills from the fish head because they will make your stock bitter.

1 whole hook-and-line-caught rockfish (about 5 pounds), scaled, gutted, and gills removed

Olive oil

Salt

2 pounds Salted Lingcod (page 117) or other fine-fleshed fish, such as sea bass

3 pounds fish bones

4 or 5 large tomatoes (about 1½ pounds)

1 yellow onion, sliced thinly

1 small leek, rinsed and sliced thinly

2 dried moderately hot chiles

3 bay leaves

3 sprigs winter savory

2 sprigs Italian parsley, leaves picked

1½ heads garlic

1 cup white wine

Pinch of saffron (about 15 threads)

A big handful of Persian mint or spearmint leaves

Bread for grilling (see page 11)

Remove the head, tail, and fins of the rockfish with scissors or a knife. Set aside for the stock. Cut the body into 1½-inch-thick steaks, leaving all the bones intact. Lightly oil the steaks, season with salt, and refrigerate until you're ready to grill.

Soak the salted lingcod in cold water for 1 to 3 hours, depending on how long it has been salted (see page 117). You can cook a piece of the fish to taste for salt and then soak longer if necessary. Cut the fish into manageable pieces for grilling. Chop the fish bones into 4-inch sections and rinse them well to get rid of all traces of blood.

Blanch all but one of the tomatoes in rapidly boiling water until the skins split open and get loose, about a minute. Drop them into ice water to cool completely. Cut out the cores, peel off the skins to use in the stock, and set the peeled tomatoes aside for the stew.

Heat a pot over medium heat, add olive oil to cover the bottom of the pot, then add the onion and leek. Stir and cook for a couple of minutes, until slightly softened. Chop the remaining raw tomato into rough pieces and add it to the pot, along with the reserved tomato skins. Tear the chiles in half and stir them in

along with in the bay leaves, the savory sprigs, and the parsley stems (keep the leaves for the stew). Cook for a few minutes, then add the fish bones and scraps and cook, stirring, until the bones look opaque, about 2 or 3 minutes.

Separate the cloves of garlic. Smash a few of the tiny inner cloves and add them to the pot, unpeeled, along with the white wine and enough water to barely cover everything. Bring up to a simmer, then turn down the heat so that the liquid barely bubbles. Skim carefully. Cut the peeled tomatoes in half through their equators and squeeze the seeds and juices into the stock. Save the rest of the tomato for the stew.

The stock will get better and stronger as it cooks, but if it cooks too much it will start tasting muddy. The window is somewhere between 30 and 60 minutes of simmering, so start tasting the stock after about 30 minutes. Strain the stock and set aside.

Pour a couple tablespoons of boiling water over the saffron threads and soak for at least 30 minutes to extract the flavor.

Build a fire to grill the lingcod and the rockfish.

Cut the peeled and juiced tomatoes into big chunks. Peel and slice about 6 cloves of garlic. Heat a pot over medium-high heat, pour in enough olive oil to cover the bottom of the pot, and add the garlic. Cook it for a moment, stirring to keep it from browning, then add the tomatoes and some salt. Cook the tomatoes for a few minutes, then add the fish stock. Pour in the soaked saffron (including the water) and use a spoonful of the fish broth to rinse the saffron cup so that you get every last bit of it in there. Bring to a simmer, cook for about 5 minutes to let the flavors come together, and taste. Add salt (or pickled chile liquid; see page 19) and taste again. If the broth is not as concentrated as you'd like, you can reduce it.

While the coals are getting ready, make the minty garlic spread for the grilled bread. This can be done on the stove or you can do it in a pan right on the grill

continued

by moving the coals to adjust the heat as necessary.

Peel and thinly slice the remaining ½ head of garlic. Heat a pan and then turn the heat down to low. Pour in enough olive oil so that the sliced garlic will be able to move around pretty easily. Add the garlic and a pinch of salt. Cook slowly, stirring with a rubber spatula and adjusting the heat so that the garlic sizzles gently for a couple of minutes. Add a splash of water and cook until the garlic is completely soft and all the water has evaporated. Take the pan off the heat, add the mint, and stir well. Set aside until you have grilled the bread.

You want to grill the rockfish at a slightly lower temperature than the lingcod, so make two separate areas of your grill setup: one medium for the rockfish and one medium-hot for the lingcod. Brush the grill and wipe it with a dry, clean towel. Because fish tend to stick, wipe the grill with oil. If you by chance have a piece of pork or beef fat, that works even better.

The rockfish is going to take a little longer to cook so start it about 3 minutes before the lingcod. While the rockfish is getting its 3-minute head start, remove the lingcod from the soaking water, pat it dry, and brush both sides with olive oil. Set the lingcod on the hotter side of the grill and cook it until you see the bottom edge of the sides starting to turn opaque.

Flip the rockfish right after you put the lingcod on the grill. Grill it on the second side for about 3 more minutes. Pull it off the heat and check for doneness by poking at the flesh next to the center bone to see if it will flake away easily. Don't be nervous if it's not done yet—rockfish on the bone can take a little longer than you think—just throw it back on and keep checking it.

Flip the lingcod over and cook it on the second side until the fish is just barely opaque all the way through. The easiest way to check it is to pull the fish off the grill and break it slightly to see what it looks like at the thickest part.

When the fish is done, the hottest part of the grill should be perfect for grilling bread; see page 11.

To serve, put a piece of grilled rockfish and lingcod in each person's bowl. Chop a few parsley and savory leaves (saved from making fish stock) and sprinkle them over the fish. Heat up the fish broth and pour it into the bowls. Smear the minty garlic on the grilled bread and serve with the stew.

WHOLE ROASTED PETRALE SOLE WITH NEW POTATOES, RADISHES, AND PRESERVED LEMON
Serves 2 to 3

When I was a kid we always ate fish whole. We caught bonito, perch, pompano, and mackerel off a jetty in Redondo Beach and my mom would bake them wrapped in tin foil with soy sauce, ginger, scallions, and sesame and serve them to us whole to dig in and make a big mess. But whole fish was also the height of luxury—on special occasions we would get one at a Chinese restaurant, steamed with ginger and scallions or fried with sweet-and-sour sauce. Either way, they were always served with the head, bones, and fins and I never had a filet (besides Filet-O-Fish sandwich) until I was an adult.

Cooking fish on the bone and with the skin is a nice safety net; it helps keep the fish juicy and flavorful. Petrale sole cooked on the bone is totally different from the dry, flavorless, boring fish I thought it was. In fact, it's so juicy that in this recipe, its juices flavor the potatoes that are cooked underneath it.

8 ounces new potatoes

Salt

1 whole petrale sole, scaled and gutted (about 1½ to 2 pounds)

Olive oil

continued

¾ cup coarsely chopped tarragon and parsley
(also good with summer savory, oregano, chives,
or basil)

White wine

½ bunch radishes

1 small clove garlic

½ lemon

1 teaspoon finely chopped Preserved Lemon
(page 26)

Preheat the oven to 400°F.

Boil the potatoes in salted water until they are done.
Let them cool, then slice them into ⅓-inch-thick slices.

Rinse the fish carefully, getting rid of any last bits of
guts, which will make it taste bitter. Lightly oil the
fish on both sides and season with more salt than
you might think it needs. Pat the herbs onto both
sides of the fish. Line your baking dish with the sliced
potatoes, splash in a little white wine and lay the fish
on top, darker side up.

Bake until the fish is just cooked through, about
25 minutes or so, depending on the size of your fish.
To tell if it's done, push your finger along the fish's
spine—you should be able to feel the flesh flaking away
from the spine under the pressure. If you poke a knife
in, the flesh right next to the backbone should be just
barely opaque. It's better to overcook the fish than to
undercook it, because when it's undercooked it has a
pretty awful texture. And because it's cooked on the
bone, it will still be juicy if it's a little overcooked.

While the fish is cooking you can prepare the radish
salad. Wash the radishes and cut them into slices or
wedges. Pound the garlic and some salt in a mortar,
then juice the lemon directly into the mortar and add
the preserved lemon. Stir in the olive oil and dress the
radishes. Taste for salt.

If you are skilled at fileting a fish, you can serve the
petrale sole and the potatoes in the dish they were
baked in. If you are worried about the bones getting
mixed in with the potatoes underneath, you can lift
the fish out of the baking dish and onto a serving
platter. Plate the potatoes on individual plates along
with some of the juices.

To filet, use a spoon to push the top and bottom fins
away from the meat. Slide the spoon along the lateral
line of the fish, pushing the top and bottom filets away
from that center bone. Separate the head, then lift
the whole spine up and away in one piece. If you want
to be fancy, you can put everything back together
again. Or you can just portion big pieces onto each
person's plate. Spoon some of the juices over the fish
and potatoes and serve the radish salad right on top of
the fish.

VARIATION

This is also really good served with farro instead of
potatoes; just splash the baking dish with some olive
oil before you put the fish in it and cook the farro
seperately.

GRILLED KING SALMON WITH HERB BROTH
Makes 4

This dish came about because I missed poaching.
Turns out you don't poach much when you cook out
of a big fireplace. I was trying to recreate the feel of
a poached salmon dish, but I still wanted to use the
fire. Slowly grilling the fish gives it just enough smoky
flavor, but it's still a delicate dish.

One rarely makes a stock out of salmon bones because
it highlights the oily, fishy qualities of the fish. Instead
of thinking of this as a stock, imagine it as a delicate
tea. It's important to remove the pot from the heat
before it even comes to a simmer and then let it steep
for only a few minutes. This brings out the sweet,
clean flavors of the fish.

The broth relies on the quality of bones, so make sure yours are very fresh. The ideal situation would be to have the bones from the salmon you are cooking, but because salmon are so large, you are probably not buying a whole fish. Talk to your fishmonger about getting the freshest salmon bones and heads.

  4 pounds salmon bones and heads

  1 small yellow onion

  1 celery stalk, or 1 branch fennel fronds

  Olive oil

  Parsley stems

  4 bay leaves

  2 medium zucchini, such as Costata Romanesco

  Salt

  4 salmon filets (5 ounces each)

  2 bunches sorrel (about 6 ounces)

  4 handfuls of sweet herbs, such as chervil, chives, chrysanthemum, parsley, basil, or Persian mint

  Lemon

Build a fire—a smallish one if you are only grilling the zucchini and salmon for dinner. If you are cooking another course after the salmon, plan accordingly.

Chop the bones into 4-inch pieces. Rinse all the bones well to get rid of any blood, and clean out all traces of gills in the heads. Peel and thinly slice the onion. Wash and thinly slice the celery.

Heat a non-reactive stockpot over medium heat. Pour in enough olive oil to cover the bottom of the pot, then add the onion and celery. Cook for 3 minutes without getting any color; the vegetables should still be a bit raw. Add the bones, parsley stems, and bay leaves, and barely cover with water. Resist the urge to add wine. Keep the heat at medium and bring the broth up to just under a simmer—no bubbles. Take the pot off the heat and let it sit at room temperature for 15 minutes. Carefully strain the broth through moistened cheesecloth.

Trim the stem ends of the zucchini, and slice lengthwise into ¼-inch-thick slices. Brush the slices with olive oil and season with salt. Brush the salmon pieces with olive oil and season with salt.

Stem the sorrel and slice the stems crosswise very thin. Tear the leaves into large pieces. Sauté the stems and leaves with a splash of olive oil and a pinch of salt until the leaves just wilt. Don't worry about the gray color—there's nothing you can do about it. Remove the sorrel from the pan and set aside.

Heat the broth on the stove (or over the coals since you are about to start grilling) and season with salt. You want to salt lightly at this point, but the broth should still taste good on its own.

Grill the zucchini slices over fairly hot coals. The goal here is to get nice brown marks on both sides and to cook the zucchini long enough that it is softened but not mushy, about 2 to 3 minutes on each side.

Set aside the grilled zucchini and move some coals away to cool the grill down a bit—you want a medium-low grill for the fish. I really like salmon grilled slowly—there are strong oily flavors that come out in salmon when it is cooked too hot. The trouble with this gentle grilling is that the fish will want to stick, so make sure the grill is well seasoned and very clean. Set the salmon on the grill and cook without moving it until the edges begin to turn opaque. Flip the pieces over and cook the other sides. Pull the salmon off when the very center is still slightly raw; it will continue to cook off the heat. The goal is to have fish that is just cooked, with very pale grill marks.

Toss the herbs with olive oil and a pinch of salt. They should be barely coated. Put a spoonful of the sorrel into warm, shallow soup bowls. Place a piece of salmon on top of the sorrel and place a few pieces of zucchini around it. Pour a small amount of broth into each bowl. Put a handful of the dressed herbs over the salmon, letting them fall into the broth. Drizzle a spoonful of olive oil into each bowl and squeeze a little lemon directly onto the fish—try not to get any in the broth.

I like this to start off tasting plain and then let the flavors build as the salmon, herbs, and sorrel start to flavor the broth in the bowl.

CHAPTER FIVE

FIRE

FIRE

In the Piedmont region of the Italian province of Cuneo, there's a small village called Verduno, and at the top sits a magnificent eighteenth-century castle. One night during my Chez Panisse era, we were there for a Slow Food dinner—it was a pretty grand affair. Alice was there. Carlo Petrini was there. The guy who invented the Hubble Space Telescope was there. Mikhail Baryshnikov was there, for god's sake. I was there to prepare a dinner for forty-five, which then became fifty, which then became sixty. It was an important meal, an occasion for Alice to put forth the Chez Panisse ideals in a memorable way. I cooked it in the driveway.

Alice and I wanted to grill pigeon, but there was no grill. So instead of working inside this marvelous building, I found a gravelly spot out front. They probably call it the courtyard—it was a driveway. I just started gathering whatever I could find: old grapewood burls to burn, some bricks by the side of the building, a couple oven grates I crisscrossed on top of each other. Then I lit the fire.

It was always sort of like this with me—cooking in some subpar, precarious way. Whether at big Chez Panisse events or at home, where our kitchen is horrible and small, I'd just end up outside, building a weird fire and cooking over that. Partly it suits my brain. Following recipes and remembering temperatures—I'm not so good at that. Which is why I'm particularly suited to cook with fire—it's entirely intuitive.

The fire also forces you to engage at a deeper level. You're tending to these mini environments, which in turn causes you to pay attention in a way you don't with a tidy stovetop and a timer. Always in the back of my head is what's happening with the heat, what's happening with the food, what temperature the food was before it went on, how many people are in the room, what the night's various dishes need, and so on. There's a string of microdecisions that, if you make them right, result in really good food—or else something burnt and terrible.

For that meal in Verduno, I'd set out to grill that pigeon—but then it occurred to me that we might as well make the stock for the fish stew on the fire, to give it this woody tinge. Then I decided to grill focaccia to accompany the stew. Then I grilled the potatoes. At some point, the sun set. Allison came by with a glass of wine and a penlight. I was cooking in the dark. I ended up cooking the whole meal outside, on this weird, thrown-together fire. I remember Baryshnikov out there, in these white jeans—how did he pull off white jeans?—smoking cigarettes and watching me cook. He gave me whiskey. I never saw the inside of the castle.

When it came time to start building Camino, I knew the restaurant had to embody that spontaneity, or what would be the point of leaving Chez Panisse? We found the space and I started playing house: moving cardboard boxes here and there to imagine how the kitchen would work. At the center would be this massive fireplace. When I finally had it mapped out in my head, we called Pascal.

Pascal Faivre is a French stonemason up in Sonoma who comes from a long, long line of stonemasons. They go back to the Crusades. At one point, he thought he was done with the business, but he just couldn't walk away. Anyway, he and I designed this ten-foot-wide limestone behemoth. The coals do most of our cooking, rather than the flames, and we can adjust them as needed. Or move these bricks over here to trap the heat. Or hang the leg of lamb over there to twist in front of the fire. For a primeval tool, a fireplace is surprisingly flexible.

Which partly explains the learning curve when you start cooking with open flames. Contrary to what many think, you can't just go by the sound of the sizzle when you throw the chicken onto the grill, for instance—just because it wasn't as loud as you were expecting doesn't mean the temperature won't be right in just a few seconds. On the other hand, you can get important information from the color of the fire, and the color of the food.

Invariably, some of our diners come in with certain expectations of open fire cooking, and we disappoint them. No burgers, no pizza, no big, smoky flavor, or macho pyrotheatrics. This idea that meat must sear over obscenely high heat—well, not always. My style of not just grilling over high heat but of cooking at different temperatures and creating different environments is a tough pill for some folks to swallow.

And that's the point. We all inherit these notions about fire, just as we do about how certain dishes have to be prepared, and the thrill is in experimenting your way away from them. Cooking is full of fun little mysteries to solve.

The Camino approach doesn't mean you need a French stonemason to install a ten-foot fireplace in your house. You don't even need a fireplace. Many of these recipes were born over something far more ramshackle in my backyard, atop old rebar we swiped from a vacant lot. You can swipe your own rebar, or build a fire on the beach, or stack bricks in a gravel driveway with Baryshnikov.

You can also just march out to your backyard. This chapter will walk you through the basics of an easy-to-build fire and how to cook over it. The point isn't to replicate the precise circumstances we have at Camino—in fact that's the opposite of the point. Fire makes you adapt and tune in. Your creativity emerges from the limitations imposed by this primitive technique. Working with recipes and perfectly calibrated ovens—sometimes it's easy to lose our connection with the food itself.

Every time you cook with fire it is going to be different. What you are cooking, your setup, your location, the condition of your fuel—these are really the fun parts. You can pretty much cook over any fire if you understand some basic principles.

BUILDING A PROPER BED OF COALS

The most important thing is to start with a proper bed of coals so that you are NEVER cooking over flames. When the fire is in a flamey state, there is soot coming off it, and that soot will stick to and flavor your food. Think about all the drunken backyard barbeques with sooty, petroleum-y, carcinogenic chicken. I realize that holds a lot of nostalgia for people, but I think it can be better.

So you should start with a thick bed of coals with no empty patches to ensure even heat.

CONTINUE MAKING COALS

You want to create a setup where you have a way to continue generating coals once you are cooking, but not expose your food to flames. This requires two stations: the fire for making coals and the grilling area with ready coals. This way you can keep your fire working and maintain some flexibility.

At Camino, we use a Uruguayan-style metal fire basket to make coals. We build the initial fire in the basket. As the fire burns in the basket, the wood breaks down into coals, which drop through the bottom. With a metal tool, we rake the coals to the nearby cooking areas. We continue adding wood to the basket throughout the night so we have a continuous supply of ready coals.

The Uruguayan basket is easy enough to make. We had a friend weld six rebar staples together with a few crossbars. He has had to make a few repairs over the years, but we also use it every night.

If you are not yet committed to cooking with fire every day, you can build a fire on the ground next to your cooking area. I did this for years at home and it works fine. The basket is just easier because you don't have to balance the wood in any careful way to allow

airflow, and it is less messy because your coals are dropping below the fire.

FLEXIBILITY AND CONTROL

If you have coals at the ready, you can easily change the temperature by increasing or decreasing the level of coals. For example, you have just grilled some steaks over medium heat because they were kind of thick. You've pulled them off the grill to rest and now you can pile up more coals under the area where the steaks were to grill some toasts on a hotter grill. Meanwhile you've had a pot of fava beans resting on two bricks over a pile of coals that are finishing up; you can eat them on the grilled bread while you grill some wedges of escarole over the descending heat, and eat *those* with the steaks, which are now perfectly rested.

Part of the control comes from understanding the heat in different areas of your setup and thinking about where your food is in relation to these various heat sources. The fire that makes the coals becomes part of the equation as well; you can move coals under any part of the grill, but it is easiest to make the hottest part of your grill closest to the fire or fire basket.

In addition to raking coals under the surrounding grills, we also put them into little piles surrounded by bricks to create cooking areas that are almost like burners. We have several of these in the fireplace at different temperatures for cooking farro, warming fish broth, or heating up beans or ragús.

You can also cook while you are waiting for the coals to be ready for the grill. You can set up bean pots near the fire while it is developing to cook fresh or dried beans. If you are making fish stew, you can make the stock in the fire and then grill the fish once the coals are ready. This will add a subtle smokiness to the fish stew that you wouldn't get if you made the stock on the stove. Plus you aren't wasting any of the heat. Peppers and whole onions can be placed directly in the coals as they start to spill away from the fire.

ADJUSTING HEAT

For the recipes in the this book, when I say a you want a "hot" grill, I mean that you should have a thick bed of coals (closer to the grill) and/or you should be grilling next to the fire source. For a "medium" grill, you will want a thinner layer of coals and to keep a little distance from the fire. For example, when grilling meat, you can point the thicker ends toward the fire, or build the coals up slightly under that end. When I am grilling, I move the food around, making microadjustments to the placement as well as to the coals. All the while, I am thinking about—visualizing even—what the heat is doing to the food. (See page 112 on how to overthink grilling squid!) It is more mental work than physical work. I have been known to walk away from the grill to watch surfing videos, but I am always thinking about the fire.

GRILL SETUP

At Camino, our grill setup is made up of cast iron gas grill replacement grates. The grates are set in frames made (by another friend) out of angle iron. We have three of these setups: one is flat and holds the grates about three inches off the hearth, and two are built on an angle so they are three inches high in the front and five inches high in the back. The slant provides some variety in height for cooking and also allows some of the fat to drip forward into a pan instead of down onto the coals. This helps prevents grease fires that will negatively affect the taste of the food (and possibly set our restaurant, or your backyard, on fire).

At home, my favorite grill to use is an antique little cast iron French grill. It has a handle like a sauté pan, four legs, and is very lightweight. I also sometimes use a Tuscan grill, but instead of using the stand that comes with it, I set it on bricks because it is easier to access the coals. I can vary the height of the bricks to achieve a slant if I'm cooking something with a lot of fat.

If you don't have a Tuscan grill, you can also use your trusty Weber or a hibachi. They can be tricky because you have to figure out a way to generate coals to add to a contained unit. With a Weber, I usually build a fire in the middle, then move most of the coals to one side for grilling. Then I put new mesquite charcoal on the other side to build up a fire. The problem is that whenever you want to add more coals, you need to remove the grill (and likely your food) for access, and you can only really use half the grill. This can work if you are not cooking that much food. Or if you need the grill space, you can use a second Weber to make coals and then shovel those over to your grilling Weber.

A hibachi has the advantage of having different configurations of removable grills, so you have more access to your coal supply. Hibachi grills are made of cast iron, which is a better grilling surface than Webers, which are stainless steel.

FUEL

At Camino, we use only orchard wood, which is easy because it is plentiful and nearby. We use a mix of almond and cherry; almond burns slowly and makes good coals, cherry is aromatic and burns quickly and very hot. Cherry helps get the almond going a little bit and can give you good heat directly from the basket.

At home, I usually have manzanita and various types of fruitwood, but you should use whatever hardwood is plentiful in your area. I also use mesquite charcoal or a mix of mesquite and wood. Mesquite charcoal is partially prepared, so it is faster, easier to light, and burns hotter. It does not give you as good a flavor as wood, it's messy, and the dust is gross to breathe. Wood has to burn completely to break down into coals, so it will take longer and need more attention. But it will smell really good and add cleaner flavor to whatever you are cooking.

Charcoal briquettes freak me out. As does lighter fluid.

I usually start my home fire with one of those charcoal chimney starters using mesquite charcoal. Once the pieces are burning well, I dump them out on the ground, add some wood (and sometimes more mesquite), and let it burn down to coals. With my home setup, I actually build the fire where the grill is going to be placed. Once the coals are ready and the grill is down, I slide a few hot coals off to the side where I rebuild the fire to supply me with coals while I am grilling. If I need more coals right away, I will continue with mesquite. Otherwise, I will maintain that fire with wood.

Whatever fuel you decide on, try to only use as much as you need. If you're inexperienced, it's better to have a bit more fire burning, but as you get better, you should try to cut it close. After seven years, Camino is a busier restaurant, but we use much less wood than when we first opened, just because we have become more efficient. If you overestimate your fire needs and create too many coals, to alleviate any guilt you have, you should use the leftover coals to cook something for the next day—a piece of meat for a salad, some peppers directly in the coals (page 63), some Smoky Eggplant (page 61), or some vegetables that will add depth to a stock you are planning to make.

ESSENTIAL TOOLS

Wire brush

Rags

Large metal spatula

Two pairs of long tongs: one pair to move wood, coals, and burning logs; the other to move food

Stick to move coals

Bricks for resting pots on or holding your grill

Chimney starter

Some sort of grill

FUN STUFF

Clay bean pots: for beans and soups

Chinese sand pots: great for farro, beans, soups, anything liquid

Cazuelas: for warming already cooked vegetables, catching juices under roasting meat

Fire basket

Metal tool to move coals: an upgrade from the stick

Wind block: bricks, cinder blocks (see below)

Notice that "wire brush" is the first item on the essentials list! I am not a neat freak about anything, but it is crucial that you cook on a clean grill. Every time you remove something from the grill you MUST prepare it for the next item that is going on it. Brush it with the wire brush to loosen any burnt pieces and caramelized juices that are stuck to the grill. After you brush the grill, you need to wipe off the loose bits with a dry rag. People tend to skip this step, but if you look at that rag after you've brushed and wiped the grill, you will see all the junk that would have gone onto your food, and you will not want to eat it. Maybe rags should be the first item on the list.

A note about wind: It can be your worst enemy. Plan for it. If you are cooking in a windy area (say, my backyard), you need to determine where the smoke is going to go and build your cooking area appropriately (just ask my neighbor about his smoky cat). Also be aware that if it is windy right where your grill is, it is going to blow the heat away. You also don't want the wind to blow the flames of your fire through your food, so build your fire downwind of your coals/cooking area.

GRILLING MEAT

The meat dishes at Camino are unique in that, because we get whole animals, we serve all the parts on the plate. Since there are only so many chops to go around, your plate will not always look like that of your dining companions, but everyone gets a mix of different parts. And those parts are cooked in different ways—legs, loins, and racks are grilled in the fireplace; shoulders and necks are cooked slowly in the wood oven.

A lot of the time spent training cooks on the grill at Camino is spent talking and observing. Because we don't actually cook from recipes at the restaurant, the cooks who do the best on the grill are the ones who have gleaned some understanding of what is actually happening between the fire and the meat. They are thinking about each piece of meat anew and making decisions about what their next move is based on the characteristics of that piece—thickness, temperature, fat content, shape, and so on. It is an exciting, dynamic, and engaged way to cook.

The fireplace at Camino is so low tech that is has more in common with a barely outfitted backyard than a professional kitchen. The recipes in this book that call for grilling meat require the same understanding of cooking with fire that I try to instill in Camino cooks—it will be different every time, but there are some basic steps for success.

The rundown is something like this: seasoning, tempering, cooking at the right temperature, resting, and carving. If you skip any of those steps, it is like tying one hand behind your back. If you follow all these steps, there is a really good chance you can cook almost any size or shape piece of meat successfully.

SEASONING

Meat tastes better seasoned ahead. My rule of thumb is the thicker or bonier a piece of meat is, the more seasoning you use and the further ahead you do it.

I always salt first so that I can control the salt level separately from other seasonings.

If I'm using dry spices (juniper, allspice, bay, caraway, cumin, coriander, mustard seed), I will toast them in a cast iron pan to release the aromas and then grind them in a coffee grinder. Then I sprinkle them on the meat and rub them in a little bit. Dry spices are particularly good with duck and pork.

Fresh herbs and garlic are good with everything. I pound the garlic (cured or green) and picked herbs (mint, lovage, savory, oregano, cutting celery, tarragon, nepitella, etc.) in a mortar and pestle, then add just enough olive oil so to barely coat the meat. Too much oil and you will start a grease fire.

TEMPERING

Meat will cook much more evenly and gently if the interior temperature is close to room temperature when it starts cooking. You are trying to manage how the heat affects the different parts of the meat and what will happen to that heat when it meets the cold interior of, say, a chicken breast. If the exterior and interior temperatures vary greatly you will have to cook the meat for so long for the inside to be done that the outside will be dried out. With a bone-in cut of meat, you have to be even more serious about tempering. Imagine that ice-cold bone protecting the meat next to it from ever getting enough heat to cook. But if the bone is 15 to 20 degrees warmer than the refrigerator, the meat can gently be coaxed to doneness.

But yes, once you've tempered the meat, you do have to cook it, even if you've had a change in plans or don't feel like it. You can eat it for lunch the next day.

TEMPERATURE

Finally, you get to grill something. You want to start with an ample bed of coals so that you can control the temperature. If you are cooking something large, or a succession of smaller things, you will need to make more coals while you are cooking.

The basic theory you want to remember is lower temperatures and longer cooking times for large or bone-in pieces of meat and high heat for small or thin cuts. Leaner meats (pork legs, beef sirloins, fish) should also be grilled at a lower temperature. The temperature is controlled by how deep your bed of coals is and the height of the grill in relation to the coals.

One of the points of cooking something on a grill is to get whatever it is nice and brown. You need to think about the brownness of the exterior versus doneness of the interior. I tend to go slower and at a lower temperature because things can get more evenly brown on the outside and still be juicy on the inside.

One of the great things about grilling is you can cook something that is thin on one end and thick on the other end. You can either build up the coals under the thick end or point that end toward the fire that is supplying you with coals. At Camino, the fire is off to the side of the grill, so you will often see pieces of meat fanning out away from the fire with the thick ends pointed right at it. This all becomes intuitive.

When is it done? This is the hard part. I recommend you poke at the meat from the moment you put it on the grill until you take it off. What you are doing when you are poking at meat is feeling whether the heat is penetrating the flesh and cooking it. You know what raw meat feels like—it is wiggly. Similarly, you know what well-done meat feels like—it is very firm. The trick, of course, is to feel what it is like when it is perfectly done. I tend to gently poke from all different directions to see how different muscle groups are acting. Sometimes a roast feels done at first, but if you very gently poke from different angles, you can feel a wiggly part in there that's still raw.

For large cuts, you can use an instant-read thermometer, but I think you should try not to rely on it. When I'm grilling, I like to daydream about how long this particular piece of meat was tempered, how hot this particular fire is, and what must be going on inside the piece of meat, all the while poking at it to see if I'm right. And *then* (and really only if it is a big

cut like a lamb leg), I will take its temperature right at the bone, at the thickest part, just to double-check.

So honestly, that's really my method—dorky as it is. In the recipes that involve grilling meat, I'll try to give you some times and temperatures as guidance, but I think you should really try to daydream about it—you will learn something that will help you the next time.

RESTING

When you pull a piece of meat off a hot grill, it is squeezing itself away from the heat. If you cut into it right away, it will be gray and overcooked on the outside, raw in the middle, and the juices will pour out of it. If you let the meat relax away from the heat, the juices will redistribute and the meat will be more evenly cooked. This step is often skipped, especially in restaurants, because cooks rarely have the time to let meat rest. It is faster to overcook the meat and slice it right away—it will look right, but it will be dry. Conscientious cooks will pull the meat off the grill a little earlier and let it rest. When they slice into it, the meat will be evenly rosy and very little juice will be left on the cutting board.

Larger cuts take a longer time to rest, smaller cuts take less time. A 5-inch-thick piece of pork loin needs to rest about 15 minutes, a leg of lamb about 25 minutes. A bone-in chicken leg or breast should rest for 15 minutes or so. A thin steak only needs a couple of minutes (especially if you aren't slicing before serving). Don't fuck up all the work leading up to this meal by rushing this stage. Your guests can have another drink.

CARVING

Slice against the grain. It's pretty easy to see how muscle fibers run along a piece of meat. If you cut with the grain, the meat will be chewier than if you cut right across the grain.

The tougher the meat is, the thinner you should slice it.

A long, thin knife is helpful, but I got away with a sharp chef's knife for years.

A WHOLE MEAL COOKED IN THE FIRE

If you are going to all the trouble to build a fire to grill something, you might as well try to cook as many things as you can in it—maybe even your whole meal.

The challenge in cooking a whole meal outside is managing time and fire—figuring out how long things need to cook, and what kinds of coals or fire you need for each item on the menu. Cooking in the fire can be slow, so you don't need to have everything prepped before you start. There are long periods of passive cooking (you can't rush the garbanzo beans!), so you can use that time to work on other parts of the meal. You can draw on your larder (see page 17) to include things that are already made. Cooking outside is part of the party, so don't forget to work in snacks for your guests when there are long pauses in cooking.

Here is a sample menu of an entire meal cooked outside in a fire. Use this as a guideline for your outdoor cookouts. There are so many factors that come into play when cooking like this that it is highly unlikely that it will ever go down exactly this way again. Don't be tied to this sequence, but look for the logic behind the decisions. The Amaro Cocktail is easy when the mix is made ahead and it will bide you lots of time and goodwill with your guests.

> Amaro Cocktail (page 246)
>
> Duck Hearts, Gizzard, and Wings Confit (page 179, but without the wings) and Sauerkraut (page 20) on Grilled Bread (page 11)
>
> Herb Jam (page 23) and aged sheep's milk cheese on Grilled Bread (page 11)
>
> Grilled Endive with Fresh Turmeric and Walnuts (page 43)
>
> Lamb Leg à la Ficelle (page 189) with garbanzo beans, grilled radicchio, and Pickled Chile Sauce (page 19)
>
> Grilled fuyu persimmons with sheep's milk ricotta and honey

The duck giblets, sauerkraut, and herb jam for the toasts are going to come from your larder so that you have some easy snacks to serve if your fire doesn't cooperate (plan for this!). For the Belgian endive salad, follow the directions on page 43, but cook each element on the grill. You'll use a small pan set directly on the grill instead of the stovetop for toasting the walnuts and cooking the turmeric—so have your glass of water ready for the tricky turmeric-garlic part. I also added onions roasted directly in the coals to this salad—why not use every part of the fire for this dinner?

The lamb leg à la ficelle uses an A-frame apparatus because it is what we had available. Any outdoor setup will work. You can use the resting time to catch up on prep if you fall behind.

For dessert, grilling fruit, in this case persimmons, is really easy. You could also grill figs, peaches, nectarines, or plums—just halve them instead of slicing. Or any of these fruits could be cooked in a *cazuela* nestled in the coals, maybe adding a little sugar to coax out the juices.

THE DAY BEFORE:

Season the lamb leg (page 189).

Soak the garbanzo beans covered in three inches of water.

Prepare Amaro Cocktail mix (page 246).

THE DAY OF:

The first tasks for your dinner party need to be done in a little bit of a rush because they will affect the timing of everything to come after. The garbanzo beans are going to take the longest to cook (2 to 3 hours), so you need to get the fire built and get them started about 2 hours before your guests arrive.

Put a couple pages of crumpled-up newspaper in the bottom of a chimney starter. Fill to the top with mesquite and light the newspaper. Once the mesquite is lit, let it burn for about 15 minutes in the chimney, and then pour the glowing coals onto the ground in your cooking area. Add more mesquite and some wood to the coals.

While you are waiting for the fire to get started, you can make the marinade for the lamb (page 189)—saving the herb stems for the garbanzo beans. Marinate and tie the lamb (page 190), and set aside a little of the marinade for a sauce. Put the soaked garbanzo beans in a bean pot with their soaking liquid, 4 cloves of slightly smashed garlic, a big pinch of salt, and the herb stems leftover from the marinade. The bean pot will crack if exposed to sudden temperature changes so place it about 6 inches away from the fire to temper for 15 minutes before moving it right into the coals. During that 15 minutes, start prepping the rest of the meal: julienne the turmeric for the salad, trim the radicchio and cut it into wedges for the main course, and prepare a *cazuela* with 2 cups of chopped canned tomatoes and their juices and 4 cloves of sliced garlic. Hold off on cutting the Belgian endive until right before you grill it.

Once the fire is roaring (though there won't be many coals at this time), hang your lamb leg. Place the *cazuela* of tomatoes under the lamb leg to catch the drippings. While the leg is cooking, turn the *cazuela* every so often to keep it from burning on the hottest side. The tomatoes will be added to the garbanzo beans once the beans are done—if you add them too early, the acid from the tomatoes will stop the garbanzos from cooking, so make sure the beans are really done. Let the garbanzo beans come to a boil and then move them to a cooler spot to maintain a simmer. The lamb leg will take about 1 hour to cook (start checking it after 45 minutes) and then it will need to rest for at least 25 minutes. Because you are going to be eating snacks and cooking other food during this time, it is likely that the leg will be resting for up to an hour or so. Create a resting area (a platter propped up by bricks) near the fire so it stays warm.

Once you have lots of coals, rake them away from the fire in a thick, even layer and set your grill on top of them to get it hot. Nestle the onions, with the skins still on, right into the coals (see Ratatouille, page 77). Turn the onions over in the coals while they cook. They are done when a skewer goes easily through them, about 20 minutes. At this point, you can also put a *cazuela* of duck giblet confit and duck fat on the grill to warm for your toasts. Brush baguette slices with a little of the warm duck fat and brush dense rye bread with olive oil and grill both breads over high heat. When the bread is done make your Amaro cocktails and assemble the toasts: sauerkraut and sliced duck giblets on the baguette with a grind of black pepper, and herb jam and thinly sliced aged sheep's milk cheese on the rye bread.

With toast or cocktail in hand, pull the blackened onions out of the coals and set aside to cool.

Peel and slice the persimmons into 1/3-inch slices. Brush with olive oil, season with a very small amount of salt, and a grind of black pepper.

Check the lamb leg for doneness and cut it down when it's ready. Let it rest while you continue cooking.

The garbanzo beans should be done at this point, but taste to make sure before you add the tomato-garlic-lamb dripping mixture to the bean pot. Let the beans and tomatoes simmer for 15 minutes, then move them away from the fire to cool.

Up until now your fire has been ascending and your grill hot. Once the lamb leg is down, you are going to be working your way through the existing coals, but keep in mind what else you need to cook in case you need to add some fuel along the way—you don't want to get caught off guard at this point.

Toast the walnuts in a small pan set on the grill over what should now be a medium-hot bed of coals. Sizzle the garlic and turmeric according to the recipe on page 43 except in a pan directly on the grill. Cut the Belgian endive into quarters and grill over medium-high heat. Peel off the burnt layer of the onions, cut them lengthwise through the root and then into wedges, which will separate into petals. Salt them a little and add them to the endive when you plate the salad.

With one eye on your coals so they don't disappear, take a break to eat the endive salad. Then up again to finish cooking. Rake some coals under your grill for medium heat. Rewarm the garbanzo beans by moving the bean pot closer to the fire. Brush the radicchio wedges with olive oil and sprinkle with salt. Grill the radicchio on the cut sides for about 3 minutes each. If they still seem too crunchy, pile them together to steam for a few more minutes. Right when you remove the radicchio, put the sliced persimmons on the grill. It's best to do this now so you can be done cooking and not have to worry about your coals dying while you enjoy your perfectly smoky meal. You can grill the persimmons over very few coals—you just want grill marks on each side. While the persimmons are grilling, slice the ricotta and arrange it on a platter. Add the grilled persimmons to the platter and set aside.

Check the garbanzo beans to make sure they are hot, and slice the rested lamb leg. Serve the sliced lamb leg on a platter with the grilled radicchio. Drizzle the extra marinade over the lamb. Put the garbanzo beans in a different serving dish, because the bean pot will be ashy and blackened. Serve the pickled chiles on the side.

Now is your chance to bask in the glory of your accomplishment—you've cooked an entire meal outside over the fire. Enjoy all the congratulatory toasts from your friends and don't worry about being too drunk—all you have left to do for dessert is drizzle honey over the persimmons and ricotta. Cheers! Here's to hoping your friends help clean up this smoky mess.

CHICKEN
AND EGG

CHICKEN AND EGG

There comes a point in every marriage—or at least mine with Allison, in the panicky, we-don't-know-what-we're-doing planning stages of Camino—when you grab a piece of paper late one night and start manically sketching chickens. Not just any chickens, but delicious chickens, cooked like they're seldom cooked these days, all miraculously fitting on the grill, then tossed upon the butcher block for chopping, and going out to many diners throughout the evening without derailing the kitchen. In retrospect, the diagram looked like an insane person's drawing. I think it sent Allison into a brief depression.

But I had my reasons. Spend enough of your life cooking this creature and two questions will haunt you: how do restaurants make money on chicken, and how do they cook it so fast? Alas, the answer is simple: Chicken is routinely flubbed on multiple fronts. When we opened Camino, we were determined to avoid several common sins.

This started with how it's prepared. Painfully, most restaurants cook the bird in advance, then blast it when they get your order; Americans' tolerance for dry, overcooked chicken has reached worrisome levels. To make matters worse, they serve the most flavorless part. To me, a boneless, skinless breast is but a joyless protein block. Finally, they are doomed from the start with the animals they buy. These factory-raised animals—loaded with hormones, lusciousness bred out of them—are practically guaranteed not to become a truly great dish.

Deciding to buy better chickens and serve their tastier parts was just a matter of making a commitment to ourselves. But figuring out a way to cook them in a restaurant setting, that was our real challenge. There was some excitement around town among chefs when a farm started offering heritage chickens. Despite our excitement, we all quickly realized that we didn't know how to cook them. Cooked like a regular chicken, the skin is rubbery and the flesh is tough. I realized I needed a way to import my personal backyard cooking technique—from raw and on the bone—to a restaurant scale. That's where my late-night chicken-cooking diagram came in. It was crazy but, several variations later, it worked.

These chickens take time and attention to bring the best out of them—so don't rush them. You have to season them ahead, temper them so they don't go onto the grill cold, and let them rest so the juices have a chance to recollect and the meat can relax. The result of all this is a consistently and amazingly flavorful chicken.

I remember one night Michael Pollan coming in, taking a couple bites and walking back to the butcher block.

"You figured out how to cook these chickens!" he said. I was psyched.

These days our regular Wednesday chicken delivery is the one stable thing in our world. Riverdog Farm in Yolo County has figured out a way to raise these birds so they're both intensely flavorful and entirely reliable. They move them around the farm regularly, so that they eat through a patch of ground, and fertilize it, and then they plant there, and so on. I like that each side, theirs and ours, has figured out a way to do chickens better.

Since figuring all this out, I've noticed something: Our chicken is especially popular with older diners and those who've traveled a bit. These are folks who've been exposed to higher quality birds, either in other countries—France, Vietnam, wherever—or in this one, in an earlier era. I love the idea of bringing back the traditional Sunday night chicken dinner, when the family gathers 'round and you cook this terrific bird, as special as any other meat you could put on a plate.

It's starting to change, happily, but for a while it was tough to find good, non-factory-farmed chicken in the States. Of course that helped devalue chicken in diners' minds. It didn't help that they'd been literally devalued: chicken is too cheap. As a result, its excellence has been obscured by its ubiquity. Chicken sandwiches, chicken soup, chicken tacos—it's everywhere and its inherent specialness has faded in diners' minds.

The exact same is true of eggs. I'm tempted to draw a crazy diagram showing just what's wrong with the system.

Americans have gotten used to those 99¢ cartons of eggs. But if you have a really good egg, where the white is thick and the yoke stands up and the flavor is bright and rich and fresh—these are another thing entirely, and paying $8 to $10 for a dozen strikes me as entirely reasonable. At that price, farmers could actually afford to raise them in the first place.

We're getting there. So much so that restaurants like Camino have to compete with shoppers at the farmers' market to get enough eggs—you should see the line at the Riverdog stand on Tuesdays just for eggs. It's tough for a farm to make it work raising just perfect eggs. We're always meeting some hippy who's decided to try it. I always tell them: grow something else as well. You can't make it just on eggs. The eggs are wonderful—until the day the farmers burn out and quit. We've already gone through three of those guys.

But we'll always keep finding a way to score excellent ones. For years, our go-to dinner at home was sautéed greens from the yard, a little rice, and a poached or fried egg. I think of eggs as no different from duck or pork. They add a lusciousness to a plate, a richness. They're a perfect luxury item.

And as with all of our humble "luxury" items, we have to wring every last drop out of our eggs. When we make ice cream and we have whites left over, you'll notice lots of egg white drinks on the bar menu. Still more left over? We make meringues, or use them to clarify consommé.

We even use the shells—Allison's favorite thing is to fill empty eggshells with confetti and smash them on diners' heads on New Year's Eve.

GRILLED CHICKEN BREAST AND LEG WITH GRILLED CHICORIES

Serves 4 to 6

1 large whole heritage breed chicken, such as Freedom Ranger (about 5 to 6 pounds)

Salt and black pepper

3 cloves garlic

2 cups herb leaves, such as sage, winter savory, or lovage

Olive oil

3 heads assorted chicories, such as escarole, radicchio, or curly endive

2 cups Fried Farro (page 8)

Start by butchering the chicken. With the chicken breast side up on a cutting board and the legs pointing away from you, start separating the legs from the breast by making a 3-inch cut to the skin between the legs and the breast (closer to the legs because you want to leave a lot of skin to cover the breast later). Next, spread the legs apart and pop the legs out of the joints. To remove legs, cut around the side of each leg, working toward the back of the chicken. Your knife should be scraping against the carcass the whole way, leaving the oysters (little knobs of meat on either side of the backbone) attached to the legs.

With the chicken still breast side up, insert a large knife into the cavity and cut along each side of the backbone, cutting through the ribs. The cuts should be about 1/3 inch from the backbone. You will end up with the backbone attached to the neck and head—it'll look like a snake. Save this for stock or voodoo.

Next, flip the chicken over. It will open up where the backbone was. Split the chicken in half right down the middle by crunching through the cartilage and breastbone with your knife. Leave the drumette attached to the breast. Cut off the last two joints for another use, or save for stock. Trim any excess skin or fat. (You could have a butcher do all this for you,

but be sure to tell him or her you want the breast left on the bone.)

Season the breast and legs with salt and pepper the day before grilling (or least two hours ahead). I like to salt separately from other seasonings because then I have more control over exactly how much of each I'm using. I tend to salt the bony side of the breast more heavily than the meaty side because the bones are protecting the meat, so less salt penetrates.

Two hours before you plan to grill the chicken, make an herby marinade: pound the garlic and a pinch of salt in a mortar, add the herbs, and continue pounding until you have a rough paste. Add enough olive oil to just moisten it. You don't want the marinade too oily or it will catch fire when it drips off the chicken. Set half aside to use as a sauce later. Rub the marinade onto the seasoned parts of the chicken. Let the meat temper at room temperature for two hours.

Build a fire to grill the chicken.

Prepare the chicories, by peeling off any tough outer leaves (herb jam!). Cut the chicories through the core into quarters or sixths, depending on their size. Wash the pieces well and shake off excess water. Brush with a generous amount of olive oil and season with salt.

Rake the coals under the grill for medium grilling. Once the grill is hot, place the breasts and legs skin side down on the grill, with the thicker parts of each piece pointing toward the fire. Because the legs will be on the grill longer than the breasts (they take a little more time to cook), you need to cook them over slightly lower heat, so put the breasts closer to the fire source (or wherever the coals are hotter) and put the legs a little further away, where the grill is not as hot.

Set a weight on top of the chicken to press the skin flat down on the grill. We usually use a broken *cazuela*, though any sort of heatproof ceramic thing will work. A brick is a bit too heavy. After 2 minutes or so, lift up the chicken and check how dark the skin is getting. It should be a light golden color. If it already has some dark spots, move it to a cooler part of the grill or move some coals away. Continue cooking the chicken skin side down and under the weight for as long as necessary to get the skin evenly brown and crispy. Ideally, when the skin is perfectly brown and the pieces are ready to flip over, the chicken will be two-thirds done. Paying attention to the skin is especially important with heritage breeds because they have thicker skin and it will be rubbery if it is not properly cooked. While they are cooking you want to rotate each piece so that the thinner side gets a little time pointing toward the fire source.

When the pieces are ready, remove the weight (you won't need it for the second side) and flip them over. Cook them at the same heat as the first side until they are done. The breasts will take about 25 to 30 minutes total cooking time. To tell when the breasts are done, gently poke, prod, and press them all over—this is the hardest part, but you will feel the flesh firm up when it's done. The legs will take about 6 minutes longer. It is more difficult to test the legs by feel, but luckily there is more leeway—they also taste good if they are cooked a few minutes past "done." Look for the tendon that runs along the length of the drumstick—once it breaks, you usually have another 5 minutes to go.

Let the chicken rest for about 15 minutes in a warm place near the fire. While the chicken is resting, brush and wipe the grill and set the Fried Farro to warm in a clay pot or baking dish on the grill.

Rake some more coals under the grill to get it a little hotter and place the chicory wedges neatly and compactly on the grill, cut side down. Keeping them close together will help create a little steam as they cook. Grill on the first side until it is fairly brown before flipping it to the next cut side. Cook for less time on the leafy side because it will burn more quickly. You are shooting for them to have good color on the outside and be slightly crunchy on the inside. The whole process should take about 5 to 10 minutes, depending on the density and thickness of the chicory wedges and the heat of the fire.

To serve, cut the butt end off of each chicory wedge and split them in half crosswise. Place all the halves on a platter. Separate the chicken legs from the thighs by cutting between the joint. Cut the breast in half through the middle of the breastbone. Arrange the chicken on top of the chicory. Add a little olive oil to the reserved marinade and drizzle it over the whole thing. Serve the Fried Farro in the dish you heated it up in.

GRILLED CHICKEN BALLOTINE WITH GREEN LENTILS AND PARSLEY ROOT

Serves 8 as an appetizer or 5 as a main course

A ballotine is a terrine made from a whole chicken that is wrapped in its own skin. This is a very elaborate and, some might say, not a very "Camino" dish. We started making ballotines at Camino because we needed to make our chicken main course a little fancier so that we could charge enough for the pricey Riverdog chickens. I turned to my fancy friend Mike Tusk. He and I both learned to make them from Jacques Pépin, but Mike went on to perfect them at Quince. My sous chef at the time, Melissa Reitz, had worked at Quince, so she showed us Mike's version of ballotines.

P.S. A really sharp knife is key.

BALLOTINE

1 large whole heritage-breed chicken (about 5 to 6 pounds)

1 leek

2 celery stalks

3 carrots

½ small bunch bitter greens (about 6 ounces), such as rapini, chicory, puntarelle, escarole, or kale

Olive oil

Salt

continued

¼ cup heavy cream

Black pepper

1 large egg

5 or 6 sprigs cutting celery, stemmed and
chopped (or parsley, lovage, or savory)

¼ cup cooked mushrooms, such as black
trumpets, king trumpets, or morels (optional)

GREEN LENTILS

½ cup celery, diced the size of green lentils

½ cup yellow onion, diced the size of green lentils

Olive oil

Coarse salt

1 cup dried green lentils

PARSLEY ROOT

1 cup peeled parsley root cut in ¼-inch rounds

Olive oil

1 clove garlic, sliced thinly

Coarse salt

½ bunch Italian parsley, picked and
roughly chopped

One of the trickiest parts of this recipe comes first.
You have to cut off the chicken skin in one whole
piece because it is going to wrap around the terrine
and hold all the meat inside. To do so, first remove the
feet and the wing tips. Set the chicken breast side
down and find the joint between the drumsticks and
the feet. Cut right through the joint. Flip the chicken
over onto its back, find the second joint from the wing
tip and cut through the joint. Once you have both feet
and wing tips removed, flip the chicken onto its breast
again. Slice down the backbone, cutting through the
membrane that attaches the skin to the flesh. Then
use one hand to gently pull back the skin while you
use the other hand to swipe the knife through that
attaching membrane as you lift the skin away from

the meat. You can also use your fingers to loosen the
skin, if that seems easier. When you get all the way to
the joints, flap the skin back and pull it off like a sock.
Be extra careful around the bony parts, like where
the wing meets the breast, because that's where the
skin really wants to tear. It's difficult to patch up a
hole in the skin, so better to err on the side of slicing
into the meat with your knife rather than ripping the
skin. Work from the back of the chicken to the front,
pulling the skin down and off the head end and both of
the wings, and moving toward the legs.

When you've got the skin off in one big piece, lay it
out flat. There will, of course, be holes where the legs
and wings were, so you'll need to cut from each joint
hole along the shortest path to the outer edge of the
skin. Once you've done this, the chicken skin will look
a little bit like Batman. Carefully trim any excess fat
and membrane.

Flip the chicken over so that the breast side is facing
up. Next, spread the legs apart and pop the legs out of
the joints. Cut around the side of each leg, working
toward the back of the chicken. Then, flip the chicken
over and look for the oysters—little knobs of meat
on either side of the backbone. Use the tip of your
knife to scoop down and around each oyster, keeping
it attached to the thigh as you cut the entire leg off
the body. Slide your knife down both sides of the
breastbone, cutting the breast meat away from the
bone. Leave the drumettes on the carcass. You should
now have one chicken carcass (including the feet and
wings), one whole piece of skin, two breasts off the
bone, and two legs still on the bone.

Now you're going to cut the meat into various sizes
for various purposes. Start with the breasts. Remove
the tenderloin, a loose piece of meat that you can
easily lift off the back of each breast. Set them aside.
Cut a long strip, about ¾-inch wide from the center
of the each breast. You want the strip to be as long
as possible as it needs to extend the whole length of
the ballotine. It's okay if the ends are a bit thinner

continued

than the middle section. These two pieces will form the center of the ballotine. Set these two long pieces aside, then put the breast trimmings in a bowl with the tenderloins.

Separate the legs and thighs by cutting through the joint. Then cut the bone out of the thigh by slicing along either side of the bone and pulling it out. Cut out the hard cartilage bit at the knee. Do the same for the drumstick. Remove all the major tendons—the thin, slippery, shiny things. If the tendons are too slippery, you can try using a towel to get a better grip. There should be about seven or eight tendons in each leg. Slice open each thigh so that it is an even, flat rectangle-ish shape, then cut the meat into ⅓-inch cubes. Slice open the drumstick into a manageable, flat piece, then finely mince all the meat. You want to cut the drumstick meat smaller than the thigh meat because it's tougher, plus it needs to be small enough that it will help hold everything together later on. At this point, you should have a bowl of breast trimmings and tenderloins, the two long breast pieces, a bowl of thigh meat cubes, a bowl of minced drumstick meat, and that big piece of skin.

Next, cut up all your vegetables. For the leek, trim the roots and cut off the top at the point just below where it branches. Dice the leek into ¼-inch pieces, put them in a bowl of water, and swish around until all the grit settles on the bottom. Cut the celery into a fine dice. Peel the carrots and cut them into a fine dice as well. It is not often that we are super precise about dicing at Camino, but this is where you want to make sure that all the pieces are evenly diced so that you don't end up with odd-size pieces in the ballotine. Lastly, pull the bitter greens off their stems and coarsely chop them.

Heat a pan over medium-high heat. Pour in enough olive oil to coat the bottom of the pan, then add the diced leek, celery, and carrot. Season with a little more salt than you would normally use. Cook for a few minutes, stirring and tasting, until the vegetables are

tender with just the slightest bit of texture. Put them onto a plate and let cool. Return the pan to the stove, pour in a little more olive oil, and add the greens. Season them with salt and cook until tender. You can pour in a splash of water if the greens are really tough and need to cook longer. Put the greens onto the plate with the vegetables and chill everything in the refrigerator until it is completely cool.

Preheat the oven to 300°F.

Combine the cream, tenderloins and breast meat trimmings, ½ teaspoon salt, and several grinds of pepper in a food processor. Blend for a few seconds, until a ball forms, then add the egg and continue blending until the mixture is smooth. You're looking for a soft, pillowy texture that can still hold its shape. Put it into a bowl and stir in the minced drumstick meat and diced thigh meat. Run your knife through the cooked greens to break up any long, stringy pieces, then add them to the bowl along with the other cooked vegetables, the cutting celery, and some salt and pepper. Mix everything together. While you're mixing, if you see any tendons, just fish them out.

To test the amount of salt in the mixture, make a little patty, wrap it in foil, and bake it until the meat is cooked through. You have to bake it in the oven and then taste it because that's how the ballotine will ultimately be cooked, and the saltiness could change if it were fried in a pan or cooked some other way.

Lay the chicken skin down on a two-foot-long piece of parchment paper. Using half of the meat mixture, form a 3-inch-wide rectangle lengthwise down the center of the skin. Using wet hands can help with the problem of the meat sticking to your fingers. Lay the two long pieces of breast meat end to end lengthwise in the center of the mixture with their thin ends overlapping slightly. Mound the remaining meat mixture on top of the breast pieces, then wrap the skin all the way around the meat. If there happens to be a crazy excess of overlapping skin at the seam, just trim some of it off. Tightly roll the parchment up around the ballotine as if you were making a burrito. Crimp the ends, then wrap the whole thing in aluminum foil (now it looks like a super burrito). You can do all this ahead and put in the fridge. Just take it out of the fridge 1½ hours before baking.

Put the ballotine on a baking rack and bake until a thermometer inserted in the very center reads 135°F, about 45 minutes to an hour. It's difficult to tell if the ballotine is done by touching it because each one ends up feeling so different. Let the baked ballotine rest, still wrapped in foil, for about 20 minutes.

Build a fire to grill the ballotine.

While the ballotine bakes and the coals are getting ready, make the green lentils and the parsley root. Heat a small pot. Sauté the celery and onion with olive oil and a pinch of salt until tender but not brown. Add the dry lentils and stir to mix. Cover with water by ½ inch, add some salt, and bring to a boil. Turn down to a simmer and continue to cook until the lentils are completely tender but not falling apart. Taste and adjust for salt. While the lentils cook, you will have to add splashes of water to keep them covered. You want to end up with the cooked lentils barely covered with water. This should take 15 to 30 minutes. Pour the lentils and their liquid into a shallow pan to cool.

To make the parsley root, heat a pan over medium heat. Add a couple tablespoons of olive oil, then add the garlic and cook just until it softens, about 30 seconds. Add the parsley root, enough water to barely cover, and some salt, and bring to a boil over high heat. Turn down to a vigorous simmer and add a couple more tablespoons of olive oil. You want the water to reduce while the parsley root is cooking, so that the cooking juices concentrate and emulsify with the olive oil. Be careful not to add too much salt, as it will get saltier as the water reduces. Once the parsley root is tender but still holding its shape, add the chopped parsley and pour everything into a shallow dish to cool.

Rake the coals under the grill for medium-hot grilling.

When the grill is hot and the ballotine has rested, unwrap the baked ballotine, pat it dry, and rub it lightly with oil so that it doesn't stick to the grill. Place the whole ballotine on the grill for just long enough to brown the skin. The grilling part usually takes only about 10 minutes, but you could also brown it in a 500°F oven. Once the ballotine is done, you have to make a decision about which vegetable juices are most valuable. To me the parsley root water is more interesting than the lentil water, but I might just as easily make a case for the opposite in the future.

So when you are ready to eat, bring the parsley root and all its parsleyed liquid up to a boil and add the lentils, leaving some of their liquid behind. Bring this mixture up to a boil, taste for salt, and look to see how juicy it is. Ideally, there is just enough liquid clinging to this mixture so it's not dry. Too loose and it will seem very bland and watery—this is the key moment! If it seems like it can take it, add a splash more olive oil.

To serve, put a spoonful of lentils and parsley root on each plate and a ½-inch slice of the grilled ballotine on top.

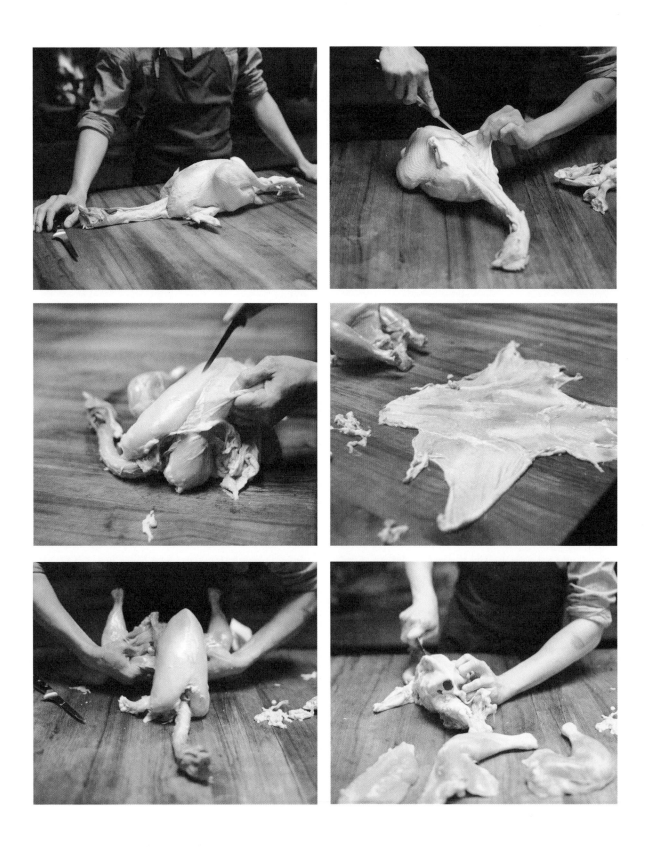

EGG TEA

Our herb situation is a little crazy. Our neighbors bring us herbs randomly and in unplanned quantities. It is not unusual to have three different people bring us lovage on the same day, and I may have ordered it from a fourth source, not knowing the plans of the other three. I love this dilemma because it forces me to find creative ways to use all the herbs. It also leaves me with a lot of herb stems after the leaves are picked off.

When you spend so much time thinking about how to use every part of a lamb, or how to get the most out of a lingcod, you can't help but extend that to everything else you do, so it seemed only logical to find a use for herb stems. This is the vicious cycle of Camino—first trying to find something to do with all the stems and then "needing" lots of stems so that we can cook eggs the way we like them. Now we fight over herb stems for Egg Tea—the special herby broth we use to poach/bake eggs next to the fire in the wood oven.

Our egg tea is decidedly NOT vegetable stock. Vegetable stock always seems sweet, where this is bright and strong with a medicinal herb flavor—though not quite Chinese medicine. It has to be really strong to impart any flavor to the egg, but strong in a clean, bright, just-steeped way, not in a muddy, boiled way.

While we are prepping, the cooks will save all of their herb stems for the cook who is working the wood oven station, because that is who is usually making the vegetarian main course. That cook will sort of curate what he or she wants for the evening—maybe adding something like turmeric peel or a cardoon leaf if it seems appropriate for the dish (see the Cardoon Gratin on page 66).

As you are prepping for dinner, collect all your herb stems in a pot. They can really be jammed in if you have a lot. Barely cover with water. Bring to a boil over high heat and then strain immediately. You can really use any herb for this—if you are able eat it for dinner, you can add it to the pot. Possible additions include:

> Artichoke or cardoon leaf (really, just one!)
>
> Turmeric peels
>
> Green garlic tops
>
> Ginger peel
>
> Fennel tops
>
> Tomato peel
>
> Mushroom butts

Do not use carrots, leeks, or onions—because then you are making vegetable stock.

CAMINO EGG

The vegetarian main course dishes at Camino often have an egg on them, but I don't think of the egg as a substitute for meat—more as the thing that is going to help tie all the vegetables together. Consider adding the egg to any of the vegetarian main courses like we did with Cardoon Gratin (page 66). It's especially good with Ratatouille (page 77).

When you're ready to cook your egg(s), preheat the oven to 400°F. Put enough Egg Tea (preceding recipe) in a sauté pan so that it will eventually cover the whites but not the yolks when you drop the eggs in. Add a splash of olive oil and heat the pan. When the liquid comes to a boil, turn off the heat and crack in the eggs. I have trouble doing more than three eggs in a 10-inch pan because they get too crowded and are hard to maneuver. And it's better to do fewer eggs in multiple smaller pans to keep the heat more even. Sprinkle salt and chopped or whole herbs directly on the egg. Put the pan in the oven and cook until the whites are set but the yolks are still runny, about 4 minutes.

HERB FRITTATA

Makes one 10-inch frittata

The frittatas we make at Camino are thin and supple, with just enough egg to bind the herbs and other ingredients together. They range from bright green to dark green depending on which herbs we add.

I hate the method of finishing a frittata in the oven; all I can think about is the already cooked egg at the bottom of the pan and how it continues to cook while it's sitting under all the egg that still needs to cook. There is no way that is not going to end up rubbery. So, to make this frittata, you have to get comfortable doing the old-fashioned Italian flipping method rather than finishing it in the oven. This is a good reason to have at least one well-seasoned cast iron pan in your kitchen. If it is maintained properly, nothing will stick to it and you can get rid of all your cancer-causing Teflon.

A trick when using cast iron with eggs is that the pan has to be hot enough so that the egg sizzles slightly when it hits the pan but not so hot that it is going to brown. Your pan should be hottish to start, but the flame should be low when you add the eggs, so the pan is cooling a bit but is still hot enough to cook the eggs. Eggs cook very evenly and predictably once you have the hang of it.

> 6 large eggs
>
> 1½ cups chopped soft herbs, such as parsley, chervil, sorrel, mint, chives, or lovage
>
> ½ cup cooled and chopped Cooked Greens (page 13)
>
> 2 tablespoons olive oil, plus more for the pan
>
> Salt and black pepper

Whisk the eggs in a bowl. They don't have to be crazy perfect—there just shouldn't be any big patches of egg white. Stir in the herbs, cooked greens, olive oil, a big pinch of salt, and a few grinds of pepper. The amount of salt will vary every time you make this frittata depending on the greens you are using, the fluffiness of the herbs, and the size of the eggs. You're just going have to take a guess, taste the raw mixture, and see you how close you are. Hopefully, your guessing ability will improve over time.

Heat a well-seasoned 10-inch cast iron pan over medium heat until it is hottish, then turn the flame to low. Splash in enough olive oil to coat the bottom of the pan, then pour in the egg mixture. There should be a nice little satisfying sizzle when the eggs hit the pan. The greens want to get all bunched up in the middle, so you have to push them toward the edges. Cook gently until the frittata is about two-thirds done. (The bottom and sides will be set but the top will still be raw.) As the frittata cooks, there will be tiny, gentle bubbles around the edges of the pan. To get ready for the flip, try shaking the pan to see if the frittata moves easily. If it won't budge, gently loosen it with a rubber spatula. Put a plate on top of the pan and quickly and confidently (!) invert the frittata onto the plate. (Don't despair if it falls apart—the egg that has yet to be cooked will hopefully seal it back together.) Put the pan back on the burner, wipe it out, and add a little more olive oil. Carefully slide the frittata back into the pan, using your hand to hold it steady, then cook the other side for another couple of minutes. Check for doneness by poking the tip of a small knife into the center of the frittata. Put the plate on top of the pan again and flip the frittata out of the pan. Serve whichever side is prettier facing up.

VARIATIONS

You can add a little sheep's milk cheese or cooked mushrooms.

EGG BAKED IN CREAM
Serves 1

We bake these eggs in the wood oven for brunch with the option of one or two eggs. If you opt for two eggs in one dish, add a little more (but not twice as much) of everything. The baking dish is important: you want something shallow, no higher than one inch, or else the egg will steam instead of bake. A 5-inch *cazuela* works well for one egg and a 6-inch *cazuela* for two.

We also serve this egg as a middle course at dinner with black trumpet mushrooms (page 66), or black truffles if we are feeling fancy.

> ¼ cup sliced leeks, white and pale green parts
>
> 1 tablespoon butter
>
> Salt
>
> Leaves from 2 sprigs thyme
>
> 1 egg
>
> Cream
>
> Pepper
>
> Grilled Bread (page 11)

Preheat the oven to 400°F.

Wash the sliced leeks by putting them in a bowl of water and swishing them around to rinse out all the grit, then lift them out of the water. Melt butter in a medium-hot pan. Add the leeks and a pinch of salt. The slices will have some water clinging to them, so you can cook them pretty hot, but don't brown them at all. If they threaten to brown, add a splash of water. When the leeks are tender, add the thyme and cook for just a moment longer.

Put the cooked leeks and thyme in the baking dish and let them cool completely in the dish. Once they are cool, spread them around, effectively buttering the dish, and create a shallow well in the middle for the egg. Gently crack in the egg and pour in enough cream to barely cover the white. Season with salt and pepper. Bake until the white is cooked through but the yolk is still runny, about 6 minutes.

Serve with grilled bread.

CONFETTI EGGS

This is just for fun—not edible! But you will no longer be able to have fun without confetti eggs. Whenever you use eggs, instead of just cracking them in half, try to tap the shell gently toward the top so you get a clean, smallish opening (about the size of a quarter or smaller). Empty out the egg for whatever culinary purpose and then rinse the shell thoroughly. Set upside-down in the egg carton to drain. When you have accumulated enough eggshells for your festivities, fill them with confetti, using a funnel made from a rolled up piece of paper. Then glue a patch of tissue paper onto the egg to patch up the hole and keep the confetti inside.

Then crack them on the heads of your unsuspecting friends and loved ones! And, as you can imagine, the clean up is impossible—you will keep finding confetti everywhere for a long time.

CHAPTER SEVEN

DUCK

DUCK

Duck is a self-esteem builder.

When chef friends come in to cook with us, I put them on duck. People who've never cooked on an open fire get to hit it out of the park all night long. Duck's the easiest thing we do. It's also the item customers seem to like more than any other.

I grew up eating at those Chinatown noodle shops with the roast ducks hanging by their necks in the window. Duck noodle soup, tea-smoked duck, Peking duck on special occasions—these were foundational. Nobody cooked duck better than those restaurants, and that's still true; they've worked it out over millennia. It's a pretty high bar, but it gives us something to shoot for.

The most important step is letting the meat rest so that overcooking isn't inevitable—that's the number-one mistake cooks make with all meat. But, of course, it starts with sourcing. Anyone with a Chinese restaurant in the Bay Area knows the Reichardt family. They began raising Pekin ducks in 1901 and became the default supplier for just about everyone. Then, in the 1980s, the great-grandson broke out.

Jim Reichardt decided he wanted to raise ducks without antibiotics or hormones, with room to roam, and in more of a natural environment. In many places around the world, this concept wouldn't have been startling—ducks had only ever been raised that way. But in the States, which had perfected all these horrible farming habits, it was a radical notion. It would be years before "free range" entered the vernacular.

Jim called his operation Liberty Ducks. The freedom, the absence of chemicals—the difference in taste was dramatic. They're bigger, leaner, and plumper in the right areas. They're more moist and more flavorful. Plus I just love having this guy walk into my restaurant every week. I've never met anyone who understands this animal better. In high school, he'd take his pet duck to his baseball games. I heard it would ride around in his convertible, wrapped in a blanket.

Ducks defy physics. If you buy a whole one, and butcher and trim it well, you're left with more fat and stock than you need for the meat you get. There's a surplus, in other words, and those extra by-products will give you an extra dish—consommé, for instance. That's how a high-end duck pays for itself. Ducks are givers.

Looking back, duck was the first food I spent my own money on, as a budding cook. It was amazing to me, wandering into these old Chinese deli places, having them spoon some of that dripping grease onto the meat for you. I can't say we cook in the Chinese style at Camino, but the influence is there. We make a similar crispy skin. And our duck with prunes is sort of Chinese-ish, except we use red wine. The way we cook a leg really slowly, the texture of our grilled duck breast—I like to think these have a trace of that thousand-year-old Chinese approach.

BUTCHERING A DUCK

If you've never butchered a whole animal, start with ducks—they are easy and very rewarding. You can use just about everything: breast, leg, and wing; liver, gizzard, and heart. On top of all that, you get the fat for cooking and preserving, the skin for cracklings, and the bones for broth, stock, or sauce. The benefit of all this far outweighs the hassle of butchering. Usually the giblets are removed, so make sure they are included with your duck.

To butcher the duck, pull the legs away from the body one at a time, and slice through the skin that stretches between the drumstick and the breast. You want to keep as much skin as possible on the breast, so make your cut close to the leg. Use both hands to pop the legs outward from the body. Press away from the breast and down, then you'll hear a pop. Cut around the side of the leg, working toward the back of the duck. Flip the duck over so the back is facing up and look for the oysters, the little knobs of meat on either side of the backbone where the thigh connects to the body. Use your knife to scoop down and around each oyster, keeping it attached to the thigh. Once the legs are removed, slice down the breastbone, running your knife along either side of it and continuing along the wishbone. It works well if you use one hand to push the breast meat away from the body and use the other hand to make scraping cuts close to the ribs. Keeping the wings attached to the breasts, cut at the joint next to the body. Once the breasts are removed from the carcass, separate the wings from the breast. Remove the last joint of the wing and save it to make stock or sauce. Trim the excess skin and fat off the breast, leaving just a ½-inch border of skin around the breast meat. If there is a pocket of excess fat or skin on the inside of each of the legs trim it off. Trim all other fat and skin off the carcass—there will be a lot around the neck. Discard any glands from the skin trimmings.

At this point, you will have breasts, legs, wings, wing tips, giblets, fat, skin, and bones—all to enjoy!

GRILLED DUCK BREAST WITH LITTLE GEMS AND ENGLISH PEAS

Serves 2 to 4

Because ducks have so much fat, many people will advise you to cook the duck breast skin side down in a cast iron pan to render some of the fat before grilling it to avoid a grill fire. If "Safety First!" is your motto, then this is a good idea. Since "Safety Third!" has always been my motto, I prefer to grill them from start to finish, but that means you have to be patient when preparing the coals to make absolutely sure there are not flames—and maybe don't do it right next to your house.

Little Gems are perfect for grilling because they stay crunchy and have a little bit of bitterness on the outer greener leaves that contrasts with the sweeter inner leaves. I've always liked the classic combination of peas and lettuce. If you are over the age of seventy-five or are French, you might have had a dish of peas cooked with lettuce at some point. This is a different take on the classic dish, in that the lettuce is grilled.

There is a perfect moment when peas are just the right size. Too small and there is nothing there; too large and they become starchy. They can be very tasty when they are starchy, but you have to cook them until they are grayish and they won't be as sweet. My friends at Riverdog Farm know exactly when they are perfect, and when they are, Camino will buy fifty pounds of peas per week. Sometimes they're so good we just serve a bowl of English peas.

2 duck breasts

1 teaspoon black peppercorns

1/2 teaspoon allspice berries

8 juniper berries

2 bay leaves, torn into small pieces

Salt and black pepper

2 heads Little Gem lettuce

Olive oil

2 cloves garlic, thinly sliced

1 1/2 cups shelled English peas

5 spearmint leaves, or use Persian mint or basil

1 sprig oregano (optional)

Brown Stock (using duck, see page 32; optional)

Duck Fat and Cracklings (page 182; optional)

To make the duck, first trim the skin around each duck breast, leaving about a 1/2-inch border around the meat. With a sharp knife (this really doesn't work with a dull knife) and a quick, light hand, score the skin by gliding your knife in 1/8-inch rows on an angle, cutting only the skin, not all the way to the meat. Do the same thing from another angle to make a crosshatch pattern. The point of this is to increase the surface area so the skin gets crisp while the fat renders a bit. I actually think it's better to skip this step completely if your knife is so dull that it just tears up the skin.

Grind the peppercorns, allspice, juniper, and bay in a spice grinder. Season the duck on both sides with salt, then sprinkle the ground spices, perhaps putting a bit extra on the skin side. Ducks are fatty and rich, so I tend to season and spice them more than I would other meats. It's best to season them the day before and keep them covered in the refrigerator. If you are in a pinch, you can season them 2 hours before cooking and leave them out at room temperature. If you seasoned them the day before, you will need to pull them out of the refrigerator to temper for a couple of hours before cooking.

Build a fire to grill the duck.

When the coals are ready, rake them under the grill for medium-hot cooking. When the grill is hot, place the duck skin side down on the grill, with the thickest part of the breast pointed toward the hottest part of the grill.

Because ducks have so much fat, some of that fat is going to drip into the coals. If the coals are not

continued

completely ready and there are any flames coming off them you will likely get a flare-up when the fat hits. If this happens, remove the breast immediately and let the flames die out. You will probably have enough time to drink a glass of wine before the grill is ready again, which might sound nice, but, really, you just butchered this duck, preserved all its innards, and made sauce out of the carcass, so be patient when preparing the coals in the first place so you don't ruin your duck breast. Flames create a sooty layer on the duck and make it taste like kerosene.

Feel free to move the breast around—the goal is nice, even brownness, not sharp grill marks. If the coals are too hot, the breast will be splotchy and flabby; if they are too cool, the meat will be done before the skin is brown. The skin side usually takes about 6 minutes to cook.

Once the skin is satisfyingly brown, flip the breasts over to the flesh side and continue to cook. It usually takes about 4 more minutes to get to my preferred duck breast temperature, which is somewhere between medium-rare and medium. You can feel the flesh side firm up when it nears medium-rare. You are shooting for the breast to have a crisp brown skin and be evenly pink throughout but completely set and not raw in the middle. The true secret to this is to pull the breasts off the grill and let them rest in a warm spot for at least 12 minutes before slicing. If you cut into them too soon, the meat will be gray on the outside and raw in the middle.

While the duck breasts are resting, grill the Little Gems. Cut the lettuces in half lengthwise, brush both sides with olive oil, and season with salt and pepper. Place the halves cut side down on a hot grill for a few minutes until they have darkish grill marks. Flip them over and grill the other side for a couple of minutes.

Heat a pan that will fit all the peas in a single, crowded layer. Add a splash of olive oil, then add the garlic and sauté it briefly but don't let it brown. Add about a cup of water, another splash of olive oil, and a pinch of salt. Bring the liquid to a roaring boil, then add the peas.

Cook them as fast as you can on the best burner on your stove. As the peas cook, keep tasting them as well as the cooking water for salt. Remember, the peas will be as salty as the water when they are done cooking, so don't overdo it early on (see Oil and Water Method, page 30). If the peas are taking too long and the water is evaporating, keep adding a splash here and there. Don't add too much or you'll end up with watery pea water instead of super tasty pea water. I don't think pea water is the right term, but you know what I mean. A perfect pea will take about 2½ minutes to cook. If they are bigger, you have to keep cooking them until they are done, even if they lose color. A gray but tasty pea is better than a green, undercooked pea. Peas can take up to 10 minutes to cook, depending on their age and size. I don't really know any way around that. You just have to taste them. A minute before the peas are done, add the mint.

To serve, slice the duck breast into ⅓-inch-thick slices on the diagonal, holding your knife at about a 60-degree angle to the cutting surface, and place slices on the plates, crispy skin side up. If you made brown stock out of the duck bones, spoon it over the breast. Cut each Little Gem half in half lengthwise and set the wedges next to the breast. Spoon the peas over the lettuces and a little bit over the breast. Sprinkle duck cracklings over everything, if you have them.

VARIATIONS

At Camino, we always serve a few slices of grilled duck breast along with slow-cooked leg, so consider serving the whole duck with peas and lettuce if you've got more people to feed. The sauce will be extra luxurious if you mix the duck leg braising liquid with the brown duck stock and reduce them together. I love duck with lettuce and peas, but because I cannot hold myself to one recipe I want to mention an alternative for seasoning that goes in a totally different, more Middle Eastern direction: a combination of caraway, chiles, cumin, and coriander; lots of black pepper; grated Seville or blood orange zest and chiles. This is more of a fall or winter seasoning and would be good with red lentils and greens.

SLOW-COOKED DUCK LEGS WITH SAVOY CABBAGE, PRUNES, AND DUCK CRACKLINGS

Serves 2

½ teaspoon whole black peppercorns

6 allspice berries

2 juniper berries

2 duck legs

Salt

Duck fat, lard, or rice bran oil

1 yellow onion, or 2 large shallots, sliced

2 celery stalks, sliced

1⅓ cups red wine

6 cloves garlic, unpeeled and lightly smashed

4 bay leaves

6 sprigs thyme

6 prunes with pits (hard to find but totally worth the effort)

2 cups brown stock (using duck, page 32; optional)

1 small Savoy cabbage (about 1½ pounds)

2 cloves garlic, peeled

¼ cup Duck Cracklings (page 182)

Polenta (page 9; optional)

Preheat the oven to 400°F.

Grind the pepper, allspice, and juniper in a spice grinder or mortar and pestle. Season the duck legs with salt and the spice mixture. This is best done the day before you cook them, but it will work fine if done 2 hours ahead.

Heat a heavy-bottomed pan over high heat. Swirl in about ¼ cup of the duck fat, then add the onion and celery. Cook the vegetables until they're brown, then spread them out in a baking dish. Pour the wine into the empty pan over low heat to deglaze. With a wooden spoon, scrape up any brown bits from the pan.

Add smashed garlic, bay, and thyme to the baking dish with the cooked vegetables. Arrange the duck legs skin side down on top of the vegetables. Pour in the wine from the pan and enough water to come two-thirds of the way up the legs. Cover tightly with foil and bake.

After 30 minutes, peek under the foil to see if the liquid has begun to simmer. If it has, reduce the oven temperature to about 300°F to keep it at the barest simmer. Flip the legs over to expose the skin, then tuck the prunes around the duck legs. If much of the skin is still under liquid, pour a little of it off (and save it for later—you'll add it back into the sauce). If the liquid isn't simmering, keep the oven at 400°F until it does, then lower the temperature, flip the legs over, and continue as above.

Now the plan is to let the skin gently brown while the legs gently cook in the gently simmering liquid. If the liquid is too hot, the legs will dry out—hence the three times "gently." If everything goes perfectly, the skin will be brown when the meat is done. Check for doneness by poking a skewer next to the bone in the thickest part of the leg; the skewer will slide out rather easily when the meat is cooked, but you don't want the meat falling off the bone. If the skin is getting too brown before the legs are done, loosely cover with foil. This whole browning and cooking process should take about 40 minutes after the legs are flipped.

When the ducks legs are done, let them cool in their braising liquid. (Slow-cooked duck legs can be made 1 day ahead and refrigerated in the cooking liquid overnight.) Once cool, take the legs and prunes out of the dish, then strain the liquid into a pot. Let it settle for 5 minutes then skim off as much fat as you can. If you made brown stock, this is when to add it to the braising liquid for a richer, meatier sauce. Over high heat, bring the braising juices to a boil and reduce by one third. At this point, taste for salt and continue reducing to about half, but stop reducing if it gets too salty.

Reheat the duck legs in the oven skin side up with the braising juices and prunes for a few minutes.

While the duck legs reheat, cook the cabbage. Start by bringing a pot of salted water to a boil. Quarter the cabbage through the stem. Cut out and discard the core. Slice each quarter into rough 1-inch pieces. Boil the cabbage for a couple of minutes, until it turns bright green and tastes sweet and no longer raw but still has a little crunch to it. Drain and spread it out on a plate to cool. Melt about 3 tablespoons of duck fat in a pan set over medium heat. Thinly slice the 2 cloves of garlic, add them to the fat, and let them sizzle for a minute or so without browning. Pour the garlic duck-fat mixture over the cooked cabbage and toss well.

To serve, arrange a duck leg, Savoy cabbage, and prunes over polenta on a plate. Ladle some of the braising juices over the duck, then sprinkle the cracklings on top of everything.

DUCK HEARTS, GIZZARDS, AND WINGS CONFIT

Confit refers to a method of preserving something in fat. It is a great way to have something on hand to avert disaster—by disaster, I mean you didn't get a chance to go to the store and you have people coming over. At Camino, disaster is averted by adding a duck giblet confit toast to a salad that is lacking something, or switching to Grilled Duck Wing Confit (following recipe) if we run out of sausages in the middle of service.

Season the parts generously with salt and a little black pepper. Cover and refrigerate for at least 2 days, but not more than 4 days.

With duck wings, I always cut off the tip of the wing and use it for stock—there is not much to eat there.

Put the seasoned meat in a small pot and add enough melted duck fat to barely cover. Bring the fat to a gentle simmer over low heat. It should bubble just a little bit around the edges of the pot. You really don't want vigorous bubbling, because then the meat will just fry and dry out. If you have trouble keeping your flame low enough, you can try setting the pot on the pilot light. The wings will take about 2 hours to cook—they should be completely tender. Gizzards and hearts take about 3 hours until they're completely tender. This is one of those things that you can leave on the back burner while you cook a bunch of other dishes and just check in with it every once in a while.

To store the duck parts, cover completely in the melted fat and refrigerate. They will taste good right away and even better after a month. They will last for a year, but remember to keep them completely sealed in fat. I would store the hearts and gizzards separately from the wings because you will use them differently. You can warm the giblets in some of the fat, then slice them, and add to a chicory salad, or put slices on top of grilled bread with some sauerkraut for a snack.

You can do exactly the same thing with chicken giblets and wings. We always end up cooking them in duck fat just because there is never enough chicken fat for storing.

GRILLED DUCK WING CONFIT WITH POMEGRANATE, CHILES, AND SESAME
Serves 6 as a snack

> 1½ cups pomegranate juice
>
> 2 or more tablespoons Chile Sauce (page 13)
>
> 1 tablespoon plus 1 teaspoon Toasted Sesame Seeds (see page 33)
>
> 8 confited duck wings (see preceding recipe)

Build a fire to grill the duck wings.

Bring the pomegranate juice to a boil in a heavy-bottomed pot and cook it until it reduces to a syrup.

continued

It should be thick but still pourable. When it's done, there should be about ½ cup.

When there are enough coals, rake them under the grill for medium-hot cooking. Place the duck wings on it so they lie as flat as possible. The trick with grilling these duck wings is that the skin is very soft at first and wants to stick to the grill. So cook them over a medium-hot fire on one side until the skin is firm and brown, about 3 or 4 minutes. Flip them over and cook for another 3 or 4 minutes. After they are brown on both sides, you can lean them up on each other to get the weird angles of the wings browned.

Remove the wings from the grill and cut at the joints. Toss the grilled duck wings in a bowl with the pomegranate syrup, the chile sauce, and 1 tablespoon of sesame seeds. Sprinkle with the remaining sesame seeds and serve. We serve this as a bar snack or as an appetizer with a puntarelle salad.

ROAST DUCK CONSOMMÉ WITH HERB DUMPLINGS AND WILD NETTLES

Serves 10

This is a fancy little dish that is the result of a lot of planning and hoarding at Camino. It's made out of leftover everything: duck carcasses, stock, mushroom butts, old bread, egg whites. At home, this will be a little more difficult, but use it as a guideline for the right moment—like when you happen to have three duck carcasses left from your duck party. You can also skip the dumplings and use some mushrooms, cooked carrot rounds, or burdock root slices cooked using the Oil and Water Method (see page 30).

I like to believe that cooking is magic, so I plug my ears when people try to tell me how the raft works in consommé. All I know is that it is a matrix of flavorful vegetables held together with egg whites that act as a filter. You thoroughly mix the eggy glop into the consommé when it is cold, and when you heat it the egg whites firm up and bring all the vegetables and other little bits along as it floats to the surface like a raft. The vegetables and ground mushrooms give structure to the raft and add flavor to the broth, and the raft makes the broth totally clear. Magic!

BROTH

3 duck carcasses

3 big handfuls of mushroom butts, or 1 handful of dried mushrooms

Duck fat, lard, or rice bran oil

2 yellow onions, sliced thinly

2 large carrots, peeled and sliced

4 celery stalks, sliced

5 bay leaves

1 head garlic, sliced crosswise twice into thirds

Handful of winter savory or thyme sprigs

Handful of parsley stems

3 quarts chicken stock or blond poultry stock (page 31)

1 bottle of white wine

Coarse salt

Brandy (optional)

RAFT

1 carrot

1 celery stalk

1 spring onion, or a handful of leek tops

1 tomato, fresh or canned

Roasted mushroom butts, left over from making the broth

1 cup egg whites (about 7 eggs; use the yolks to make ice cream!)

HERB DUMPLINGS

About ½ loaf of day-old bread

3 eggs

⅓ bunch scallions

Duck fat

Salt

4 confit duck gizzards or hearts

1½ cups mixed picked herbs, such as lovage, cutting celery, mint, nepitella, summer or winter savory, chervil, or parsley

Pepper

½ pound wild nettles or Savoy spinach (optional)

Preheat the oven to 450°F.

To make the broth, use a cleaver to chop the duck carcasses into 3-inch pieces. Roast on a sheet pan, turning often, until quite brown, about 30 minutes. Keep an eye on the pan—you don't want it to turn too dark, because you will be getting a lot of the flavor from the pan when you deglaze it.

While the carcasses cook, toss the mushroom butts with enough duck fat to coat, and roast them until they're fairly brown, about 7 minutes. If you are using dried mushrooms, don't roast them.

Heat your biggest pot over medium-high heat. Add enough duck fat to generously cover the bottom of the pot, then add the yellow onions and carrots and cook them, stirring, until well browned. Again, keep an eye on the bottom of the pot to make sure it's not getting too dark. Then add the celery, the roasted duck carcasses, and two-thirds of the roasted mushrooms, reserving the rest for the raft. With a wooden spoon, try to break up the carcasses and smash them down a little. That way, it'll take less stock to cover them and you'll end up with a really rich broth. Add the bay leaves, garlic, herbs, enough stock to barely cover (if you don't have enough stock to cover, you can top it off with water), wine, and a small handful of coarse salt.

While the stock is heating up, deglaze the mushroom roasting pan and the duck roasting pan by pouring a ladleful of the stock into each pan. Heat each pan on the stove to loosen the browned bits. Scrape them up with a wooden spoon and add the liquid and the browned bits to the pot. This stage is critical because much of the flavor and color of your broth comes from these pans.

Once the liquid in the pot comes to a boil, turn it down to a simmer and skim off any foam and fat on the surface. Continue simmering for 2 to 3 hours, skimming occasionally and tasting every so often for that perfect moment where it tastes really good, but doesn't taste bony. The bones will have fallen apart and added a little gelatin to the broth, which gives it some nice body. When the broth tastes right, strain it into another pot. Let it settle for a minute, then hold your ladle so that the lip is parallel with the surface of the broth. Make a little swirling motion and carefully lower the ladle just barely enough that the fat falls into the ladle—you don't want to lose any of the precious broth that you've worked so hard to make. Ideally, at this point you want to refrigerate the stock for a few hours—it is easier to clarify from cold—however, when I don't have time, I go straight to the clarifying stage, and it works (sorry, Escoffier).

To make the raft, peel the remaining carrot and cut it into a fine julienne. Julienne the celery and the spring onion as well; it doesn't have to be perfect, but the pieces have to be small enough that they will float. Chop the tomato; if it is a fresh tomato, you can leave the skin on. Grind up the reserved roasted mushroom butts in a food processor; if you are using dried mushrooms, you can pulverize them to a powder in a spice grinder.

Whisk the egg whites until they are a little past frothy and just beginning to turn white. Whisk in the ground mushroom butts, chopped tomato, and julienned vegetables. Pour this gloppy mixture directly into the broth and whisk it vigorously—it will now look ruined. Put the pot on the stove over medium heat. Stir occasionally until the raft starts to form. As the egg white mixture starts to solidify, it will collect all the bits and proteins in your stock and float to the surface, like a raft! When the broth is simmering, you will

continued

see bubbles rise around the edges of the raft. When this happens, turn the heat to low and use your ladle to make a little hole in the center of the raft. Dip the ladle into the hole, scoop up some liquid, and pour it over the top of the raft to help firm it up. Let it simmer gently for about half an hour. What you will now have is a firm raft of all the detritus in your stock with clear broth below (miraculously).

At Camino, we use a large, clear, food grade hose to siphon the broth out. I realize that siphoning boiling broth out of a hose is scary and it is probably unlikely that you have such a thing, so you can use a large ladle or small saucepan to carefully scoop the broth out into another pot, straining through a strainer lined with several layers of moistened cheesecloth. You should try not to disturb the raft too much. There will be some cloudy broth at the bottom of the pot—strain that part into another container to use for poaching the dumplings.

If the broth isn't very clear, feel free to strain again, using fresh cheesecloth.

At this point, correct the seasoning of the consommé. Take your time getting the salt right. If it tastes flat, consider adding a splash of white wine. If it still isn't there yet, add a small amount of brandy. But really just a splash—it is easy to go overboard and ruin the whole thing.

To make the dumplings, take the crust off the day-old bread, tear it into manageable pieces, and grind it in a food processor until fairly fine—you'll want to end up with about 2 cups. In a bowl, beat the eggs and vigorously mix them with the bread.

Clean the green onions and slice thinly crosswise. Sauté them with a little bit of duck fat (or other fat) and a pinch of salt until they just wilt, 30 seconds or so. Slice and then chop the giblets into small pieces. Chop the herbs. Add the green onions, giblets, and herbs along with a good pinch of salt and a grind or two of

pepper to the eggy breadcrumbs. Mix the whole thing together, really working the egg into the bread.

Test the mixture by making a few dumplings the size of a small cherry and poaching them for 4 or 5 minutes in salted simmering water. If you have trouble forming them into balls, add more dry breadcrumbs. If they fall apart when you cook them, try adding a little more egg. Dumplings are tricky because the moistness of the day-old bread varies. You will have to be flexible with the amount of egg based on the moisture in the bread.

Once the test dumplings are holding together and they taste good when poached, form all of the mixture into balls and let them chill in the refrigerator for 10 minutes. You should have about forty dumplings. At this point you can prepoach batches of the dumplings as much as 2 hours before you plan on serving the consommé. If you saved the slightly cloudier dregs of the consommé, you can use that to prepoach the dumplings—otherwise use salted water. Bring the liquid up to a simmer and carefully put the dumplings in (don't crowd the pot too much—you want them to float freely). After they float to the surface, cook the dumplings for 1 minute more, then skim them out and set aside.

When you are ready to serve, place the dumplings in warm bowls and heat up the consommé. Once it is at a simmer, add the wild nettles and cook for a quick 15 seconds. Pour the pristine consommé over the dumplings, making sure that each bowl has some greens in it.

Pat yourself on the back and drink a glass of sherry.

DUCK FAT AND CRACKLINGS

This is the best and most satisfying way of using the skin trimmings and fat from your duck butchering project. You'll get about 1/2 cup of cracklings and 1 1/3 cup of duck fat from one 5-pound duck. Cut the skin and fat into roughly 3/4-inch squarish pieces.

Place them and all the fat in a heavy-bottomed pot with 2 inches of water. Cook over medium heat, stirring and scraping the sides occasionally, until the fat bubbles. Reduce the heat to medium-low and continue cooking for about 2 hours. While the fat cooks, it will look cloudy at first, but then it will turn clear, which means all the water has cooked out. The key at this point is to not let the skin pieces stick to the bottom of the pan. If they do, they'll brown and then the beautiful, clear fat will brown as well. (It's not the end of the world if this happens, but the fat will take on a decidedly brown flavor.)

Eventually, the skin pieces will get crispy and turn golden brown. When they do, lift them out of the fat with a slotted spoon and place them on a rack to cool. Strain the fat into a heatproof container (hot fat is hot enough to melt plastic). Let it cool and store it, covered, in the refrigerator. Duck fat will keep for weeks.

To make the cracklings, take the pieces of golden brown skin and crisp them on the rack in a 325°F oven for a few minutes. Once they are totally crispy, remove them from the oven and let them cool. Toss with salt and serve as a snack or atop any duck dish or sprinkled in a chicory salad. Duck cracklings will keep, covered, in the fridge for a week or so.

POTATOES FRIED IN DUCK FAT
Serves 6

When I cut potatoes, I always imagine an old grandmother in a curlicue apron or an army cook sitting on an upturned bucket. What they have in common is that they are holding the potato in their hand and turning it as they cut toward themselves. This sounds super un-pro and possibly dangerous, but you get the benefit of being able to make all different shapes (some with pointy ends) that will make for crispy bits. The important part is that all the pieces are about the same thickness so they cook at the same rate.

I like them roughly 2 inches by 1 inch, but you can also just cut everything into a 1-inch dice, if you are no fun.

> 3 medium floury potatoes, such as russets or Yellow Finns (about 1½ pounds)
>
> Coarse salt and fine salt
>
> Duck fat

Peel and cut the potatoes. Put the cut potatoes into a pot and just cover with cold water. Add a handful of coarse salt. Bring to a boil and reduce the heat to simmer until the potatoes are cooked all the way through. It might seem like a good idea to undercook them a little bit since you're going fry them in duck fat, but if the centers aren't done, the potatoes end up leathery, so make sure they really are cooked all the way through.

Carefully lift the potatoes out of the pot and spread them on a plate to cool. Don't worry if there are some potato nubbins that broke off from the larger pieces; they'll all get brown and crackly, and a difference in size is actually nice.

Melt enough duck fat in a cast iron pan set over medium-high heat to reach about ¾ inch. If you don't have enough duck fat, you can add in some rice bran oil or lard. When the duck fat is hot but not smoking hot, add the cooked potatoes in a single layer and let them sizzle in the hot fat, without stirring them, for a couple of minutes. The potatoes will start to brown on the undersides and around the edges. If they don't, turn the heat up a little. As they start to brown, turn the potatoes so they cook on all sides. Use a slotted spoon to lift the potatoes out of the fat and put them on a plate lined with a paper towel. Sprinkle liberally with fine salt and serve. If you need to fry in multiple batches, you can strain the fat and reuse it. After about three batches, the fat might be done.

CHAPTER EIGHT

LAMB

LAMB

If you own a vineyard in Napa, it's going to need weeding, and if your vineyard needs weeding, lambs do yeoman's work, and if you need lambs you call Don Watson and his Woolly Weeders. I don't own a vineyard, but I call Don regularly. Turns out the Woolly Weeders are delicious.

At Camino, each of our meats comes from a single person who specializes in that meat. Don's our lamb guy. Lamb is underused in this country, because generally it's subpar. Fatty. Uninteresting. Don's are another animal entirely: sweet and full of flavor. I pay more and they're worth it.

The lambs are reliable, too, which is no small thing. They vary with the season, but I know what I'm going to get every time. Once a week, or two, or four, Don walks in with this beast over his shoulders. I order them whole and I order them big. "If you can't deal with a whole lamb, you can't deal with me," he says.

Different parts of a lamb want to be cooked in different ways, and our kitchen is set up nicely for all of it— starting with the big butcher block in front of the fireplace, where we break them down. We usually do it at the end of the night when our diners are finishing their meals, which tends to either fascinate them or freak them out. There are places—macho-er places— that thrive on those reactions, on the drama of the hacksaw. To me, it's just logistics. You have a big thing that needs to become many smaller things, and you have a narrow window in which to do it.

Cooking lamb draws on all our skills. The only equipment I have in my fireplace is the bar I had installed for dangling lamb legs in front of the fire.

We braise the shoulders, ribs, and shanks in the wood oven in the morning, using residual heat. We grill the racks and loins over slightly hotter heat. The bones make the sauce. And the leftover bits from last night's dinner service become tomorrow's ragù—it's literally made from scraps. It almost always sells out.

The way we cook lamb, we're sort of curating it all night long. You have to carve it thoughtfully, so you have the right amount of the different pieces left over. It's technique overlaid on economy, and if we didn't do it this way, it would be a money loser, just like Don would lose money if his animals didn't also do weeding.

In the end, this is one of my favorite things about lamb: the challenge. If you're careful, one lamb yields enough sauce for one lamb, and the number of dishes you get lets you continue to buy this high-quality piece of meat. It's a closed system. When I'm at the fire, I'm constantly seeing where we are within this system—how much of the different pieces are left, how far the sauce is going, and so on. I can't ever remember people's names, but I can judge quantities of lamb with great accuracy.

As Allison says, this is poor-people cooking. We're not poor. We just don't have any money.

LAMB LEG À LA FICELLE

Serves 8 to 10

This is the hardest and the easiest recipe in this book: hard because you have to actually build something, and easy because once you have your setup, the cooking is very passive—just a spin of the leg. Since the setup is sort of a production, you definitely want to bust this out for a dinner party. A leg will serve at least eight hearty eaters, and it is perfect because once your guests arrive, the hard work is done and you can enjoy the party. The main thing to know for the setup is that you need to build a tall, narrow fire by leaning pieces of wood vertically against each other. The fire does not have to be huge—just tall enough so that the hottest part of the flames come up to the thickest part of the leg. You will want to hang the leg as low as possible (preferably with a dish of beans, farro, or vegetables under it to catch the drippings) so you don't have to have a really tall fire. The lamb leg is going to dangle about an inch or two away from this fire, basically being cooked from the side (think about it almost like a vertical rotisserie, but with string as your only equipment).

INDOOR SETUP

At Camino, we had a bar installed across the width of the fireplace with hooks hanging on it to tie the strings to. We move the fire basket forward so it's close to the hanging leg and use that as the heat source. For parties, we have had up to eight legs cooking at the same time. Very dramatic!

If you have a fireplace that you want to cook out of, find something on or above the mantel to attach the string to. This could be something architectural or it could just be a hook that holds whatever painting you have above your fireplace. With this method, you are going build the fire more forward in the fireplace because the lamb leg will be dangling right in front of, rather than inside, the fireplace. Place a pan underneath the leg to catch the drippings, ideally filled with cooked beans, but mostly to protect your floor.

NOTE

Experiment with building a fire in the front of your fireplace to make sure that the chimney will still draw well, so your house won't fill with smoke. Also, make sure your chimney is clean.

OUTDOOR SETUP

More likely you will try this outdoors. In this case, you just need to find a patch of ground where it's safe to build a tall fire and where you can arrange a way to hang a lamb leg next to it. I've seen people jam a piece of rebar into a retaining wall so that enough length pokes out to accommodate the leg, then build a fire next to it.

At a party once, someone made a small A-frame structure, almost like pup tent frame, that I was able to hang four legs from and then build the fire adjacent to the frame. Romantically, you could hang the leg from a tree so long as the branch is high enough that it will not catch on fire and the tree broad enough that you can build the fire away from the trunk. Now that you know what you are shooting for, you will have to figure out the appropriate configuration for your cooking site.

> 1 lamb leg on the bone (about 6 pounds), aitch bone (pelvic bone) removed
>
> Salt and black pepper
>
> 1 bunch mint, stemmed
>
> 3 cloves garlic
>
> Olive oil

The day before you plan to cook the lamb, season it heavily with salt and pepper. At least 2 hours before cooking, make the marinade. Pound the mint and garlic together in a mortar, pour in enough olive oil

continued

to moisten it, then rub the minty garlic mixture all over the leg.

Normally, when you cook meat with fire, you have two elements you can play around with—you can adjust the fire and you can move the meat around to focus more heat to different parts. Because the lamb leg will be spinning in midair, you can only adjust the fire, so it is a good idea to tie the leg, making it as compact and tidy as possible to help it cook evenly. Your butcher can do this for you, or . . .

To tie the leg, start by making a loop of twine around the leg just below the bump of bone that you can feel on the shank side of the leg. Tie it off with a square knot that has a double loop in it, for extra support. Hold the uncut piece of twine in the palm of your hand, then twist your wrist away from the leg twice to create another loop of twine around your hand. Stretch open this second loop, slip it under the leg, and pull it up near the first loop. Pull the uncut piece of twine to tighten the loop securely around the leg. Then repeat the looping process a couple more times so that there are three or four loops of twine around the thickest part of the lamb leg. Tuck the flap of meat at the end of the leg up and over the exposed leg bone and hold it there with one hand. Using the other hand, stretch the twine down and around that flap in the direction perpendicular to the orientation of the other loops. Then flip the leg over, pull the twine all the way to the shank bone and cut it off there. Slip the cut end over and under the lowest loop, pull it tight, then slip the end over and under the topmost loop and pull it tight. Make a final square knot somewhere between the top and bottom loops to tie off the twine. Double knot it, to be sure.

A whole leg of lamb is a big and bony piece of meat, so it'll need to be pulled out of the fridge to sit out at room temperature to temper for three to four hours before you cook it.

Once you have figured out your cooking apparatus, build a wood fire. Let it go for a bit so you develop some coals; this will help keep the fire going if you need to adjust it. Next, hang the leg. Using a double length of regular COTTON (!) butcher's twine, tie one end around the shank of the leg, running the twine under the tendon. Tie the other end of the doubled twine to the support that your lamb will hang from. Once you have the leg tied up, give it a little spin. It's important for the leg to spin straight so that it doesn't start swinging.

Fix the fire so some pieces of wood are tilted vertically, so the flames really climb up. The fire should be very close to the leg—an inch or two away. Move away any coals that have fallen under the leg—keep an eye out for these—you don't want coals under the leg or it will get overcooked in that one spot.

The leg will continue to spin and unwind on its own, getting slower and slower until it needs a little nudge again. You will need to pay vague attention to it so it doesn't come to a complete stop or get snagged on a piece of wood in the fire—it will turn black very quickly if that happens. So, keep an eye out as you sip your wine and tell stories about other large animals you have cooked with fire.

After about 20 minutes, the leg should start getting brown. If the browning is not even, adjust the fire. After about 45 minutes, stick an instant-read thermometer into the thickest part of the leg, touching the bone. Once it reads 115°F, you can pull the leg down, but you should really poke around and find the lowest temperature, to ensure that it's really done, because you really only have one shot at it. If you have a good fire and a large lamb leg, it should take about 1 hour. If it's windy or you didn't temper the leg enough, it could go to 1½ hours.

When you hit the right temperature, pull the leg off and let it rest in a warm spot for at least 25 minutes. Don't skimp on this part: remember, the larger the piece of meat, the longer rest time it needs. An overcooked leg will still be pretty good after it rests for 30 minutes and a perfectly cooked leg will be too raw if you try to cut into it in 10 minutes. After the leg is rested, cut the strings off.

continued

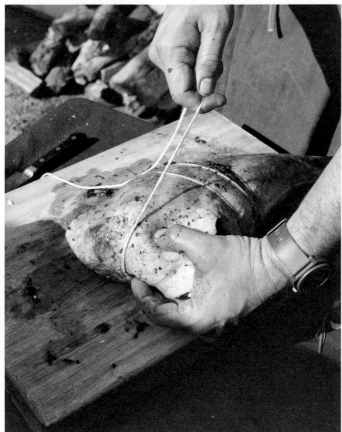

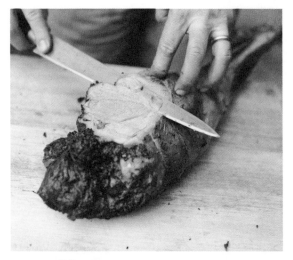

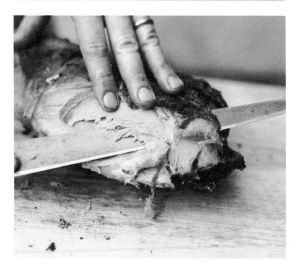

CARVING

Carving skills are important but, honestly, you just cooked a lamb leg on a string (possibly hanging from a tree)! You have earned the right to carve it however you want. However . . .

I find it helpful to visualize the leg in three different sections:

1. The biggest, bulgiest muscle—this will be the rarest meat.

2. The muscle exactly kitty-corner to this on the other side—this meat will be more well done but still very juicy.

3. The very end of the leg (the part that was flapped over when it was tied, but is now unfolded)—this will be either medium or well-done depending on your fire.

Because each of these muscles will be different, carve a little from each section in fairly thin slices with a sharp and longish knife. When carving, don't be tempted to hold the shank end up—leave the leg flat on the table. When you start hitting bone or cartilage, change the angle of the knife a bit. Only rotate the leg when you are moving on to the next muscle. When you really get down to the end, the meat at the shank end tastes pretty good if you carve it perpendicular to the bone. After you have carved everything, refrigerate the leg—there will probably be a lot of meat left on the bone that you can use to make ragù tomorrow.

Serve the sliced lamb leg with Ratatouille Cooked in the Fire (page 77), Red Lentils (page 10), and Chile Sauce (page 13).

GRILLED LAMB RACK WITH FRESH SHELL BEANS, TOMATILLOS, AND MINT

Serves 3 to 4

The tricky part about grilling a lamb rack is that one side of the cut is completely protected by the ribs. You want to get the skin side brown (medium-hot grill) and you want the meat on the bone side to be medium rare without burning the bone (slightly cooler grill). I recommend flipping the rack over a few times while you are cooking so that you can see how quickly the skin is browning and still keep an eye on the condition of the bone. When you flip it to the skin side, move it slightly toward the fire; when you flip to the bone side, move it slightly away from the fire. The rack should take about 20 minutes to cook, but with all the flipping and moving you want to keep track of how long each side is on the grill—they should both be on for about same amount of time.

If possible, ask your butcher for a rack that has not been Frenched which means the meat between the ribs has not been cleaned off—tasty!

Tomatillos de Milpa are usually smaller, drier, and sweeter than other varieties and they work particularly well for roasting. Other varieties are less intense, but are still delicious.

> 1 lamb rack (1 to 1½ pounds)
>
> Salt and black pepper
>
> 1 bunch Persian mint or spearmint
>
> 8 cloves garlic
>
> Olive oil
>
> 2 bay leaves
>
> 3 cups shelled fresh beans (from about 3 to 5 pounds in the pod), such as cannellini, borlotti, flageolet, or cranberry—do not mix before cooking!
>
> 1 pound Tomatillos de Milpa or regular tomatillos

The night before you plan to cook, season the lamb generously with salt and pepper. Pick the mint leaves, saving the stems for the beans. Pound the mint leaves and 2 peeled cloves of garlic together in a mortar, pour in enough oil to moisten, then rub the minty-garlic-oil marinade all over the lamb.

Let the meat temper at room temperature for 2 hours before you cook it. While it tempers, you can cook the fresh shell beans: tie the mint stems and the bay leaves together with kitchen twine. Put this herb bundle in a pot, along with the shelled beans and a big pinch of salt. (If you're using some combination of different varieties of shell beans, you'll want to cook each variety separately as they will each take a different amount of time to cook). Add 2 cloves of garlic, slightly smashed but not peeled. Pour in enough water to cover by 1 inch, and bring up to a low simmer. While the beans are cooking, check for salt by tasting the cooking water and the beans. The beans will become as salty as the water, so think ahead to the final seasoning. Cook until the beans are tender and have no starchy raw flavor, anywhere from 10 to 20 minutes. Let the beans cool in their liquid until you're ready to serve them.

Once the beans are cooking, build your fire for grilling the lamb. If you want cook the beans in the fire, see the technique used for garbanzo beans in the "Fire" chapter.

Preheat the oven to 500°F or as hot as it will safely go. The tomatillos only take about 12 minutes to roast, so you can cook them while the meat is still tempering and the coals are developing.

Peel the husks off of the tomatillos and rinse them in several changes of water to get rid of the sticky film. If they are the small Tomatillos de Milpa, put them in a baking dish in a single layer, lightly coat with olive oil, and sprinkle with salt. If you are using a larger variety, cut them in half first and proceed. Roast the tomatillos until they get a little bit brown and start to give off juice, about 12 minutes. Set the roasted tomatillos aside in their baking dish to cool. If they are very juicy at this point, you can pour off those juices into a small

continued

pan and reduce them for a few minutes to concentrate the flavor and then add it back to the tomatillos.

Once the tomatillos are cool, roughly chop them so you have a mixture of large and small pieces—make sure not to lose the juices while you chop.

Peel and slice the remaining 4 cloves of garlic. Heat up a pan over medium heat, then add enough olive oil to coat the bottom of the pan. Add the sliced garlic and cook it for a minute or so, shaking the pan often so the garlic doesn't burn. If the garlic threatens to brown at all, add a small splash of water to the pan. Once the garlic is tender, add the mint and continue to cook for another minute. Scrape the garlic and mint mixture directly into the tomatillos and mix. Taste for salt and acidity. If the tomatillo mixture is very tart, a splash of olive oil will smooth out the flavor.

When the coals are ready, place the lamb rack on the grill, skin side down, with the rib bones pointed away from the fire. After 3 or 4 minutes, flip the rack over onto the bone side moving it to a slightly cooler spot on the grill. Check the skin; it should just be starting to get brown. Adjust the heat of your grill, building up the coal bed or cooling it down, as necessary. After 3 or 4 minutes on the bone side, flip the rack over onto the hotter part of the grill, this time with the bones pointed toward the fire—with this turn you are continuing to cook the whole rack but concentrating on browning the fat on the top of the ribs. If they are not sitting flat on the grill you can weigh them down with a *cazuela* or other weight. Once the fat is fairly brown, another 3 to 4 minutes, flip the rack over and poke the meat to see how done it is. Now is the time to gauge how done the meat is compared to how brown the skin is and adjust your fire accordingly. It could be that the skin is plenty brown, in which case, move the rack away from the heat and let it coast slowly to medium-rare on the bone side. Or it could be that the skin is not brown but you can feel the meat firming up, in which case build up the hot side of your grill for the next turn.

The point is that you are constantly monitoring the doneness of the flesh versus the brown-ness of the skin. This is the intuitive part of cooking with fire—and it takes practice. But you don't have to always practice on rack of lamb—it is the same principle with steak or duck or pork loin.

When the rack is done, take the meat off the grill and let it rest for at least 12 minutes in a warm place. While the meat is resting, reheat the beans and the tomatillos (either on the stovetop or in the waning heat of your grill). Cut the rack between the ribs and arrange on a platter. Spoon the minty tomatillos over the chops and serve with the fresh shell beans.

———

SLOW-COOKED LAMB SHOULDER WITH GREENS, YOGURT, CHILES, CILANTRO, AND BASIL
Serves 6

This recipe calls for lamb shoulder, but it's really very flexible—you could also use just ribs, bellies, or even necks.

    1 bone-in lamb shoulder (about 7 pounds)

    ½ teaspoon peppercorns

    ½ teaspoon cumin

    ½ teaspoon caraway

    ½ teaspoon fennel seed

    2 dried moderately hot chiles

    Olive oil

    Salt

    1 yellow onion

    1 carrot

    2 celery ribs

    Lard or rice bran oil

    2 tomatoes, fresh or canned

    ½ bottle white wine

continued

1 small bunch cilantro

1 small bunch basil

6 cloves garlic

1 (2-inch) piece of ginger

1 cup whole milk yogurt

⅓ cup Chile Sauce (page 13)

Cooked Greens (page 13)

The night before, season the lamb shoulder. Toast the pepper, cumin, caraway, and fennel seed in a heavy pan until they are shade darker. Grind the spices in a spice grinder and set aside.

Tear up the chiles into small pieces including the seeds and ribs and grind them in a spice grinder until you have a coarse texture. Mix the chile powder with the spices.

Rub the lamb shoulder lightly with olive oil and season fairly heavily with salt. After the lamb is salted, season with two-thirds of the spice mix. Rub all the spices in, cover the lamb, and refrigerate overnight.

The next day pull the lamb out to temper while you preheat your oven to 400°F.

Peel the onion and carrot. Slice the onion, carrot, and celery into ¼-inch pieces. Heat up a wide pan to medium-hot. Put enough lard or rice bran oil to cover the bottom of the pan and add the sliced vegetables along with the remaining spices. Sauté the vegetables until they are brown and stick to the bottom of the pan. Roughly chop the tomato and add to the browned vegetables. When the tomato releases its juices, scrape up some of the brown bits. Keep cooking until the pan browns again.

Pour the vegetables into a roasting pan or baking dish. Deglaze the sauté pan by putting it back on the stove, add a splash of white wine and scrape up any brown bits. Pour the juice over the vegetables.

Pick the leaves from the cilantro and basil and set aside.

Add the herb stems to the vegetables. Lightly smash the unpeeled garlic and add it to the pan. Slice the unpeeled ginger into ⅛-inch slices and add to the pan.

Set the lamb shoulder on top of the vegetables, skin side down. Pour the rest of the wine into the pan. Add enough water to bring the liquid up so three-quarters of the lamb is covered.

Put the lamb in the oven, uncovered, and cook until the liquid begins to simmer, then turn the shoulder over. At this point, turn the oven down to keep the liquid barely bubbling. You'll likely have to adjust the oven temperature thoughout the cooking process to maintain this temperature—it's important that it never comes to a boil or it will dry out. About every 15 minutes, pull the pan out of the oven and flip the meat over. Notice that each time you do this the exposed parts are getting a little browner and then when you turn them over that brown-ness gets introduced to the liquid in the pan. All that roasted flavor is building in the cooking liquid along the way. Keep cooking this way until the meat is tender. The best way to tell if the meat is done is to poke the flesh with your metal tongs to see if the fibers are breaking down. You should feel a little resistance, but you should be able to poke through. Some folks use a skewer or a sharp knife for this, but when I've done it this way I can't help but think I'm just piercing through fibers that are not fully cooked. The shoulder should take about 4 hours to cook.

If you have time, let the shoulder cool in the pan at room temperature, flipping it over once in a while when you walk by. The meat will be a little bit juicier if it cools in its own juices but, if you are pressed for time you can skip this step.

Pull the shoulder out of the pan and set aside. Strain the braising juices, allow to settle for 5 minutes and skim off the fat. Now you have 3 options:

· You can reduce the braising juices to make a thin but tasty sauce.

· You can put the vegetables you strained out of the braise through a food mill, add them back into the braising juices, and reduce for a rougher textured and flavorful sauce.

- If you made a brown stock out of extra lamb bones, you can mix it with the strained braising juices and reduce for a thicker and more luxurious sauce.

However you finish the sauce, check for salt before you reduce very much because some of the salt on the meat will have seasoned the braising liquid.

While the sauce is reducing, pull the meat off of the bone in large pieces. Cut those pieces into big chunks across the grain. If you have a fire going, you can grill them and get the exterior crispy. If not, just warm them in the sauce.

At some point during the braising or reducing process, make a Chile Sauce (page 13). Quickly chop the cilantro and basil leaves and stir into the chile sauce adding some olive oil.

Serve the lamb on a platter with bowls of Cooked Greens (page 13), yogurt, and the chile and herb sauce (page 14) on the side. This would be great with the addition of red lentils or Fried Farro (page 8).

―――――

SPICY LAMB RAGÙ
Serves 6 to 8

I think of ragù as a strategy for dealing with a mix of leftover meat. Since we get whole animals at Camino, in one night we will serve all the various parts of an animal each cooked in an appropriate way. For example, with lamb, we'll cook legs à la ficelle (page 189), grilled racks (page 193) and saddles, and braised shoulder (page 194), neck, ribs, bellies, and shanks. At the end of the night, there are always some random bits of all these different meats leftover that we use to make ragù.

The technique is straight-up Italian in that you are going to make a *soffritto* and deglaze the pan several times. For this recipe we are using lamb, but the technique is the same for other meats. When we make

lamb or goat ragù, we veer toward using chiles, strong spices, and minty herbs, but with pork and beef we usually use more herbs and less spices. For chicken, duck, or rabbit ragù, cooking the meat goes a lot faster.

Since whatever grilled or roasted meat you're using (leg, rack, saddle) is leaner and will likely only be cooked to medium or medium-rare, you will need to cook it really slowly and for a long time to get it tender. Any braised meat you have on hand (shoulder, neck, ribs, belly, shank) has already been slow-cooked, so you will add it to the ragù closer to the end. Use the proportions as a guideline for whatever amount of leftover meat you have.

If it's cold out, a ragù like this is good with Red Lentils (page 10) or Polenta (page 9). If it's warm, or you just want a lighter dish, it's good with a thick slice of Grilled Bread (page 11).

   1/2 teaspoon coriander seeds

   1/2 teaspoon caraway seeds

   1/4 teaspoon fennel seeds

   2 dried medium-hot chiles

   Various cuts of leftover medium-rare meat from 1 lamb (about 2 pounds)

   2 large yellow onions

   3 celery stalks with their leaves

   2 carrots, peeled

   5 tomatoes, fresh or canned

   Cloves from 1 head garlic, peeled

   Lard or rice bran oil

   1/2 bottle white wine

   Various cuts of leftover braised meat from 1 lamb (about 2 pounds)

   A handful of chopped herbs, such as lovage, parsley, mint, oregano, or cutting celery

Toast the coriander, caraway, and fennel seed in a heavy pan until they are shade darker. Grind the spices in a spice grinder and set aside. Tear up the

continued

chiles into small pieces including the seeds and ribs and grind them in a spice grinder until you have a coarse powder. Mix the chiles with the spices.

Cut all the medium-rare meat off the bone. Most of the connective tissue and little pieces of fat are really good for ragù, but remove the larger yellow tendon that runs along top of the spine. Also remove pieces of cartilage and any little bits of bone. Dice all the meat into ¼-inch cubes. I know this seems small, but we want to the ragù to melt together, and any big pieces of this leaner meat will stand out as dry. Dice the onion, celery, carrots, and tomatoes about the same size as the meat. Save the juice from the tomatoes for the *soffritto*. Thinly slice the garlic.

Heat a wide pan over high heat. Add enough lard or other fat to cover the bottom of the pan. This is a good place to use animal fat as your cooking medium. Add the diced meat in one layer along with a good pinch of the spices. Quickly brown the meat over high heat. It doesn't need to be evenly brown, just some good brown parts here and there and a good bit of caramelized juices stuck to the pan. Keep an eye on the color of the pan. The browned bits in the pan are as important as the browned meat, so remove the pan from the heat if it is getting too dark.

Depending on the size of your pan, you may have to brown the lamb in several batches. If this is the case, you should deglaze the pan in between each round. To do this, remove the cooked lamb from the pan, pour off the fat, and add a splash of white wine. With a wooden spoon, scrape up all the brown bits and pour the whole thing over the already browned lamb. Then start the next batch as above.

Once all the diced lamb is cooked, remove from the pan and set aside.

The success of the ragù depends on the careful browning and deglazing of the *soffritto*. This is where you are developing the flavor, and if you skimp at all, your ragù will end up tasting boiled and not fully pulled together. This is where the dish becomes something bigger than the sum of its humble parts. It is frugal grandmother cooking at its pain-in-the-ass best.

Return the pot to the stove over high heat, add enough lard to generously cover the bottom of the pan, and add the diced onions, celery, and carrots. Add the rest of the spice mix and stir. As soon as the vegetables start to brown, turn the heat down to medium-low and continue to brown, carefully stirring and scraping until it almost looks burnt. Add the garlic, cook it for a few minutes, then add the diced tomatoes but not the tomato juice. The tomato will keep the garlic from burning and deglaze the pan a bit. Keep stirring and scraping, letting the vegetables brown again. Repeat this process, this time adding the tomato juices: scrape, deglaze, and brown again. Now you can add the diced and browned meat and all the juices from deglazing the pan earlier. Pour in some wine and enough water to not quite cover. Bring to a gentle simmer.

Cook the ragù very slowly and gently, scraping the sides and bottom of the pot every so often and adding splashes of water as needed. Cook until the meat is tender, which should take anywhere from 1 to 2 hours.

While it simmers, pick leftover braised lamb off the bone. If it's been braised long enough that the connective tissue is tender, it can all be added, except for that same yellow tendon that you will find on the back of the neck. Cut the meat across the grain into rough 1-inch pieces. Since this meat is already tender, it's nice to have it in bigger pieces so you end up with some textural diversity.

Add all of the braised meat, plus enough water so that it will be barely covered. Bring up to a boil and cook until the meat is heated through. Taste for seasoning. Add the herbs and taste again. Pour the ragù into a shallow pan to cool. If there is a lot of visible fat on the surface, skim some of it off.

Believe it or not, it is ready to serve. Refrigerated, it should keep for 3 or 4 days. You can freeze it for up to a month.

CHAPTER NINE

PORK

PORK

I do not have a pig tattoo. No bacon obsession, either, or any of those other goofy, bro-y feelings about pork. Pork has become a fixation in recent years, too often with unfortunate results. That big flavor gets used to mask imperfect vegetables, or else to unwisely obscure something delicate and great. Pity the overshadowed shell bean.

That said, I do love pork. Like duck, it's an insanely versatile animal, one central to my palate since childhood. I was a fat kid, and I ate pork all the time growing up. I remember my mom explaining the subtleties and nuance of its complex appeal: *it just tastes better.*

At Camino, pig is the largest animal we buy. Riverdog Farm, out in Yolo County, sends us a whole one every couple of weeks, plus some additional shoulders for our brunch sausages. If you're one of the diners who have developed a chemical dependency on our pork, Riverdog deserves a lot of credit. But in a larger sense, a healthy part of our pork success is owed to a weird day in Iowa many years back.

I was at Chez Panisse at the time, and a few of us had flown out to cook a dinner for the farmers whose hogs we were buying. It was a crazy trip. My co-chef Cal Peternell and I were cruising around outside Des Moines in this big white Lincoln Continental. Cal's friend Bobby was driving—this private eye dude barreling down the highway with a cigarette in one hand and a joint in the other.

Before the dinner, we headed out to visit Paul Willis's hog farm. But on our way, we made a very different stop, at one of these strange, tarp-covered structures we saw scattered around the area. They were hog confinement farms—something I'd heard of but never seen. We snuck on to the land, skidded up to one of the huts in a cloud of dust. Nobody was around, so we lifted one of the tarps.

I'll never forget what I saw. Staring back at us were the pink, beady eyes of these miserable, shit-covered, diseased-looking creatures standing on metal grates. I would've signed my life savings over to PETA in that moment. But it wasn't just the pigs. In the distance were these horrible evaporation ponds full of crap. And all around were acres of soy and corn—pure monoculture. The whole system was broken. We climbed back in the car feeling awful, and kept feeling that way until we got to Paul's place.

If there's such a thing as pig Shangri-la, this was it. We pull up and here's this guy in a straw hat and overalls with a parade of happy pigs trailing behind him. I didn't know pigs could frolic. Paul knew each one individually. He explained to us how the composting action under their straw beds kept them warm at night. Not a fence in sight. "They have a great life, and one bad day," he told me.

It was pivotal for me. From then on, Allison and I vowed never to buy meat if we didn't know where it came from. It made life difficult—my restaurant-going life, my taco-eating life. Years later, that experience led me to another vow: to buy Riverdog's pigs.

The pigs weren't even that great at first. But Tim and Trini, who run Riverdog, are good people; they're local, and I dug their ecosystem. If they'd commit to perfecting their operation, I said, I'd commit to supporting them. It paid off. Today their animals are meaty, full of good fat, and have a nice range of sizes. They gambol around on this lovely farm, eating organic whey and culled, organic vegetables. They have one bad day.

When it comes time to cook them, they're just right for our approach. A lot of newer pork varieties are bred for leanness, but lean pork is hard to cook right— you need that intramuscular fat. We grill the leg muscles throughout the night; sometimes we grill big chunks of loin, too. We braise the ribs, then grill them crispy. The bellies are roasted in the wood oven; or put into our sausage; or braised, then sliced and grilled. The head and trotters are made into fritters. Too much pork left over? Pancetta and ham.

Most restaurants get to do none of that—they just buy pork chops. They miss the fun of utilizing all these different skills to cook all these different parts. It's a constant puzzle. You're figuring out how not to waste anything, and at another level you're taking part in this delicious alternative to a nondelicious, screwed-up system.

And pork just tastes better.

PORK SHOULDER COOKED WITH MILK, LEMON, AND MYRTLE, WITH TURNIPS

Serves 6

This is a take on the classic Tuscan dish of pork cooked in milk, lemon, and sage, but I swapped out the sage one day when Annabelle, my long-time friend of La Tercera and Star Route Farms, foisted a bunch of myrtle on me. Myrtle tastes like pine-ier bay, and it brings out the sweetness of the pork and the milk. The lemon adds a little tanginess and, be aware, it curdles the milk, providing a rich but somewhat ugly sauce for the pork. We often serve this with turnips and white polenta or boiled or grilled potatoes to fully commit to the beigeness of the curds.

4 pounds pork shoulder

Salt and black pepper

3 lemons

Lard or rice bran oil

6 cloves garlic, peeled and smashed gently

3 sprigs myrtle

1½ quarts whole milk

TURNIPS

2 bunches Tokyo or scarlet turnips, with tops (about 2 pounds)

2 cloves garlic

1 bay leaf

Olive oil

Salt

3 cups Brown Stock (using pork, page 32; optional)

Cut the pork shoulder into 3-inch pieces, making sure there are seams of fat or connective tissue running through each piece. This will ensure the meat stays moist during the long cooking time. Season with salt and a little pepper and refrigerate overnight.

On the following day, let the pork stand at room temperature for an hour or so to temper before cooking.

Use a vegetable peeler to remove wide strips of zest from the lemons, then squeeze the juice from the lemons. It should make about ⅓ cup.

Heat a large heavy pan over high heat for a minute or two. Add enough lard to coat the bottom of the pan and put in the pieces of pork in one layer. I usually crowd the pan pretty good, but if you find that juices are coming out of the pork, remove a piece or two so the pan will heat up again (this is key because you really don't want to stew the meat yet—just brown it). Turn the meat a few times to brown as many sides as you can. Keep an eye on the color of the pan. The browned bits in the pan are as important as the browned meat, so remove the pan from the heat if it is getting too dark.

Depending on the size of your pan, you may have to brown the pork in several batches. If this is the case, deglaze the pan in between each round. To do this, remove the cooked pork from the pan, pour off the fat, and add about a cup of water. With a wooden spoon, scrape up all the brown bits and pour the whole thing over the already browned pork. Now heat the pan, put in more lard, and brown the rest of the pork.

Once all the pieces are browned, pull them out of the pan, turn off the heat, and pour off all but about 2 tablespoons of fat. Add the lemon zest, garlic, and myrtle—there should be enough residual heat in the pan to sizzle these ingredients for a moment. If the pan is so hot that the garlic threatens to get more than barely brown, quickly pour in a little milk to stop the cooking. Leaving the zest, garlic, and myrtle in the pan, add all the pork back into the pan along with enough milk to almost cover. Add the lemon juice and bring up to a very gentle simmer. The milk will curdle immediately, but don't worry, that's supposed to happen. Every now and then, turn the pieces of pork over in the milk and continue at a very low simmer. If it cooks too fast, the pork will dry out, even with your creative butchering. Cook until the pork is very tender but not quite falling apart, anywhere from 2 to 3 ½ hours.

While the pork is cooking, get started on the turnips.

You are going to use the Oil and Water Method (see page 30) to cook the turnips, but in this case, you are going to cook two things—the turnips and their greens—so you will be building on the cooking liquid as you go. The advantage is that the greens will be cooked in water that has been infused with turnip flavor. Try to find turnips with beautiful tops, the variety doesn't really matter. The trick with turnips is trimming the tops so they cook quickly and keep their bright green flavor.

Cut the leaves off right where they meet the stem. Trim the remaining stems off of the turnip, leaving about 1 inch attached. You are essentially removing the stringy, nonleafy midsection of the stem from the leaves and the turnips. Wash the leaves and set aside.

If you are using Tokyo turnips, you don't need to peel the skin. If you are using scarlet turnips or another variety with thick skin, you should peel all but a little at the top of the turnip. Cut the turnip vertically into ⅓-inch slices with the little bit of stem still attached. Wash the sliced turnips—washing after cutting helps get the dirt that is often stuck in the stems.

Heat up a wide pan with ¾ inch of water, the bay leaf, a big splash of olive oil, and a big pinch of salt. Once the water is boiling rapidly, add the turnip slices in one packed layer. Cook over high heat until tender. Remove the turnips from the pan with a slotted spoon and spread out to cool. Repeat if you couldn't fit all the turnips in one batch.

Add a little more water to the oil-water mixture and bring to a boil again. Add a mounded layer of turnip greens to the pan and stir while the leaves wilt. They should be done when the leaves are wilted, but if the turnip leaves are a little tough, keep cooking until they are tender. Lift the greens out of the pan and spread them out to cool. Repeat if you couldn't fit them in one batch.

Once the pork is done, if you have time, let it cool in the pan at room temperature, flipping it over once in a while when you walk by. The meat will be a little bit juicier if it cools in its own juices but, if you are pressed for time, you can skip this step.

Once the pork is cool, lift it out of the liquid, let the liquid settle for a few minutes, then skim off the clear fat that floats up to the surface. Whatever you do, don't strain the braising liquid—the weird milk curds are the best part.

If you are using brown pork stock to enrich your sauce, now is the time to add it. Reduce the milky liquid with the brown stock until the sauce has a velvety texture but is not too salty.

If you are not using brown stock for the sauce, just reduce the milky liquid to concentrate the flavor but stop before it gets too salty.

When you are ready to serve, return the pork to the pan to warm it up in the reduced sauce. Reheat the turnips and their greens in the turnip cooking liquid. I would serve the pork and the milky sauce in one family-style platter with all the curds and the turnips and greens in another bowl and let people make their own plates—it can be challenging to make this plate look good (beige!), but the big platter is dramatic.

GRILLED PORK LOIN WITH FAVA BEANS, SUMMER SAVORY, AND CHILES

Serves 6 to 8

When we butcher pigs at Camino, we like to remove the ribs from the loin to cook separately. This leaves us with a boneless pork loin that is no fun to cook whole, so we cut it into fat steaks with a little of the belly attached. After we cook it, we cut it into thick slices. Cooking it like this leaves you with plenty of crispy brown parts on each slice. This is, of course, best seasoned the night before, but it will be fine as long as it's seasoned at least two hours before cooking.

Fava beans are one of my favorite things. Some folks think they are too much work, but I disagree—you just have to find a way to shell them while you are sitting down, drinking tea, and reading the paper. Look for the largest beans possible that are still bright green in the pod, you will probably have to pop a few out at the market to check, unless you really know the farm well. Fava beans are best peeled twice—even the little ones benefit from a second peeling. This is great with Polenta (page 9).

3 pounds boneless pork loin

1 tablespoon black peppercorns

1 teaspoon juniper berries

1 teaspoon allspice berries

6 bay leaves

Salt

3 pounds medium to large fava beans in the pod

A few sprigs of summer savory or winter savory

½ cup olive oil

½ cup sliced green garlic, white and lighter green parts, or 3 cloves garlic, sliced thinly

½ cup Chile Sauce (page 13)

The night before you're going to cook the pork, cut the loin into 2-inch-thick steaks. Trim the outer edge if there is more than ½ inch of fat. Grind together the peppercorns, juniper, allspice, and 4 of the bay leaves into a coarse powder. Season the pork pieces liberally with salt and the spice mixture. Cover and refrigerate overnight. Pull the pork loin out of the refrigerator to temper 2 hours before cooking.

Build a fire to grill the pork.

While you are waiting for the coals to get ready, start in on the fava beans. Put a large pot of unsalted water on to boil (salt doesn't penetrate the fava bean skin so don't waste it). While the water is coming to a boil, pop the favas out of the pods. Now you are going to blanch the shelled beans to make it easier to peel the skin. You want to blanch them enough to loosen the skin but quickly enough to keep them bright green, so you want to keep the water at a rolling boil the whole time. Blanching the beans in batches rather than all at once will help maintain the water temperture. Put the beans into the water and check a bean after 30 seconds to see if the skin is loosening, it could take up to a minute or so.

Once the skins are just loose, pull the beans out of the water with a strainer and immediately plunge them into ice water. Keep them in the ice water for a few minutes to ensure that they are cooled all the way inside that insulated bean. When they're cool, remove the beans from the ice water and start popping them out of their skins. The easiest way is to break the skin slightly with your thumbnail and squeeze the bean out. Pop all of the beans out of their skins and set them aside.

When you are ready to cook the pork, rake the coals under the grill for medium-hot grilling. Let the grill heat up for 5 minutes. Put the pork on the grill with the belly end pointed toward the hottest part of the fire. Flip the meat over every few minutes, adjusting the proximity to the fire depending on the color of the meat. Throughout this process, you should also

continued on page 210

be checking for doneness by poking the meat in various places to see how it's firming up.

Shoot for cooking the pork to medium, which means still pink in the middle but completely set. Once the pork is cooked, take it off the grill and let it rest in a warm spot for at least 15 minutes.

While the pork is resting, cook the fava beans. Pick the savory leaves off of the stems. If you are using summer savory, keep the leaves whole; if you are using winter savory, give them a rough chop.

Heat a pan over medium heat, add half of the olive oil and all of the green garlic, and cook for a minute. Add about ½ inch of water to the pan along with a big pinch of salt and the bay and savory leaves. Turn the heat to high and bring to a rolling boil. Add the fava beans and keep the heat high. After the beans have cooked for a minute, add the rest of the olive oil and start tasting for doneness. Favas can take anywhere from 2 to 6 minutes to cook. If the pan starts drying out before they're done, add a little splash of water. The goal is to have just enough water left in the pan at the end of cooking that the oil emulsifies with it. If all of the water evaporates, the beans will feel greasy and fried; if there is too much water the beans will feel boiled.

Slice the pork on the diagonal into ½-inch slices and serve with the favas and the chile sauce.

LARD

When we butcher a pig, we always use some of the fat to make sausages or terrines, and we render the rest into lard. It's a great fat for browning vegetables and meat for ragùs and braises. You can also use it in pastries, like Doughnuts (page 231).

To render pork fat, cut it into ¾-inch pieces and place those in a heavy-bottomed pan. Add about 1 inch of water to the pan. Cook over low heat, stirring

occasionally until the fat is very clear, about 1½ to 2 hours. Pour fat through a fine strainer, discarding all the solids. Do not pour the fat into a plastic container while it's hot—it will melt it. The lard should keep for at least 2 months stored in the refrigerator.

PIG'S HEAD AND TROTTER FRITTERS
Serves 15

This recipe is really two in one. You could just stop after you make the terrine, slicing it like headcheese and serving it with some pickles and mustard. Or you could continue on and make fritters. One pig's head will make a lot of fritters, so you might be able do a little bit of both. The fritters are great as a snack with mustard or horseradish. Or you can serve them as part of a salad with leftover roast pork and Sauerkraut Salad (page 58).

    1 whole pig's head

    1 pig's trotter

    Rice bran oil, for seasoning and frying

    Salt

    Black pepper

    8 large carrots, peeled

    3 yellow onions, halved

    1 bunch celery with leaves attached

    1 head garlic, halved crosswise

    10 bay leaves

    ¾ teaspoon whole allspice, cracked

    ¼ teaspoon whole cloves

    1½ bottles white wine

    Egg whites

    Breadcrumbs (see page 33), for coating

Cut the tongue out of the pig's head and set aside. Saw the head in half with a hacksaw (unless your kind butcher will do that for you) and discard the brain. (Why discard the brain? I just don't like it, but if you do, save it for that brain omelet you've been wanting to make.) If your pot is not big enough to accommodate the halves, you can quarter the head by separating it at the jaw.

Rub the head, tongue, and trotter with a little rice bran oil and season with a generous amount of salt and a less generous amount of pepper. Refrigerate, covered, for 2 days.

Put the pig parts in a very large pot with the carrots, onions, and outer celery stalks (reserving the tender inner stalks for later), garlic, bay, allspice, cloves, and wine. Pour in enough water to barely cover. A pig's head never seems to fit perfectly in any pot—there will always be a few parts sticking out of the liquid, so carefully turn the head over every so often while it cooks. Bring to a boil, then lower the heat to a very gentle simmer. Skim off any foam that rises to the surface. When the carrots are no longer crunchy, after about 40 minutes, fish them out and put them on a plate to cool.

Continue to simmer until the tongue is completely tender but not mushy, about 3 hours total. Pull out the tongue and let it cool a bit. While it is still warm, use your fingers to peel off the skin; set the peeled tongue aside. At this point, you want to start checking the head for doneness by using metal tongs to poke the cheek, which is the biggest muscle in the head and takes the longest to cook. You'll know the cheek is done when the tongs easily pierce through the skin and fat, then resist slightly as they hit the cheek meat. You want to feel that resistance—you are not waiting for the meat to be falling off the bone. Metal tongs are the perfect tool for this because they are blunt. If you use a skewer or a knife it will be hard to know if the muscle fibers are breaking down.

Remove the pig's head and trotter from the pot and set aside to cool. Strain the cooking liquid into another pot, discarding all the vegetables. Save this valuable liquid—you will need a little bit for the terrine, but the rest can be used to reinforce pork braises or for soup.

When the meat is cool enough to handle, pull it off the bone in large chunks. The ears and snout have a lot of cartilage, so you want to cut them into thin slices. The tip of the ear is more tender than the base; if the base of the ear is so tough that you have to force your knife through it, discard it. Cut meaty pieces like the cheek and parts of the jowl into 1/3-inch cubes. Cut the skin and fat into even smaller cubes. If the pig is particularly fatty, you should use only about three-quarters of the fat for the terrine. Discard the teeth and bones.

Cut the trotter, which will be mostly skin, into small cubes.

Quarter the cooked carrots lengthwise, then slice them crosswise into 1/8-inch pieces. Cut the reserved, raw inner celery stalks and leaves into 1/8-inch pieces. Finally, slice the tongue into 1/3-inch pieces.

Combine the chopped meat, skin, and vegetables in a large bowl. Like anything fatty, the meat mixture must be seasoned generously. Stir in lots of salt and black pepper. Toss well, then taste. When the mixture tastes salty enough, add another big pinch of salt—undersalted pig's head is NOT good. Pour in 1/2 cup of the warm pig's head stock, then put the mixture in one or more baking dishes, filling each dish to a depth of about an inch. Put a sheet of plastic wrap directly on the meat, using your hands to gently smooth the surface. Chill it for a few hours or overnight in the refrigerator.

After the mixture is chilled, either serve the terrine or go on to make fritters with it. To make fritters, cut the terrine into 1-inch cubes. (I recommend that you only cut up what you are going to serve because the terrine will hold for about 5 days if it is uncut.) Whisk the egg whites just until frothy. Dip the cubes in the egg whites, then roll them in the breadcrumbs. Heat rice bran oil to 325°F and deep fry the fritters in batches until golden brown. Serve immediately.

CHAPTER TEN

DESSERT

DESSERT

Early in our relationship, Allison requested that I make her a birthday cake. It wasn't a crazy request—she was having a birthday. But I was petrified. I felt like I was about to take the SATs. My mouth actually started twitching.

Like many savory types, I'd always been terrified of desserts. But I had a few days' notice, so I started asking people for advice. I asked way too many people. In the end, I picked a recipe for chocolate cake. It was great. I mean, it was good. The lights in our dining room are dim.

I've improved since then.

Actually, I love the desserts at Camino, but we took a roundabout way getting here. Early on, we hired a pastry chef, which seemed like the logical thing to do if you intend to make pastries. It *was* a logical thing to do, and together we made the latter portion of our menu as exciting as the rest. The plates were simple and high level: small, sweet bites and, oftentimes, fruit. It was the kind of dessert we ourselves wanted to eat at the end of the night. Strictly forbidden were refined sugar, cornstarch, bleached flour, shortening, corn syrup, and any other unholy ingredient delivered to us from big ag. It was incredible.

There was only one problem, which came to light when our pastry chef eventually left. It became clear to us that we were a bunch of clueless savory cooks with no idea how to make all those desserts. But as it happens, cluelessness can be a great asset.

Rather than attempting to mimic the technique of a trained pastry chef—among other things, I'd have to learn how to measure—we just used our own techniques. Because the desserts were made by the same folks making our savory dishes, a wonderful consistency came to run through our meals. Our wood oven–roasted apples, our hazelnuts, our buckwheat tart—you can draw a line back from these through our entrées and our appetizers and our cocktails.

Of course, that consistency extends to our obsession with reusing and repurposing. We're thrilled that we can avoid the great crime against humanity that is a bar's waste of eggs by making ice cream whenever we want (shockingly, a lot of fancy bars chuck the egg yolk after they've made your frothy egg white drink). The same goes for candied citrus peel and other tricks for wringing extra life out of fruit. This isn't thrift for thrift's sake: It lets us spend more on better ingredients in the first place.

Desserts, for some reason, are particularly vulnerable to the whims of fashion. We never wanted a trendy dessert menu. Our approach has always been grandmotherly—maybe "timeless" is the word we should use—and that, in turn, makes for a great guiding principle where sweets are concerned. All we had to do was embrace what we'd thought was a weakness. And keep birthday cakes to a minimum.

GRILLED FIG LEAF ICE CREAM AND GRILLED FIGS

Makes about 1½ quarts of ice cream

Allison and I have lived in the same house for a long time, and we planted a fig tree probably twenty years ago. It is tall and leafy, but it barely gives any fruit, and what fruit it does produce is pretty bad. We have just accepted that it is a "fig leaf tree." And now we can never move because we use the leaves for cooking all the time, and we really like this ice cream (which Allison invented).

I would not build a fire specifically to grill fig leaves for this ice cream—try to work it in when you are grilling something else.

5 (6-inch) fig leaves

2 cups whole milk

1 cup sugar

Salt

9 large egg yolks

2½ cups cream

Figs

Pepper

Olive oil

Grill the fig leaves shiny side down, on a clean, hot grill. After about a minute they'll start to curl and turn dark brown at the edges. Flip and grill them for another minute or so on the second side, until the leaves have a few black spots. Let cool, then crumble them into a bowl.

Bring the milk, sugar, and a pinch of salt to a simmer. Pour it over the crumbled leaves and let them steep for about 3 minutes and strain. If the leaves steep too long, the milk-sugar mixture gets this funky, vegetal, medicinal flavor instead of the floral coconut flavor you're going for.

Pour the cream into a bowl and get your straining setup ready, because you're going to need to move quickly at the end of this next part. You'll need a rubber spatula and a fine-mesh strainer set over the bowl of cream.

Whisk the egg yolks until smooth. Heat the milk-sugar mixture back up to just under a simmer. Whisk a ladleful into the yolks to temper them, and then whisk the tempered yolks back into the rest of the milk-sugar mixture. Cook over low heat, constantly scraping the bottom of the pot with a rubber spatula until the liquid thickens slightly and steam forms on the surface. This happens in a couple minutes, or when the liquid reaches 170°F. Be careful because if you do this step too hot or for too long, you'll end up with scrambled eggs.

Strain the custard into the cold cream and stir, then refrigerate until completely cold, at least two hours. Freeze the ice cream according to the directions on your machine.

Raw figs are great with grilled fig leaf ice cream, but if you have a fire already going, you might as well grill the figs. Cut ripe figs in half lengthwise, brush with a little olive oil, and season with a grind or two of black pepper. Grill cut side down on a medium-hot grill for 3 or 4 minutes, or until the flesh browns a bit. Flip them over and let them cook for another minute. Serve with the grilled fig leaf ice cream and little drizzle of olive oil.

PU-ERH ICE CREAM WITH POACHED QUINCE AND PRUNES

Makes about 1½ quarts of ice cream

We went to a tea tasting with Chinese tea expert David Hoffman of The Phoenix Collection, and he mentioned that his friend made ice cream with *pu-erh*. I loved the idea of taking something so earthy and dirty and making a dessert out of it. He gave us a bag to try it out. I should mention that *pu-erh* (like all tea) ranges in price, so keep your expensive stuff for drinking and try this recipe with something less pricey.

Pu-erh doesn't have a lot of tannins, which is why you can steep it a long time for flavor without it turning bitter (think about going to dim sum and having the water sit in the pot with the leaves for hours while you eat dumplings). Because ice cream has so much fat and sugar, I like to add a little bit of a more tannic tea (like black Yunnan) to strengthen the *pu-erh*'s composty, earthy, fermented qualities.

The poached quince and prunes are almost completely lifted from Fergus Henderson's *Beyond Nose to Tail*. I really like English desserts for their sense of practicality and lack of indulgence. You may have trouble finding prunes with pits, but it won't be the same without them—pitted prunes get mushy and fall apart when you cook them. You can also serve the fruit with sheep's milk ricotta, rice pudding, another ice cream, or just on its own.

ICE CREAM

2 cups whole milk

1 cup sugar

Salt

¾ ounce pu-erh

1 tablespoon black Yunnan tea or other non-flavored black tea

2½ cups cream

9 egg yolks

POACHED QUINCE AND PRUNES

2¼ cups sugar

1 cup white wine

7 cups water

6 or 7 medium quince (about 3 pounds)

3 bay leaves

2 sprigs winter savory or thyme

15 prunes with pits

To make the ice cream, combine the milk, sugar, and a pinch of salt in a heavy-bottomed pan and bring up to just under a simmer. Turn off the heat and add both teas. Let steep for one hour, then strain.

Pour the cream into a bowl and get your straining setup ready, because you're going to need to move quickly at the end of this next part. You'll need a rubber spatula and a fine-mesh strainer set over the bowl of cream.

Whisk the egg yolks until smooth. Heat the milk-tea-sugar mixture back up to near a simmer, whisk a little bit of the mixture into the yolks to temper them, then whisk the tempered yolks back into the milk. Cook over low heat, constantly scraping the bottom of the pot with a rubber spatula until the liquid thickens slightly and steam forms on the surface. This happens in a couple of minutes, or when the liquid reaches 170°F. Be careful because if you do this step too hot or for too long, you will end up with scrambled eggs.

Strain the custard into the cold cream and stir. Cool in the refrigerator for at least 2 hours, then make ice cream according to the directions on your machine.

To make the poached quince and prunes, put the sugar, wine, and water in a large non-reactive pot. Peel, quarter, and core the quince. Tie the peels and cores in cheesecloth along with the bay leaves and savory, and toss the bundle into the pot. If you don't have cheesecloth, as I often don't, just put everything in the pot—you can fish it out later. Bring the mixture up to a boil and add the peeled quince. Cook at a very gentle simmer until the quince is tender. Cooking time for quince seems to vary from 20 minutes to 1½ hours. When they are done, remove the quince from the pot and add the prunes to the poaching liquid. Cook until the flesh starts to loosen from the pit, about 30 minutes. Remove the prunes from the pot and set them aside with the quince. Strain the liquid, discarding the cheesecloth bag. Take one-third of the liquid and reduce it until it is sweet enough and the texture is right for saucing the ice cream.

To serve, scoop the ice cream into bowls along with a couple pieces of fruit and a little bit of the reduced cooking syrup.

You can store the quince and prunes covered with the unreduced syrup for up to a week. If you have leftover reduced syrup you can pour a little in a glass with some sparkling wine and a twist for an easy cocktail.

JAGGERY ICE CREAM WITH PERSIMMONS AND SALTY WALNUTS

Makes about 1½ quarts of ice cream

Jaggery is unrefined sugar from South Asia. It tastes like rough molasses and smells like *agricole* rum. You find it in Indian and Pakistani stores—it comes in different shape blocks and a range of color. I usually like the darkest and strongest smelling ones.

    1¼ cups jaggery

    5 tablespoons water

    9 egg yolks

    2½ cups cream

    2 cups whole milk

    2 tablespoons sugar

    Salt

    ½ cup walnuts

    Olive oil

    2 Fuyu persimmons

To make the jaggery syrup, bring the jaggery and water to a full boil. Cook over medium-high heat until the jaggery dissolves completely and thickens up a little bit, and you see evenly sized bubbles all over the surface. Let cool slightly. Most of the syrup will be added to the ice cream, but reserve a few tablespoons for drizzling when you serve it.

Whisk the egg yolks until they're smooth.

Pour the cream into a bowl and get your straining setup ready, because you're going to need to move quickly at the end of this next part. You'll need a rubber spatula and a fine-mesh strainer set over the bowl of cream.

In a heavy-bottomed pot, heat up the milk, sugar, and ½ teaspoon salt to almost a simmer.

Whisk a ladleful of the milk and sugar mixture into the yolks to temper them and then whisk the tempered yolks back into the rest of the milk and sugar mixture. Cook over low heat, stirring constantly with a rubber spatula, scraping the bottom, until the liquid thickens slightly. Look for steam rising to the surface; this happens in a couple of minutes, or when the liquid reaches 170°F. Add a ladleful or two of custard to the jaggery syrup to temper. Stir well, then pour the tempered jaggery mixture back into the custard.

Give it a stir and then strain the custard directly into the cream. Stir, then refrigerate until completely cold, at least 2 hours. Freeze the ice cream according to the directions on your machine.

Spread the walnuts on a baking sheet and toast them until they are a shade darker, about 8 minutes. Once they are cool, taste to make sure they are crunchy. If not, pop them back in the oven for a little longer. Rub off the skins with a towel and toss them with a small amount of olive oil and a pretty good sprinkle of salt. Peel the persimmons and cut them into wedges. Scoop the ice cream into bowls. Set a few persimmon wedges next to the ice cream scoops, sprinkle with walnuts, and drizzle with the reserved jaggery syrup.

INDIVIDUAL RHUBARB-BUCKWHEAT TARTS

Makes 6

Back when I was a line cook at Chez Panisse, Jacques Pépin came to do a week of menus upstairs in the café. When I say do a week of menus, I actually mean he worked side by side with us all day long and showed us some of his famous techniques—butchering a chicken, making onion soup and apple tart. For the apple tart demo, he tasted the apples to see how much sugar to add and he made the dough without measuring, relying only on what the dough felt like as he added the butter and water. That dough went on to be the dough that Chez Panisse uses for all their fruit tarts. I did not work in the pastry department at Chez Panisse—so tidy and all that measuring!—but the demo had a huge impact on me. Jacques approached the dough like a savory cook—it wasn't precise measurements that made it good; it was all the decisions he made along the way. This recipe is basically that same recipe but with the addition of buckwheat flour. Buckwheat doesn't have gluten, so it helps keep the dough tender and adds a nutty flavor.

BUCKWHEAT DOUGH

3 tablespoons buckwheat flour

1⅓ cups all-purpose flour, plus more for rolling

1½ teaspoons sugar

Pinch of salt

9 tablespoons unsalted butter, chilled

Ice water

RHUBARB

½ cup whole almonds, raw

1½ cups plus 2½ tablespoons sugar

3½ tablespoons all-purpose flour

Salt

2 pounds rhubarb

3 tablespoons melted butter

Whipped cream or ice cream, for serving

To make the dough, mix together the buckwheat flour, all-purpose flour, sugar, and salt. Cut the butter into ½-inch pieces and add about half of them to the flour. Toss to coat the butter in the flour mixture, then gently press each butter piece between your fingers. You want to flatten all the pieces and start to break them up into many uneven pieces that will melt in the oven to create flaky dough. After you've touched just about every piece, add the other half of the butter and press those into the flour mixture. The idea is to have lots of irregular pieces—some butter from the first round will be small and some butter from the second round will be larger, but nothing should be bigger than a pea.

Drizzle in 5 tablespoons of ice water. Using your hands, scoop and lift the flour mixture, letting it gently fall between your fingers until the water is evenly distributed. What you are trying to do is add as little water as possible to just make the dough hold together. You are doing everything you can to not develop gluten, so you want to be careful about how you handle the dough. Too much squeezing and pressing leads to gluten development, which leads to tough tart dough. That said, you do need to test to see if your dough will hold together, so grab a little handful of dough and squeeze gently. If it doesn't clump and stay together, keep adding water, a few drops at a time, until it does. Of course, it's easy to make this dough super wet, and with lots of water it rolls out easily and looks really nice—but it will be tough. Form the dough into a ball, press it into a disk, wrap it in plastic, and then pat the sides to smooth out the edges. Put it in the refrigerator to chill for at least 1½ hours. (The dough can be made ahead and frozen for up to 1 month.)

Cut the dough into six equal pieces, each weighing about 2 ounces. On a floured surface, roll each piece out to an 8-inch circle about 1/16 of an inch thick. Sometimes streaks of exposed butter will cause the dough to stick. If this happens, just scrape it up, flour the surface a bit more, and start rolling again. It's okay to patch any holes, but don't fold and reroll or the dough will get tough. Stack the rounds between sheets of parchment and put them in the refrigerator to chill for at least 30 minutes.

Make the almond flour by grinding almonds in a food processor until fine. Mix in 1/3 cup of sugar, 1/3 cup of flour, and a pinch of salt. To make the rhubarb, trim both ends of the rhubarb. Discard the leafy ends (the leaves are mildly poisonous), but reserve the funny-shaped root ends in a pot—you will need them to make the glaze. Cut each stalk lengthwise into two long pieces, then cut crosswise on an extreme diagonal into 1/4-inch-thick slices that are 1 1/2 inches long. Put the rhubarb in a bowl and toss with 2 tablespoons of sugar and 2 tablespoons of flour.

Line a baking sheet with parchment paper. Set the dough rounds on the baking sheet and sprinkle 1 tablespoon of the almond flour in the center of each round to help absorb the excess juices that form while baking. Pile a handful of rhubarb slices on top. Use one hand to lift and fold the edge of the dough toward the center and the other hand to tuck pieces of fruit under the edge. You want to create an undulating edge that's about an inch wide. Rather than overlapping the dough onto itself, use fruit to build a tall, warbly border. Be careful that the dips and valleys in the crust aren't too deep because then the juice will run out and burn. I like the crust to look really rough and decidedly uneven, like you put no effort into it—but, of course, you did. If the dough gets too soft and wiggly to work with, just place it in the freezer for a few minutes. Pile any remaining rhubarb slices in the center of the tarts, then chill the tarts in the refrigerator for at least 20 minutes.

While the tarts chill, preheat the oven to 425°F.

Brush all the tart crusts with the melted butter and sprinkle with 1/2 tablespoon of sugar for each tart. Bake for 20 minutes, then remove them from the oven and sprinkle 2 tablespoons of sugar in the center of each tart. This looks like a lot of sugar, but rhubarb needs it. Return the tarts to the oven and bake for another 25 minutes or until the bottoms are browned

and crisp. This dough tastes best when pretty brown so try to push this to almost too dark.

While the tarts finish baking, make the glaze. Add 3/4 cup of water and the remaining 1/4 cup of sugar to the pot with the rhubarb end pieces. Cook over medium heat until the liquid turns clear and thickens, about 20 minutes. Strain out the rhubarb.

When the tarts are done, immediately transfer them to a rack and let cool. (This buckwheat dough really wants to get soggy, so it's very important to cool the tarts on a rack.) Just before serving, brush the rhubarb with the glaze.

Serve with whipped cream or ice cream.

VARIATIONS

Other fruits don't need as much sugar as rhubarb, nor do they require that you add any sugar during the baking process.

FOR CHERRY, PLUOT, NECTARINE, OR APRICOT TARTS:

Sprinkle a tablespoon of almond flour on each dough round. Put the fruit on top of the almond flour (cherries whole and pitted; apricots halved, cut side up; pluots and nectarines sliced into 1/2-inch wedges). Chill for 20 minutes, then brush the crusts with butter and sprinkle with sugar. Start with 3 tablespoons of sugar sprinkled on the fruit but adjust according to the fruit's own sweetness. Bake at 450°F for 30 to 40 minutes.

FOR APPLE-CALVADOS TARTS:

Peel and core the apples (Sierra Beauties, Gravensteins, or other tart baking apple) and slice them into 1/2-inch wedges. Cover the peels and cores with sugar and water and cook to make a syrup. Loosely arrange the apples on the tart dough, brush the apples with butter, sprinkle with sugar, and fold the edges up and around. Chill for 20 minutes, then brush the crusts with butter and sprinkle with sugar. Splash a little Calvados over the apples and bake at 450°F for 30 to 40 minutes. Serve with the syrup drizzled on top and whipped cream with a little Calvados mixed in.

CANDY PLATE

Sometimes at the end of a meal I just want a chunk of really good chocolate—not a slice or a bar, but a broken chunk. The fancier version is the complete candy plate: a chunk of chocolate, a couple pieces of candied citrus peel, and a shard of sesame candy. This is when your larder comes in handy. If you have these things on hand, you always have a sweet treat to serve.

CANDIED CITRUS PEEL

It doesn't matter to me if candied peel is the by-product of a delicious glass of juice or if a delicious glass of juice is the by-product of candied peel. The point is, with some foresight almost any citrus can yield more than one use: juice, peel, and don't forget the cooking syrup for your cocktails (see page 238).

Juice the citrus with a reamer-style juicer so that the peel is not crushed. Cover the peel with cold water and bring to a boil. Drain off the water and repeat this process four times (five times if you are using grapefruit or pomelo because the flesh is more bitter). On the last time, let it keep going at a low simmer until the peel is soft enough that you can pierce it easily with your thumbnail—this takes longer than you might think. I have paid dearly for not cooking it long enough with a compost bin full of leathery peel.

Once the peel is cooked, drain it and let it cool. Then use a spoon to scrape out all of the stringy membrane, but leave the pith. Cut the peel into ¼-inch to ½-inch-wide strips.

Now make a syrup with a ratio of 4½ cups of sugar to 2 cups of water. You'll need enough syrup to cover the strips of peel. I've made the mistake of only making enough syrup to barely cover the peel, because I was trying to not waste too much sugar, and I've lost those batches because the peels end up burning. You really do need enough syrup so that the strips of peel can move around freely. (As a guideline, 4½ cups of sugar and 2 cups of water makes enough syrup to cover the peels of three grapefruits.)

Make the syrup in a heavy pot and then add the peel to it. Bring the whole thing up to a medium simmer and keep cooking until the syrup reaches 230°F. We don't often use thermometers at Camino, but this temperature is actually super critical. What you are doing is cooking all the water out and getting the syrup to a high enough temperature that it will be firm when it cools. It will hover somewhere around 225°F for an eternity, but be patient.

Once the syrup hits 230°F, take the pot off the heat and set it aside to cool for a bit, then scoop out the peel and spread the pieces on a wire rack. Let them dry overnight, or for at least 5 to 6 hours. (Obviously, save the syrup for cocktails. If you accidentally burn the peel, taste the syrup once it cools because it still might be good—we had a nice run of cocktails with burnt orange syrup in them.)

Drop the dry pieces of peel into a bowl of sugar, separating them so that they don't stick together in a giant clump, and toss them around so they're thoroughly coated. Shake off any excess sugar and store the candied peel in a sealed container in the refrigerator. It will last for a couple of months, though it does get a little harder and tougher toward the end of its life.

SESAME CANDY
Makes 1 large sheet

This recipe is adapted from the *The Good Cook*, a series of instructional cookbooks edited by Richard Olney and published during the late 1970s and early '80s by Time Life. Making desserts really stresses me out, but this recipe has no precise times or temperatures—perfect for me!

continued

Melted butter, for brushing

3 tablespoons honey

3 tablespoons brown sugar

Salt

1/2 cup black Toasted Sesame Seeds (page 33)

1/2 cup white Toasted Sesame Seeds (page 33)

You'll want to get your workspace ready before you start making the candy because once it is ready to be rolled, you have to move quickly. Tear off two 24 by 18-inch pieces of parchment paper and brush them with melted butter on one side. Put the parchment on a flat surface and have a rolling pin nearby.

Combine the honey, brown sugar, and a good pinch of salt in a small pot set over medium heat. Cook the honey and brown sugar, swirling the pot every so often but not stirring with any utensil. Let it cook for 3 to 4 minutes, taking note of the color, size of the bubbles, and smell. Soon, the color darkens, the bubbles get smaller, and it smells toastier. Keep cooking past this point until the mixture looks foamy and tight and smells slightly burnt.

Remove the pot from the heat and stir in the toasted sesame seeds with a heatproof rubber spatula. Plop the mixture on one piece of buttered parchment, cover with the other piece of parchment, and immediately start rolling it out with a rolling pin. Moving as quickly as you can before the candy sets, trying to get it as thin as possible. Let cool completely, remove the parchment paper, and break the candy into large shards.

Sesame candy should keep, tightly sealed in a jar, for at least a couple of days.

YOGURT-SESAME PUDDING
Serves 6

1 1/2 sheets gelatin

1/2 cup whole milk

6 tablespoons sugar

1/8 teaspoon salt

1/2 cup cream

1 cup plus 2 tablespoons whole milk yogurt

2 tablespoons Toasted Sesame Seeds (see page 33)

Submerge the sheets of gelatin in ice water one at a time to hydrate. Ice water is key because otherwise the gelatin might melt into the water. It will only take a few minutes for the sheets to become soft and pliable.

Pour the milk, sugar, and salt into a pot and bring to a simmer on medium heat. Stir to dissolve the sugar, and then remove from heat. Remove the sheets of gelatin from the ice water, wring them out like paper towels, and add them to the hot milk. Stir to dissolve.

Whisk the cream and yogurt together in a bowl, then whisk in the hot milk-gelatin mixture. Don't let the milk cool for too long before mixing it with the yogurt because the gelatin might start to set before you want it to.

Break up all but 2 tablespoons of the toasted sesame seeds in a mortar and stir them into the yogurt mixture. Taste the mixture—if your yogurt isn't tangy to start, you can add a squeeze of lemon to brighten it up.

Pour the yogurt-sesame mixture into glasses, ramekins, or a baking dish, and refrigerate for 6 to 8 hours until set. When you are ready to serve, sprinkle with toasted whole sesame seeds. Our favorite is to serve it with sliced citrus, but it is great with different fruit all year round—especially strawberries, peaches, or figs.

TUNISIAN ORANGE CAKE WITH DATES AND YOGURT

Makes one 9-inch cake

A few years ago, I appointed myself as the pastry chef. This is a hysterical idea since I can't follow a recipe. Invariably, I would fuck everything up—especially cake. During this period, there were so many cakes of shame that I could only serve for staff meal. It was during one of these pastry panics (compost bin full of cake, opening in an hour) that I came across this recipe in Darina Allen's *Ballymaloe Cookery Book*. It is the perfect Camino cake—it uses breadcrumbs (good use of leftovers, plus the added bonus that you can't overwork the gluten) and the zest AND juice of the citrus, and if you make two cakes, you won't even have any leftover random half a lemon. Plus you will have some leftover cake for breakfast—it keeps for nearly a week.

2/3 cup olive oil, plus more for the pan

3/4 cup whole almonds

1/2 cup Breadcrumbs (see page 33), ground fine

1 1/2 teaspoons baking powder

1 1/3 cups sugar

4 large eggs

1 orange, zest and juice

1/2 lemon, zest and juice

2 whole cloves

1 cinnamon stick

Plain yogurt, for serving

Dates, for serving

Preheat the oven to 350°F. Line the bottom of a 9-inch round cake pan with parchment paper, then brush the parchment and sides of the pan with olive oil.

Spread the almonds on a baking sheet and toast them in the oven until they are a shade darker, about 8 minutes. Set aside to cool for a few minutes. Grind in a food processor until fine.

Sort through the breadcrumbs and pick out any particularly big pieces. Mix together the crumbs, ground almonds, baking powder, and 1 cup of the sugar.

In another bowl, whisk together the eggs, olive oil, and the zest of the orange and lemon. Pour the egg mixture into the breadcrumb mixture and stir, then scrape the batter into the cake pan. Bake for 40 minutes, until evenly brown and set. Remove from the oven and let the cake cool in the pan for at least 30 minutes.

Meanwhile, make a citrus syrup by combining the cloves, cinnamon, juice of the zested orange and lemon, and remaining 1/3 cup sugar in a small pot. Cook over medium heat until the sugar dissolves and the syrup thickens, about 3 minutes.

When the cake is cool, remove it from the pan and poke a bunch of holes through the top of the cake with a skewer. Drizzle about half of the citrus syrup over the cake—this will help it keep for a few days. Serve each slice of cake with dates, a spoonful of yogurt, and a drizzle of the syrup. It's also good with any stone fruit or citrus segments.

If you don't finish it all, it is best to store it at room temperature covered in foil, not plastic.

DOUGHNUTS

Makes 12 to 15

This recipe is directly lifted from our dear departed friend Marion Cunningham's *The Breakfast Book*. We use lard where she uses vegetable shortening. If you don't have lard, don't use shortening; use butter instead—vegetable shortening is a crime. We usually fry these to order at brunch and serve them with fruit. Because this is a yeasted dough and needs time to rise, we make the dough the night before. That means when we run out, we run out. But if we don't run out, we serve them for dessert that night at dinner.

The tricky part of this recipe is to avoid developing too much gluten. Use a wooden spoon and don't try to make the dough perfectly smooth.

- ½ cup whole milk
- 2 teaspoons dry yeast
- ¼ cup lard or butter
- ½ cup sugar, plus more for tossing
- 1 cup water
- 1 whole nutmeg, for grating
- 2 eggs
- 4 cups all-purpose flour, or as needed, plus more for rolling
- 2 teaspoons salt
- Rice bran oil, for frying

Heat the milk in a pot until just warm, not hot—under 100°F! Pour the milk into a large bowl and add the yeast. Stir to dissolve, then let sit for about 5 minutes.

In a small pot over low heat, combine the lard, sugar, water, and a few scrapings of nutmeg. Heat gently until the lard and sugar have dissolved. Remove from the heat and let cool, but not so much that the lard starts to solidify.

Once the yeast is bubbling a bit, add the cooled lard-sugar mixture and the eggs, and whisk to combine.

Add 2 cups of the flour and the salt, and gently mix until incorporated. At this point, add more flour ½ cup at a time, gently incorporating it into the mixture. Stop when you have a very soft but cohesive dough. My co-chef Michael's method for testing the moisture of the dough is ridiculous, but it works: Take a wooden spoon, and starting from the side of the bowl, pull the spoon (with the dough) to the center of the bowl. It should take just under three seconds for the dough to move back into its original place. He actually counts "one-Mississippi, two-Mississippi, THREE," so you know this timing is crucial. If the dough takes less than three Mississippis, it needs a little more flour. Adjust by adding flour or water accordingly.

Put the dough in a large greased bowl, cover with plastic, and either leave out at room temperature until it doubles in size, or let rise overnight in the refrigerator. Overnight is actually preferred if you can manage it—your doughnuts will taste better.

Turn the dough out onto a floured surface. At this point the dough will be a sticky mess. Sprinkle generously with flour and roll out the dough with a rolling pin until it is ½-inch thick. Cut the dough into 2-inch, vaguely diamond-y shapes. Put the pieces 1 inch apart on a baking sheet lined with parchment brushed with rice bran oil. Brush the tops lightly with oil, cover with plastic, and refrigerate for about an hour. Take the tray out of the refrigerator 15 minutes before you are ready to fry.

Pour rice bran oil into a pot to a depth of at least 4 inches, and heat to 365°F. Fry only three doughnuts at a time—you don't want to crowd them. Flip them over as soon as they are golden brown. Don't worry if the dough is sticking to your fingers and making warbly shapes—those are the best ones. Cook until the other side is brown, remove with a slotted spoon (giving it one whack to drain), and toss in a bowl of sugar to coat. Serve with fruit.

CHAPTER ELEVEN

COCKTAILS

COCKTAILS

Oh, the Camino bar! Our first vision for it went something like this: one bottle of each kind of spirit, a really simple menu, a place to enjoy a Negroni before dinner.

Then we met Thad Vogler, and our lives were forever altered.

Thad threw down the gauntlet: he challenged us to operate our bar the way we operate the kitchen—to put the same consideration into purchasing, ingredients, and politics that we had applied to the rest of Camino.

I distinctly remember a preliminary meeting and dinner at our house where Thad shamed us for the "absolute shit alcohol" we had in our liquor cabinet. He gave us a lecture about how people (us!) were so enamored with local, organic farm and food movements, but they completely ignored the opportunity to see spirits as agricultural products—even though we all know that spirits are made from fruits and grains that have to be grown somewhere, somehow. It doesn't make sense to buy organic vegetables from the farmers' market, to boycott Monsanto, to reuse your plastic bags, and then to drink alcohol made with GMO corn in an industrial still owned by a multinational corporation.

We felt so lame. How had we had ignored something so obvious for so many years?

Thad completely changed our idea of what the Camino bar could be. The bar could share the same philosophy and commitment to craftsmanship as the kitchen and, in keeping with our contrarian natures, we'd enjoy a little "fuck you," aimed at the corporate world of industrial spirits. Who wouldn't love it? Some rules were laid down:

> Use spirits that are traceable to the crop they're made from.
>
> No liquor made in industrial stills.
>
> No GMO products.
>
> No artificial coloring.
>
> Only organic citrus from California.
>
> Only independent distributors.
>
> Make cocktails that highlight the spirit in the drink.
>
> No goofy names.

With rules like these, we eliminated 98 percent of all spirits, pretty much anything anyone had ever heard of, and we opened ourselves to the world of grower-produced spirits, spirits distilled by orchardists and farmers as a form of preservation of their crops. We also opened our doors to customers who were pissed that they could not get the brand of alcohol they had been ordering in bars and restaurants forever. It turns out that even people who go out of their way to support small, independent businesses are very attached to brand-name liquor. We were so naïve. We actually got yelled at; fingers were wagged in our faces.

But the idea was that the cocktail list would be in scale with the dinner menu—in other words, small. We were committed to the idea that Camino should feel like you are coming to our house for dinner (after we upgraded our liquor cabinet, of course) and we are offering you a few cocktails that night—cocktails that we've measured and tested and perfected. We just wanted to present something delicious in the way cocktails are meant to be enjoyed—in a transitional moment before a meal where you relax and shake off the stress of the day.

Over time, our recipe list has developed, and our current bar manager, Tyler Vogel, has made it his mission to further connect the bar to the kitchen by using fresh herbs in drinks, making bitters and syrups, and using up every drop of anything left in the pastry department. He runs the bar with the same ingredients used in the kitchen and with the same level of refinement and balance.

And what did we do with all of our "shit liquor"? We ended up giving it to a Camino waiter who was in charge of drinks for her week at Burning Man—recipes NOT included.

It can be expensive to set up a home bar. At Camino we have a pretty small selection of each type of spirit, but each one has a certain characteristic that works for the specific recipe. We've highlighted the characteristic of the spirit in each recipe in case you can't find the exact brand (or if you need to start working your way through your shameful stash of industrial spirits), you will know what you are looking for. A home bar setup will always be different from a restaurant bar, but there are a few basic tools that you need:

Jiggers	Bar towels
A cocktail shaker	Good ice
A mixing glass	Juicer
A bar spoon	Peeler
Hawthorne strainer	Muddler
Small fine mesh strainer	Bitters bottles (or droppers)

MEASURING

Measuring is key. You will be shocked by the difference in a drink if you come up short in a pour or you get sloppy and let some dribble out of the jigger. All the measurements in these recipes (except for Gran Classico in the Camino Negroni) call for the meniscus (curve caused by surface tension) to develop at the top of the jigger. So hold your jigger steady while you pour and look for that perfect moment—it will really make a difference to the drink.

Always measure into the shaker or mixing glass before you add the ice so dilution doesn't start before you are done measuring.

ICE AND DILUTION

All these recipes call for large solid ice cubes. We use a Kold Draft ice machine that makes 1¼-inch dense square cubes. The machine is ridiculously expensive and breaks all the time but somehow still seems worth it. For home, ice cube trays will work better than your automatic ice maker. Ice is a key ingredient to all cocktails! Be sure that they are fresh and don't have that freezer smell.

When you are shaking or stirring a drink, you are chilling it and diluting it with the water that melts off the ice cube. The timing of your shake or stir is crucial to the final drink: overdiluted drinks will taste too tart, underdiluted drinks will taste flabby and sweet—both in ways that cannot be corrected by changing the measurements. Use the timing in these recipes as guidelines. They are based off of Tyler's unusually powerful shake and brisk professional stir (if you saw him you'd know what we mean). Another excellent Camino bartender, Martha, will shake for a slightly longer time because she is a normally proportioned person, but really it is just a matter of few seconds' difference. You will likely have to adjust the timing for your ice and the strength of your shake. If you want to be really nerdy you will make the same drink and adjust the timing to see what results you get—this will help you see where you fall on the Tyler-Martha spectrum.

SHAKING

When you shake a cocktail you are chilling, diluting and aerating the drink. Imagine the ice breaking as it hits each end of the shaker and the liquid gathering momentum as it sloshes around. You need enough ice to chill your drink, but you need room for the liquid to move—approximately 4 to 5 Kold Draft cubes or 7 regular ice cubes. Try to get some distance with your shake, don't keep it tight and close to your body. Something that sets Camino drinks apart is a sense of lift and movement on the palate that comes from a strong, confident shake.

Drinks with egg whites start with a dry shake (without ice) to give the egg whites their silky texture. Adding the spring from your Hawthorn strainer to the shaker during the dry shake will help you develop some volume with the egg whites and incorporate the ingredients so your drink doesn't separate too quickly. If you don't use the spring, you'll need to shake for longer.

Since egg whites are hard to measure, use a maple syrup dispenser so you can sort of cut the whites as you pour it out. Or you can double the recipe, using the white of one egg and drink with a friend.

DOUBLE STRAINING

When you shake a drink, the ice is being shattered. All of our shaken drinks are double strained so that you don't get little chips of ice in your final drink. That way the intended dilution is maintained from the first sip to the last. The Hawthorne strainer has a spring on it that makes it fit snugly to any glass or shaker so you can tip the shaker and pour your drink. To double strain, set a fine-mesh strainer over the glass you are serving in to catch citrus pulp and any stray ice.

STIRRING

For stirred cocktails, fill your mixing glass up to the top with ice—you don't want the ice floating in the spirit. The motion is all in the wrist, not the shoulder. Clues for timing will be visual (level of liquid in mixing glass) and tactile (temperature of your mixing glass). When you taste, taste for dilution and temperature— you want your cocktail cold enough that it will not dilute too fast if you are serving it on the rocks.

ON THE ROCKS

Drinks served on ice are meant to stay cold and to further dilute as you drink them. They should taste great when you first sip them but develop as time passes. It is important to use fresh ice (not the ice you stirred with) so that second dilution starts with the coldest ice and goes slowly.

GARNISH

Camino is a minimal garnish bar—mostly citrus twists or straps, occasionally an herb leaf. The point is that the garnish needs to add something—but not too much—to the drink. A twist is about ½ inch by 2 inches and a strap is ¾ inch by 2 ½ inches and includes a little more pith. Both are twisted over the final drink so the oils are released into the drink. Be warned that if you use a different citrus garnish than what is called for, it will drastically change the drink—not always in a bad way but more than you would think.

BAR LARDER

It is a good idea to start stocking a bar larder. Some of these items will share space with your kitchen larder, just like at Camino. You can really build up your bar larder if you are into it, but if you start with grenadine, orange bitters, gum syrup, and orange syrup, you can make a pretty wide variety of drinks using different spirits in different combinations. The Gin Martini, Gin Drink with Borage, Gin Fizz, Aged Rum Drink, Tequila Drink with Lovage, Mezcal Drink, Mezcal Sour, and the Freedom each use at least one of these larder items.

GRENADINE

16 ounces pomegranate juice

6 ounces sugar

¾ ounce lemon juice

Zest of ½ an orange (with some pith)

Over medium heat reduce the pomegranate juice by half. Remove from heat, but while it is still hot, add the sugar, lemon juice, and orange zest. Stir until the sugar is completely dissolved.

Strain through a fine mesh strainer and store in a bottle in the refrigerator.

ORANGE SYRUP

The orange syrup we use at Camino is the byproduct of making candied peel (see page 224)—it's just the leftover concentrated citrus-infused simple syrup. It will add another layer of depth to your cocktail, but you could use simple syrup in its place—or, even better, a mixture of half simple syrup and half gum syrup with a few drops of orange bitters.

GUM SYRUP

Gum syrup is a sweetener made from the resin of the acacia tree. It adds texture and body to a cocktail where simple syrup just adds sweetness. We've tried making gum syrup ourselves but with inferior results, so we get gum syrup from our friend Jennifer Colliau at Small Hand Foods who makes old-fashioned syrups for cocktails. If you are interested in stocking up your bar, start here: www.smallhandfoods.com. In a pinch, when a recipe calls for gum, you can substitute simple syrup.

ORANGE BITTERS

For all our bitters we use a 172-proof organic neutral grape spirit from Marian Farms in Fresno. Any high proof neutral grain alcohol will work.

2 cups dried orange peel

1 tablespoon whole cardamom

1 tablespoon ground caraway

1 tablespoon ground coriander seed

1 teaspoon whole cloves

Neutral spirit

Put all the ingredients into a 1 quart mason jar or other sealable non-reactive container. Cover with neutral spirit and let sit for 2 weeks. Shake or stir daily.

After 2 weeks, strain the peel and spices and set the liquid aside, covered. Put the solids in a small saucepan. Mash the mixture with a wooden spoon, add ½ cup of water, and simmer for 5 minutes. Let the mixture cool, put in a covered jar, and let sit at room temperature for 2 days.

Strain the spices and add the infusion to the spirit. Add ¼ cup sugar and stir until dissolved. Strain one last time—you can use a paper coffee filter for best clarity. Bitters will keep forever but are best stored in a cool, dark place.

GIN MARTINI

2 ounces Hans Reisetbauer Blue Gin (or other floral and delicate gin)

½ ounce Dolin dry vermouth

1 dash Orange Bitters (page 238)

Lemon for garnish

Measure all the ingredients into a mixing glass. Add enough ice to fill the mixing glass. Stir for 9 seconds then strain into a 5-ounce glass. Garnish with a thin lemon twist.

GIN DRINK WITH BORAGE

Borage is an herbaceous plant that grows all over the East Bay in a kind of weedy way. The leaves have a cucumber flavor and the flowers are sweet. The flavor is pretty mild so it requires a little muddling to bring out the oils in the leaves. The blue star-like flower make a pretty garnish and is edible—just pull off any surrounding greens as they can be a little prickly.

3 medium-sized borage leaves

1½ ounces Leopold's gin (or other citrusy London dry gin)

¾ ounce lemon juice

½ ounce gum syrup (see page 238)

Dry sparkling wine

Muddle the borage leaves in the cocktail shaker until they are a little frothy. Measure in the other ingredients except the sparkling wine. Add ice and give it a short shake, about 5 seconds, because you will further dilute with sparkling wine. Double strain into a 5-ounce glass, top with sparkling wine, and garnish with a borage flower, if you have it.

GIN FIZZ

This drink requires a dry shake to get the egg white frothy. For an infinitesimal improvement, try adding the cream after dry shaking because the egg whites will be easier to aerate without the additional fat.

1½ ounces Leopold's gin (or other citrusy London dry gin)

¾ ounce lemon juice

½ ounce grapefruit juice

½ ounce orange syrup (see page 238)

½ ounce egg white

½ ounce cream

Dry sparkling wine

Measure all ingredients, except the sparkling wine, into a cocktail shaker and shake for 15 seconds without ice. Add ice and shake for another 4 seconds. Double strain into a 7-ounce glass. Top off with sparkling wine. Do this part slowly so you get a beautiful foam on top.

VARIATION

If you happen to have grapefruit syrup (because you candied grapefruit peel instead of orange), you can use that for this drink, but substitute orange juice for the grapefruit juice. As long as one of those is orange, the drink will still work. You can also use lemon and lime juice interchangeably in this drink.

AGED RUM DRINK

This drink is basically a sour with the addition of tea, but it kind of comes off as a punch. The *pu-erh* gives it an earthy foundation, and the grenadine provides some tartness.

  1½ ounces La Favorite Vieux rum (or another rum from Martinique or Venezuela, something with a hint of tobacco and bread)

  ¾ ounce lemon juice

  ½ ounce pu-erh tea, brewed strong and chilled

  ½ ounce Grenadine (page 238)

  2 dashes Orange Bitters (page 238)

  Orange for garnish

Measure all ingredients into a cocktail shaker. Add ice and shake for 4 seconds—yes, a pretty short shake because the tea will already be diluting the drink. Double strain into a 7-ounce glass over ice and garnish with a thick orange strap.

TEQUILA DRINK WITH LOVAGE

Because lovage is pretty powerful, the leaves are shaken with all the other ingredients, not muddled like herbs in other drinks. It has a refreshing celery flavor mixed with more Middle Eastern spices.

  2 to 3 medium-sized lovage leaves

  1¾ ounce Herencia tequila blanco (or other sweet, herbaceous tequila)

  ¾ ounce lemon juice

  ½ ounce Dolin dry vermouth

  ½ ounce gum syrup (see page 238)

Measure all ingredients into a cocktail shaker. Add ice and shake for 10 seconds. Double strain into a 7-ounce glass over ice, and garnish with a lovage leaf.

MEZCAL DRINK

This is a variation on a sour with the addition of apple juice. Our apple juice has a spiciness to it that, with the smokiness of the mezcal, gives the drink a wintery feel but still remains refreshing.

  1½ ounces Benesin mezcal (or other smoky, sharp mezcal)

  ¾ ounce lemon juice

  ½ ounce unfiltered apple juice (we prefer Gravenstein)

  ½ ounce Grenadine (page 238)

  Lemon, for garnish

Measure all ingredients into a cocktail shaker. Add ice and shake for 10 seconds. Double strain into a 7-ounce glass over ice and garnish with a thin lemon twist.

MEZCAL SOUR

This is another drink that requires a dry shake to get the egg white frothy. You'll taste the smokiness of the mezcal, but it will be smoothed out by the richness of the egg whites.

  1½ ounces Benesin mezcal (or other smoky, sharp mezcal)

  ¾ ounce lemon juice

  ½ ounce orange syrup (see page 238)

  ½ ounce egg white

  Orange for garnish

Measure all ingredients into a cocktail shaker and shake without ice for 20 seconds. Add ice and shake for another 10 seconds. Double strain into a 5-ounce glass and garnish with a thin orange twist.

FREEDOM

This is the one drink that has broken the "no goofy names" rule. It started as "Nonalcoholic Cocktail," then became "Alcohol-Free Cocktail," then the "Freedom from Alcohol," which shortened to "Freedom" and finally made it onto the menu under that name. We always have a nonalcoholic cocktail on the menu, and though there are several different recipes, it is always has the same name.

We make this the same way as a shaken drink, paying close attention to the balance of the ingredients. In some ways, it is more difficult to get it right than a cocktail based on a spirit. When it comes out wrong, it tastes like Snapple—the ultimate diss to a Camino bartender.

> 3 to 4 large sorrel leaves
>
> 3 ounces oolong tea, brewed strong and chilled
>
> ¾ ounce lemon juice
>
> ¾ ounce gum syrup (see page 238)
>
> Lemon peel, for garnish

Muddle sorrel in a cocktail shaker. Measure the remaining ingredients into a cocktail shaker. Add ice and shake for a little longer than most drinks to get the sorrel incorporated, about 15 seconds. Double strain into a 7-ounce glass. Garnish with a lemon strap.

AMARO COCKTAIL

The Amaro Cocktail is sort of the staff favorite. It's a great lighter-weight cocktail that is especially good for a party because the mix can be batched out ahead. Come the cocktail hour (see "Fire" chapter, page 125), you can just add sparkling wine and a twist, and you are ready to go. You can make a bottle of the amaro cocktail mix and add it to the refrigerated section of your bar larder.

Amari are bitter Italian herbal liqueurs that vary in alcohol content and bitterness. This cocktail has been so fine tuned that I can't really make suggestions for substitutions. The initial financial outlay for this cocktail is on the higher side because it requires more ingredients than our other recipes. But the good news is that you have two years to save up while you are waiting for your nocino to become drinkable.

To batch a 750ml bottle of Amaro Cocktail mix, about 13 drinks:

> 9 ounces Cardamaro (Made from cardoons in Piedmont, Italy. It's minty, light and fresh. And bitter.)
>
> 9 ounces Cocchi Americano (citrusy, light, sweet, but forwardly bitter)
>
> 5 ounces Cocchi Torino vermouth (darker, woody, minty with sassafras, cola, and green herbs)
>
> 1 ounce Dolin dry vermouth (on the sweet side, dried herbs and lemon)
>
> 1 ounce Lazzaroni fernet (DRY! licorice, hyssop, mint. Smells like a Chinese herb shop)
>
> 1 ounce homemade Nocino (page 27)
>
> ½ ounce Orange Bitters (page 238)

Measure all ingredients into a 750ml bottle, give the bottle a shake to mix, and store in the refrigerator indefinitely until you are ready to use.

To serve, pour 2 ounces of chilled Amaro Cocktail mix into a 7-ounce glass filled with ice. Top off with dry sparkling wine, about 2 ounces. Garnish with a thick lemon strap.

To make just one drink:

> ¾ ounce Cardamaro
>
> ½ ounce Cocchi Americano
>
> ½ ounce Cocchi Torino
>
> 1 barspoon Dolin dry vermouth
>
> 1 barspoon Lazzaroni fernet
>
> 1 barspoon homemade Nocino (page 27)
>
> 1 dash Orange Bitters (page 238)
>
> Dry sparkling wine
>
> Lemon peel, for garnish

Measure each ingredient except the sparkling wine directly into a 7-ounce glass filled with ice. Give it a quick stir just to chill—not to dilute—and top off with dry sparkling wine, about 2 ounces. Garnish with a thick lemon strap.

─────

VARIATION

Using the amaro mix, you can approximate a Cuba Libre (yes, occasionally we will accommodate such a request—but only using our acceptable ingredients, AKA NOT ACTUAL COKE).

Measure 1 ounce of El Dorado 12 Year Rum, 1 ounce of Amaro Cocktail mix, additional ½ ounce Cocchi Torino, and 2 additional dashes of orange bitters, into a 7-ounce glass, then top off with dry sparkling wine. Garnish with at least one lime wedge for squeezing. The El Dorado 12 is rich, sweet, and molasses-y enough to hold up to the other ingredients.

─────

CAMINO NEGRONI

Our original idea of having a bar with no artificial ingredients ruled out Negronis because Campari, the main ingredient, is bright orangey-red in a pleasing but not natural way. But our true original idea was also built around the Negroni, so we had to find a way to replicate the drink with different ingredients. Tyler came up with this recipe, and once you get used to the Camino version, you can actually taste the chemicals in the original.

> 1½ ounces Voyager gin (or other grainy London dry gin)
>
> ¾ ounce Dolin sweet vermouth
>
> ¾ ounce Gran Classico (a rooty, bittersweet, slightly medicinal, dense bitter from Switzerland)
>
> Bitter orange, for garnish

Measure all the ingredients into a mixing glass. Add ice, and stir for 15 seconds. Pour into a 7-ounce glass filled with ice and garnish with an orange twist.

ACKNOWLEDGMENTS

Thanks to Danielle Svetcov for the smarts, dorky enthusiasm, and handholding all the way to the bitter end; Jenny Wapner for helping us see Camino as a book, not just a restaurant; Chris Colin for the words (his own and for making ours sound not idiotic); Yoko Takahashi for the pictures (for shooting on film and for liking the burnt stuff); Maria Zizka for the most stressful part—the recipes; Martha Chong for the letters; Emma Campion and Nami Kurita for really listening to us and designing the book we wanted; Aaron Wehner and Ten Speed Press for publishing cookbooks that have a point of view; Celia Sack, champion of cookbooks; Irving Place Studio for the plates that we all reached for to the point of redundancy; Vanessa Vega and Phillip Baltz for getting the word out; and Fletcher and Lye for beautiful places to write when our own home was too distracting.

Thanks to John Chalik, Richard and Lucy Chen, Troy Chevalier and Grace Wang, Richard Engle and Paula Horowitz, Lia and Guy Fernald, Suzanne Goin and David Lentz, Dick and Gretchen Grant, Vincent Madrigal, Chris McGovern, Todd Robinson, Phoebe Rossiter, Michael and Sylvie Sullivan, Emily Wilson and James Bullard, Paige Witte and Will Forney, and Rudy Zucca for believing in Camino before it existed.

Thanks to Anthony Fish, Pascal Faivre and Dmitra Smith, Jon Sarriugarte, Evan Shivley, and Cynthia Warren, for making Camino look like Camino.

Thanks to the farmers who work harder than any of us: Annabelle Lenderink for friendship, information, and wisdom about way too many vegetables. And for trading vegetables for dinner in the early days when Camino had no money; Kristyn Leach for inspiring us all by finding the most difficult way to farm one acre of land; Tim and Trini for the pigs and the peas and the bulk of vegetables that we serve at Camino; Lori at Blue Heron for perfect butter lettuce and tiny scallions; Didar Singh for the very best fruit all year round; Andy Griffin and Julia Wiley for the first little goats, the lectures, the vegetables, and the Mystery Boxes; Stu Slafter for the weird and awesome deliveries; and special thanks to best neighbors Chris Hwang and Tim Drew who will grow anything in their backyard and let us have lamb cookouts there too.

Thanks to Paul, Tom, Dave, and Carlos from Monterey Fish Company for the local fish and for looking out for us on Crab Monday.

Thanks to Alice Waters for her singular vision, for demanding beauty and whimsy in the kitchen, and for making it possible for Russ to work with such talented and fun people during his time at Chez Panisse: Tony Brush, Mike Tusk, Suzanne Goin, John Luther, Sylvan Brackett, Catherine Brandel, Phillip Dedlow, Amy Dencler, Gordon Heyder, Kelsie Kerr, Leah Puidokas, Lindsay Shere, Peggy Smith, Fritz Streiff, Alan Tangren, Jerome Waag, Beth Wells, and so many others. To David Tanis for hiring Russ, teaching him how to cook, and being his cooking hero. And very special thanks to Gilbert Pilgram and Cal Peternell for true collaboration in the Chez Panisse kitchen and for true friendship outside of it.

Thanks to Liz Prueitt, Lindsey Tusk, the Goin sisters, Judy Rogers, and Gilbert Pilgram (again) for ushering Allison into the restaurant world and for inspiring us to open our own restaurant.

Thanks to Oakland for the Lake, the Rose Garden, the Segway tours, and the wild turkeys that stroll by the restaurant. Thanks for speaking out against injustice and for bringing us the best regulars and best employees—we are proud to have settled here.

Thanks to Blake Brown, Libbey Goldberg, Melissa Reitz, and Carri Wilkinson for the early days in the Camino kitchen and to Thad Vogler for his vision for the Camino bar. Thanks to all past, present, and future employees who choose to work at such a ridiculous restaurant, especially Penny Dedel and Fabian Ortiz who have been with us since day one and with whom we plan to grow old.

And huge thanks to Michael Tsai, Brian Crookes, Tyler Vogel, Sean Ward, and Rachel McCabe for taking charge while we wrote this book and for making Camino a better restaurant while we weren't looking.

ABOUT THE AUTHORS

Russell Moore and Allison Hopelain are husband and wife and co-owners of Camino. Together they stand at the center of the Bay Area's vibrant food scene. Russell cooked at Chez Panisse for twenty-one years. His recipes from Camino have been featured in the *New York Times* Magazine, the *Art of Eating*, and *Food & Wine*, and on the Cooking Channel and the *Today* show. Allison is general manager of Camino. They live in Richmond, California.

INDEX

MEASUREMENT CONVERSION CHARTS

VOLUME

U.S.	IMPERIAL	METRIC
1 tablespoon	½ fl oz	15 ml
2 tablespoons	1 fl oz	30 ml
¼ cup	2 fl oz	60 ml
⅓ cup	3 fl oz	90 ml
½ cup	4 fl oz	120 ml
⅔ cup	5 fl oz (¼ pint)	150 ml
¾ cup	6 fl oz	180 ml
1 cup	8 fl oz (⅓ pint)	240 ml
1¼ cups	10 fl oz (½ pint)	300 ml
2 cups (1 pint)	16 fl oz (⅔ pint)	480 ml
2 ½ cups	20 fl oz (1 pint)	600 ml
1 quart	32 fl oz (1⅔ pints)	1 l

TEMPERATURE

FAHRENHEIT	CELSIUS/GAS MARK
250°F	120°C/gas mark ½
275°F	135°C/gas mark 1
300°F	150°C/gas mark 2
325°F	160°C/gas mark 3
350°F	175 or 180°C/gas mark 4
375°F	190°C/gas mark 5
400°F	200°C/gas mark 6
425°F	220°C/gas mark 7
450°F	230°C/gas mark 8
475°F	245°C/gas mark 9
500°F	260°C

LENGTH

INCH	METRIC
¼ inch	6 mm
½ inch	1.25 cm
¾ inch	2 cm
1 inch	2.5 cm
6 inches (½ foot)	15 cm
12 inches (1 foot)	30 cm

WEIGH

U.S./IMPERIAL	METRIC
½ oz	15 g
1 oz	30 g
2 oz	60 g
¼ lb	115 g
⅓ lb	150 g
½ lb	225 g
¾ lb	350 g
1 lb	450 g

All rights reserved.
Published in the United States by Ten Speed Press, an imprint
of the Crown Publishing Group, a division of Penguin Random
House LLC, New York.
www.crownpublishing.com
www.tenspeed.com

Ten Speed Press and the Ten Speed Press colophon are
registered trademarks of Penguin Random House LLC.

Library of Congress Cataloging-in-Publication Data
Moore, Russell (Chef)
  This is Camino / Russell Moore and Allison Hopelain with
Chris Colin and Maria Zizka; photographs by Yoko Takahashi.
    pages cm
  1. Cooking, American—California style. 2. Cooking—
California—San Francisco. 3. Camino (Restaurant)
I. Hopelain, Allison, 1967- II. Colin, Chris, 1975- III. Title.
  TX715.2.C34M665 2015
  641.59794—dc23
                        2015013757

Hardcover ISBN: 978-1-60774-728-4
eBook ISBN: 978-1-60774-729-1

Printed in China

Design by Emma Campion and Nami Kurita

10 9 8 7 6 5 4 3 2 1

First Edition